# THE WORD'S GONE GLOBAL

### EXPLORING BIBLE VERSIONS
#### updated

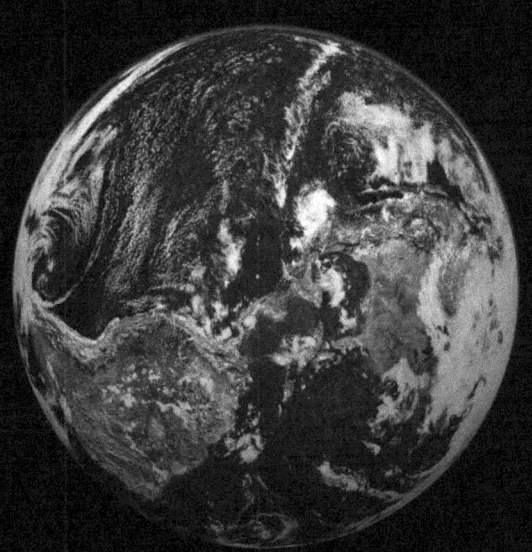

### Steve H Hakes

**Books by this author:**
Vampire Redemption
Vampire Extraction
Vampire Count
Vampire Grail
Vampire Shadows
Israel's Gone Global
Prayer's Gone Global
Singing's Gone Global
The Word's Gone Global
Revelation's Gone Global
The Father's Gone Global
Revisiting The Pilgrim's Progress
Revisiting The Challenging Counterfeit
Salvation Now and Life Beyond

# The Word's Gone Global

## Exploring Biblical Versions

~

Steve H Hakes

Copyright © 2017 by Dr. Steve H Hakes

All rights reserved. No part of this publication may be reproduced, stored in a retrieval system, or transmitted in any form or by any means (for example, electronic, photocopy, and recording) without the prior permission in writing from the copyright owner. The only exception is brief quotations in printed reviews. All lyrics are property and copyright of their owners, and those provided here are for educational purposes only.

Paperback ISBN: 978-0-9957013-3-5
Hardback ISBN: 979-8-4489222-3-7
Kindle ISBN: 978-0-9957013-2-8
V251128114022

Scripture quotations marked...

**ESV** are taken from The Holy Bible, English Standard Version Copyright © 2001 by Crossway Bibles, a division of Good News Publishers.

**GNB** are taken from the Good News Translation in Today's English Version—Second Edition Copyright © 1992 by American Bible Society. Used by Permission.

**NIV** are taken from the Holy Bible, New International Version® NIV®. Copyright © 1973, 1978, 1984, 2011 by Biblica, Inc.® Used by permission of Biblica, Inc.® All rights reserved worldwide.

**NKJV** are taken from the New King James Version®. Copyright © 1982 by Thomas Nelson, Inc. Used by permission.

**NLT** are taken from the Holy Bible, New Living Translation, copyright © 1996, 2004. Used by permission of Tyndale House Publishers, Inc., Wheaton, Illinois 60189. All rights reserved.

**NRSV** are taken from the New Revised Standard Version Bible: Anglicised Edition, copyright © 1989, 1995 the Division of Christian Education of the National Council of the Churches of Christ in the United States of America. Used by permission. All rights reserved.

**TNIV** are taken from the Holy Bible, Today's New International Version®. TNIV® Copyright © 2001, 2005 by International Bible Society®. Used by permission of Zondervan. All rights reserved worldwide.

Thanks...
- to the inspired writers.
- to John Wycliffe, William Tyndale, and Gregory Martin, pioneers of the English text.
- to Anne, my wife, for her love and support.
- to Charlotte (BA), my daughter, for painstakingly proofreading for initial publication. Any imperfections introduced are mine.

# Contents

|  |  |  |
|---|---|---|
|  | Preface | 10 |
| **PART 1** | **SPREAD THE WORD** | **11** |
|  | Prologue | 11 |
| Chapter 1 | **Islam and Infallibility** | 13 |
| Chapter 2 | **Global Go-Power** | 19 |
|  | Eastern Orthodoxy (Greek) | 20 |
|  | Western Roman Catholicism (Latin) | 24 |
| Chapter 3 | **Bibles for the Masses?** | 28 |
|  | From Majority Text to Textus Receptus: Check Mate? | 35 |
|  | The Terrific, Terrible, or Tentative, TR? | 42 |
| **PART 2** | **KING JAMES: A NEW HOPE?** | **52** |
|  | Prologue | 52 |
| Chapter 4 | **A New Fight** | 53 |
|  | King's Champion | 53 |
|  | Church Shenanigans | 55 |
|  | Eclectic Emergence | 57 |
|  | KJV Transmission | 60 |
| Chapter 5 | **Neomisian Flames** | 63 |
|  | C4 Jerome | 63 |
|  | C14 Wycliffe | 64 |
|  | C15-6 Erasmus | 64 |
|  | C15-6 Tyndale | 64 |
|  | C16-7 Bancroft | 64 |
|  | C19 Burgon | 65 |
|  | C20 Revised Standard Version | 66 |
| Chapter 6 | **James Immortal, Others Immoral?** | 67 |
|  | Greedy Graspers? | 67 |
|  | A Bloody Nose for a Bloodless Bible? | 71 |
|  | Sneaking in Sin? | 72 |
|  | Sslipery Ssnake? | 73 |
|  | Witch Westcott; Heretic Hort? | 75 |
|  | Edwin Palmer—Anonymous Arian? | 77 |
|  | Homosexual Homily? | 79 |
|  | Alexandrian Anarchists? | 85 |
|  | Fire Fighteth Fire? | 87 |
| Chapter 7 | **The KJV Lacketh...** | 90 |

|  |  |  |
|---|---|---|
|  | Justice | 90 |
|  | Greek | 91 |
|  | Understanding | 94 |
| **Chapter 8** | **Voices in the Wilderness?** | **97** |
|  | Conclusion | 98 |
| **PART 3** | **TRANSLATING THEOLOGY** | **100** |
| **Chapter 9** | **God's ID** | **100** |
|  | Tyndale | 103 |
|  | From Tyndale to KJV | 104 |
|  | From KJV to Today | 107 |
| **Chapter 10** | **Who's for Huiology?** | **113** |
|  | Deificity of God's Son | 113 |
|  | Christological Terms | 123 |
|  | The Incarnation | 130 |
| **PART 4** | **TODAY'S ENGLISH VERSIONS** | **136** |
| **Chapter 11** | **Textual Criticism and You** | **136** |
| **Chapter 12** | **Genesis of the NIV** | **144** |
| **Chapter 13** | **Attack of the ESV** | **147** |
|  | Engaging? | 147 |
|  | Literally Literal? | 152 |
|  | Clever Construction? | 153 |
|  | *Sarx* Appeal? | 157 |
|  | Ale and Arty? | 162 |
|  | Impossible Task, Needless Attack? | 165 |
| **Chapter 14** | **Gender Agenda?** | **170** |
|  | Nuances or Nuisances? | 178 |
|  | Giddy Guidelines | 181 |
|  | *Barnasa* | 185 |
|  | Overwriting Individuality? | 188 |
|  | Attack on the ESV | 191 |
|  | Hail Mother God? | 196 |
| **Chapter 15** | **Good Diversity** | **200** |
|  | Is *John* Up To Date? | 201 |
|  | Philosophy or Polytheism? | 206 |
|  | Book Conclusion | 211 |

| | English Versions Compared | Year |
|---|---|---|
| CEB | Common English Bible | 2011 |
| CEV | Contemporary English Version | 1995 |
| CJB | Complete Jewish Bible | 1998 |
| CSB | Christian Standard Bible | 2017 |
| EEB | Easy English Bible | 2024 |
| EJB | English Jubilee Bible | 2020 |
| EOB | Eastern Orthodox Bible | 2008 |
| ERV | Easy-to-Read Version | 2006 |
| ESV | English Standard Version | 2016 |
| FBV | Free Bible Version | 2018 |
| GNB | Good News Bible | 1992 |
| GWT | God's Word Translation | 2020 |
| HCSB | Holman Christian Standard Bible | 2009 |
| ISV | International Standard Version | 2014 |
| KJ21 | 21st Century King James Version | 1994 |
| KJV | King James Version | - |
| LEB | Lexham English Bible | 2012 |
| LSB | Legacy Standard Bible | 2021 |
| LSV | Literal Standard Version | 2020 |
| MEV | Modern English Version | 2014 |
| MSG | The Message | 2018 |
| NABRE | New American Bible Revised Edition | 2010 |
| NASB20 | New American Standard Bible | 2020 |
| NASB95 | New American Standard Bible | 1995 |
| NCB | New Catholic Bible | 2019 |
| NCV | New Century Version | 2005 |
| NET | New English Translation | 2017 |
| NIV11 | New International Version | 2011 |
| NJB | New Jerusalem Bible | 1985 |
| NKJV | New King James Version | 1982 |
| NLT | New Living Translation | 2015 |
| NLV | New Life Version | 2003 |
| NOG | Names of God Bible | 2011 |
| NRSV | New Revised Standard Version | 1995 |
| NRSVU | New Revised Standard Version Updated | 2021 |
| NWT | New World Translation | 2013 |

| English Versions Compared | | Year |
|---|---|---|
| REB | Revised English Bible | 1989 |
| RNJB | Revised New Jerusalem Bible | 2019 |
| RSV | Revised Standard Version | 1971 |
| TLV | Tree of Life Version | 2015 |
| TVB | The Voice Bible | 2012 |
| WEB | World English Bible | 2020 |

## Biblical Abbreviations

Ac. *Acts*  
Am. *Amos*  
Chr. *Chronicles*  
Col. *Colossians*  
Cor. *Corinthians*  
Dan. *Daniel*  
Dt. *Deuteronomy*  
Ec. *Ecclesiastes*  
Eph. *Ephesians*  
Est. *Esther*  
Ex. *Exodus*  
Ezk. *Ezekiel*  
Ezr. *Ezra*  
Gal. *Galatians*  
Gen. *Genesis*  
Hab. *Habakkuk*  
Heb. *Hebrews*  
Hg. *Haggai*  
Hos. *Hosea*  

Is. *Isaiah*  
Jas. *James*  
Jg. *Judges*  
Jhn. *John*  
Jl. *Joel*  
Jnh. *Jonah*  
Job *Job*  
Jos. *Joshua*  
Jr. *Jeremiah*  
Jude *Jude*  
Kg. *Kings*  
Lk. *Luke*  
Lm. *Lamentations*  
Lv. *Leviticus*  
Mic. *Micah*  
Mk. *Mark*  
Ml. *Malachi*  
Mt. *Matthew*  
Nah. *Nahum*  

Nb. *Numbers*  
Neh. *Nehemiah*  
Ob. *Obadiah*  
Phm. *Philemon*  
Php. *Philippians*  
Pr. *Proverbs*  
Ps(s). *Psalm(s)*  
Pt. *Peter*  
Rm. *Romans*  
Ruth *Ruth*  
Rv. *Revelation*  
Sam. *Samuel*  
Sg. *Song of Songs*  
Ths. *Thessalonians*  
Tm. *Timothy*  
Tts. *Titus*  
Zc. *Zechariah*  
Zp. *Zephaniah*  

## Grades[1]

| Percent | 100-95 | 94-90 | 89-85 | 84-80 | 79-75 | 74-70 | 69-65 | |
|---|---|---|---|---|---|---|---|---|
| Letter | A+ | A | A- | B+ | B | B- | C+ | |
| Point | 4.3 | 4 | 3.7 | 3.3 | 3 | 2.7 | 2.3 | |
| Percent | 64-60 | 59-55 | 54-50 | 49-45 | 44-40 | 39-27 | 26-14 | 13-00 |
| Letter | C | C- | D+ | D | D- | U+ | U | U- |
| Point | 2 | 1.7 | 1.3 | 1 | 0.7 | 0 | 0 | 0 |

---

[1] For handier sorting in tables, I advise using A1/A2/A3 and B1/B2/B3, etc, for grade letters. I have put these here in the more familiar forms of, eg, A+/A/A- and B+/B/B-. For grade points, I round final totals to the nearest 0.5 points.

# **Preface**

I love Jane Austen's *Pride and Prejudice*. It has a pivotal dialogue between the proud but good Mr Darcy, the prejudiced but good Elizabeth, and the social climber Miss Caroline Bingley, who seeks to marry Darcy. The topic is accomplishment among middle to upper class women of their generation. Darcy says that though he knows many women, few are socially *accomplished*. Elizabeth replies that he must be using a narrow definition of accomplishment. Miss Bingley, playing to her own strengths, pipes up that "a woman must have a thorough knowledge of music, singing, drawing, dancing, and the modern languages, to deserve the word; and besides all this, she must possess a certain something in her air and manner of walking, the tone of her voice, her address and expressions, or the word will be but half-deserved." Darcy sends her an ice-code message: "She must yet add something more substantial, in the improvement of her mind by extensive reading." Elizabeth uninterested in impressing him, laughs aloud that she is "no longer surprised at your knowing only six accomplished women. I rather wonder now at your knowing any.... I never saw such a woman. I never saw such capacity, and taste, and application, and elegance, as you describe, united." (Austen 1980:34)

Searching for the ideal English version of Holy Writ is perhaps as endless as Darcy's quest for a socially accomplished woman—give up and marry Elizabeth! After all, all Bible translations are but secondary attempts to convey Scripture. Yes, all reflect the imperfections of *lingua anglica*; none the perfections of the *lingua angelica*. But all having strengths and weaknesses, some are more of Elizabeth than Caroline standard; as in George Orwell's *Animal Farm*, some are more equal than others. I have sought to chart their comparative accuracy, but they must add to accuracy, style—and different styles will appeal to different readers.

C S Lewis said that Christianity "always remains intellectually possible; it never becomes intellectually compulsive" (Lewis 1975:94). Understanding the Bible helps Christians and non-Christians to understand Christianity, God's highest revelation to us. Understandable versions help us to understand God.

Steve H Hakes: mallon.detc@gmail.com

# Part 1     Spread the Word
## Prologue

It's good to see how passing on the Word to different peoples and generations, has been done. Many saints and scholars we've never heard of, perished in the process, for it isn't only in our days that the Bible has been a target for 'political' correctivists seeking to reshape society into their own image and to bully God's people out of truth. Christian blood has often seemed cheap. Yet their blood, sweat, and tears, has blessed the globe. They have left their mark on faithful transmission, and on making the Bible readable for all people. Truly we stand on the shoulders of martyrs.

The Bible is a unique category among world literature, for God was its active general editor, not simply its source of inspiration. Its types of speech were those that its original audience could relate to, to let them understand its message, written by those who understood them. "To deemphasise either side of [the] authorship [of this divine-human book] is a mistake" (Elwell 145). It's a kind of incarnation.

To focus on authentic Scripture, I exclude the deuterocanonical[2] writings and preclude all others from top-level inspiration. God's revelation has extended beyond Scripture (Heb.1:1), and other spiritually insightful writings exist, such as Plato, the Vedas, and *Pilgrim's Progress*, but all are subject to the OT/NT scriptures (Dt.13).

'General editor', means written by God's determination. It does not that mean each line carries his endorsement. For example, both Job's wife's bad advice to curse God and die, and Satan's evil advice to Jesus to worship him, were recorded by God's will. But that's never meant that he has agreed with them! Some have claimed that if from God, the autographs (that is, the original writings as they left the pens of the inspired writers) would have been supernaturally preserved letter for letter, word for word, without deviation. This idea neither fits Scripture, nor the history of transmission. Letters by Paul as inspired as *Colossians*,

---

[2]  In this context, *deuterocanonical* means second in inspiration. In some discussions it simply means second in time yet authentic Scripture.

## Prologue

have long perished in the Jewish Wars. And we find that the vast manuscripts we have vary, yet hold an amazing agreement in details.

This shows either God's *indirect* or *interactive* transmission, in that he so impressed his people with its worth that they, even risking their lives, sought to faithfully and frequently transmit the text. With all human endeavour, mistakes crept in, but the tenacity of the true text allows scholars to trace back to the autographs themselves. So, while the original parchments and papyri might have sunk beneath the sands of time, beyond reasonable doubt we have 100% of all basic teachings, and can be almost totally sure about even the few differences of text, none of which undermine major teachings.

Certainly, variations to the original text have occurred. If we speak about the Hebrew Bible, we should understand that there are many variations of the text. If we speak about the Greek Bible—the Septuagint/LXX text—we generally mean many Jewish variations of their Greek OT.[3] If we are speaking on the Aramaic Targums, we are speaking about many Jewish variations of the Aramaic OT. By the Old Latin Bible (*Vetus Latina*),[4] we are speaking of many unprofessional Christian Latin variations before the Vulgate (*Versio Vulgata*).

---

[3] Some say it was a non-Jewish version, perhaps written by Origen. The KJV translators located what was commonly called "the translation of the Seventy Interpreters", as made in Egypt before the incarnation, an imperfect translation yet inspired by God to help prepare the way of the lord of Jews and Gentiles. They seemed to imply that the KJV, which they humbly offered to God as an imperfect offering, would similarly have a high impact on society because it was in the language of a great Empire, as had been the Septuagint. And they argued with Epiphanius and the Fathers, that the Septuagint, the star in Origen's Hexapla, was exceptionally good. The 'Seventy' "did many things well, as learned men; but yet as men they stumbled and fell, one while through oversight, another while through ignorance, yea, sometimes they may be noted to add to the Original, and sometimes to take from it; which made the Apostles to leave them many times, when they left the Hebrew, and to deliver the sense thereof according to the truth of the word, as the spirit gave them utterance. This may suffice touching the Greek Translations of the Old Testament" (*Translators to the Reader*: Preface to the KJV, 1611).

[4] Basically, a collection of Greek to Latin translations, done by individuals for their local churches.

# Chapter 1   Islam and Infallibility

"When I was an atheist, I had to try to persuade myself that most of the human race have always been wrong about the question that mattered to them most; when I became a Christian, I was able to take a more liberal view. But, of course, being a Christian does mean thinking that where Christianity differs from other religions, Christianity is right and they are wrong. As in arithmetic—there is only one right answer to a sum, and all other answers are wrong: but some of the wrong answers are much nearer being right than others" (Lewis 2002:35).

It's true that there's no reason to turn off whenever you hear the term, *Islam*, but it's also true that it's a very silly idea that in reading a book you must never 'skip'. Sensible people skip freely when they come to a chapter that they find is going to be of no use to them. But if you interact with Muslims, you may find this chapter helpful. Even if you have never heard the word *halal*, you might also find it surprising to see that Islam can agree with a basic principle of biblical accuracy, an ancient agreement many Muslims seem to be unaware of, namely, the tenacity of the authentic text.

Islam is a significant religion and has a place for the Bible, though it sidelines it. Its place for the Bible, specifically its authentic text, is my focus here. However, what bias do I bring to this section? It might help to briefly put my position here. I am sympathetic with an early Christian position about Muhammad, namely, that he was a prophet from God for the Arabic people. Now prophets are fallible, and can move from divine revelation into human error, understandably simplifying things to gain converts. I believe that heaven and hell are valid concepts. Later, facing militant Islam, many Christians deemed Muhammad to be the hell-bound antichrist.

I assume neither that I will, nor that I won't, meet him in heaven. I sincerely feel that he would have spoken better had he understood Christianity better. Even the prophet John had a fundamental misunderstanding of Christ (Mt.11:3). Islam can command social coherence, and coherence can be good, but I do not hold that Islam saves in any ultimate sense. I do hold that some people, whether Animists, Atheists, Hindus, Judaists, Muslims, whatever, can be both helped and hindered by their faith, can love God, and can have ultimate salvation alongside their faith: pie in the sky when they die.

## Islam and Infallibility

To some extent, all religions are secondary *vis-à-vis* God. For all its benefits, under Islam people cannot know God as their father: steak on the plate while we wait.[5] I recommend the terms *iSLaM* and *MuSLiM*, in that the core *SLM* meaning is submission and obedience. Christianity is the true *islam* (submission) under Christ; Christians are the true *muslims* (submitted): Jesus messiah is *lord*, to the glory of the God the father. Oh, that we lived better as obedient children, and less "cold our warmest thoughts".[6]

Yet—I merely face an obvious objection at this point—should one be tolerant with the intolerant, benign with the malign? To many Evangelical Christians, Islam is almost the Great Enemy. Unlike Christianity, which is no longer under Sinai's justified and extremely limited war policy (Yahweh War)—being transethnic with true turf only in heaven—Islam has a mix of war/peace policies, not so clearly demarcated, and is much more socially based, allowing for global take-over. Some say its militant texts came after its peace texts, so have more relevance. These tend to be Islamists rather than Muslims, to use a differential from Ed Husain's *The Islamist* (2007:70).[7]

I am a *via media.* I do not support the radicalism which advances by the bullet (or by excessive immigration birth rate), but have some sympathy towards Islamists who wrongly believe that Christianity and the West are one, and that the West's moral perversity requires a militant response, Christians being fair targets since deemed the unfair culprits. Ironically, Christians, being increasingly persecuted in the West for defending morality, become increasingly persecuted by Islamists as if defending the immorality their governments bless.

Despite the fact that my brother David, had he not skived off his Twin Towers job that day, might have been a 9/11 fatality, I have never assumed that Osama bin Laden was hell bound. I am concerned that if we demonise the sincerely wrong, we might be demonising ourselves, as well as overlooking the fact that insincerity can be more demonic. But before the CIA knock on my door, let me add that I

---

[5] Contrasting Eternal Life 1 to Eternal Life 2, see my *Israel's Gone Global* ch.11-2.
[6] C18 John Newton's hymn, *How Sweet the Name of Jesus Sounds*.
[7] We speak of nominal Christians (Christian only by name) and committed Christians ('Born Anew' Christians, biblically the only sort of Christian).

have always deemed Osama's response to the West as sincerely fighting evil with evil, and that my death as a Christian would have seemed sweet in his eyes. I wish that Christians, Judaics, and Muslims, stood together ideologically against the secular humanist West. After all, we all understand that God is one and is to be obeyed—ethics is deontological, contrary to relativism.

If converts from Islam bring a witness of general peacefulness within Islam, I for one do not see that we need to assume that all witness to peacefulness must be a lie (*taqiyya*) to deceive non-Muslims—converts would spill the beans. I hope I've said enough of my opinions, which will win me few friends in any camp, to help you to judge any bias I bring to this section. Against correctivists, we must learn, or remember, that discrimination in itself is a good thing, and rightly judge each other rightly.[8] So, what does the Qur'an (Koran) say about the biblical text?

The Qur'an has about 20 verses that perhaps speak of the Bible's reliability, which include the claim that it witnessed to Muhammad.[9] Well, if the Bible does or ever did, it has kept its secret well. To Muslim scholars who have investigated this claim, the Bible's lack of explicit reference to Muhammad is a serious problem that they have tackled in different ways. One way has been to deny biblical reliability. Is asserting Bible unreliability a cop out, or the sad fact of the matter? Key qur'anic words include *akhfa* (to conceal), *baddala* (to substitute), *katama* (to cover up), and *nasa* (to forget). But "the strongest verb is without doubt *ḥarrafa* (to give something a wrong direction)" (Moucarry 47). We can speak of *twisting* a text. The 4 qur'anic texts that make this charge are looked at below.[10]

---

[8] If we know someone to be a dreadful liar, should we not mistrust them?

[9] For a fuller look at the Qur'an and Hadith references to this debate, along with Islamic scholarship and attempts to marshal agreed OT text for Islam, see Moucarry. A *Gospel of Barnabas* seems to have been written by a C16 Italian newly converted to Islam: contrary to Islam, it has Jesus denying his messiahship, and contrary to geography, it places Nazareth on the shore of Lake Galilee—it is about 10 miles away.

[10] Some translations put 5:13 as 5:14, and 5:41 as 5:44.

## Islam and Infallibility

The position of Fakhr-ul-Din al-Razi (1149-1209), one of the top Muslim scholars, was basically that the Bible witnessed to Muhammad, that Allah had preserved his holy words in the text, and that therefore if People of the Book disagreed with Islam, they disagreed with the very text they read. Muslims who accept that *explicit* reference to Muhammad were never present, can fall back on the idea that *implicit* references to Muhammad are present, for example assuming that what we may call 'messianic' texts prophesied Muhammad, not Jesus.

- Sura 2:75 speaks of the Israelites/Jews[11] having wilfully distorted Scripture (God's *kitab*)—perhaps meaning they heard yet twisted the Torah's witness to Muhammad, or reduced laws such as the penalty for adultery. If the text *is* about the OT (Tanak), Razi allowed that the OT *text* might have been distorted (though certainly not so much to become untruthful), but that it was far more likely that *interpretation* (*fi l-m ʼna*) of it had become distorted to the point of falsification.
- Sura 4:46 speaks of some Jews evilly twisting (*ḥarrafa*), perhaps changing, words/commands.[12] Razi argued that just possibly, during a spiritually low ebb, Jewish scholarship managed to make changes that the general Jewish population didn't detect and later generations didn't reverse. Or perhaps these Jews were misquoting Muhammad. On balance, he suspected that without corrupting the OT, these Jews were heretics who *distorted* biblical interpretation to confuse Muslims.
- Sura 5:13 speaks of Jews violating their covenant, being hardened by God, misinterpreting, decontextualising, and forgetting, text. Razi held that they misrepresented Allah's authentic text.

---

[11] It is better to speak of Jews in Muhammad's time, and Israelites in Moses' time. It is not always clear whether Islamic texts mean Israelites or Jews. Judaism is not the religion of the Jews, but a religion from the Jews of AD 70: its believers are Judaics, whatever their ethnicity. An Arab may be a Judaic, and an ethnic Jew may be a Muslim.

[12] Since the Hebrew for Dt.5:27's "we will listen and obey" (*we-shamaʼnu we-ʼasinu*) sounds very similar to the Arabic for "we have heard but refuse to heed" (*samiʼna wa ʼasayna*), Muhammad might have thought the Israelites' response to Moses was negative rather than positive (Moucarry 53.4).

- Sura 5:41 speaks of Arabs and Judaics undermining Islam, and of Jews displacing words. Whether this text meant the Jews preferred more their leaders to their scriptures, or that they were deliberately unfair mediators of Islam to other peoples, is unclear. Razi favoured the idea that it spoke about substituting rabbinic teaching for Scripture. He said that by replacing the OT penalty of stoning for adultery,[13] with mere flogging, the Jews showed they skipped commands they didn't like.

If the situational context of these texts was Muhammad's Jewish problem in Medina, then they are about the OT text relating either as to an alleged witness to Muhammad, or to the issue of stoning adulterers to death. Razi held that "Scripture that has been passed down by means of successive transmission is not liable to textual corruption" (Moucarry 52)—the true text sticks. The charge that the Bible (OT and NT) is textually corrupted in order to remove witness to Muhammad is favoured more by later Islam, perhaps because the text *as is* doesn't meet expectations. Is it a case that, if your sword breaks, you draw your dagger?

Many Muslims are unaware of the earlier position of Islamic scholars such as Razi, Baqillani (950-1013),[14] Avicenna (980-1037), Ghazali (1058-1111), and more recently Muḥammad ʿAbduh (1849-1905). True, some early Muslim scholars (for example, Ibn Ḥazm (994-1064) and Al-Juwayni (1028-85)) argued that the biblical text had been significantly corrupted, and some who think this think the Bible has inner contradictions. But good Islamic scholars have said that Allah gave,

---

[13] The socio-spiritual reasons for Sinaitic penalties during Sinaitic times made sense, were justified, and arguably offered a better conceptual package deal for that society than what the West offers. It taught sin to be valid, and to exist in the sexual arena, truths we avoid if we avoid Truth. The penalty of *physical death* was understood to allow alternatives, the cutting off of excommunication /banishment. Indeed, physical death, the doorway to true destiny, is not so bad in itself, though the path and destination can be painful and the apprehension taxing. Yosef, planning to divorce Maryam his wife, was pronounced just (Mt.1:19: *dikaios*), that is within the permitted Sinaitic framework, which may be why Islam has written him out of the story. Sinai, now invalid, was not barbaric, and offered a rich social life.

[14] He allowed some textual change for the OT once its monarchy failed.

thus protected, the biblical text. And they have also noted the unlikeliness that an inspired and established text, widely spread out geographically, could have been significantly rewritten with earlier truth lost forever (textual tenacity: *tawatur*).

It is also fair to mention here that Islam accepts that miracles can substantiate written revelation. This is not to say that they accept that all claims about miracles are true, that false miracles cannot happen, or that every true miracle confirms all miracle workers' claims to have written or spoken God's message. As one philosophy professor argued, miracles can happen, divine revelation can be given, and there is no good reason to assume that God might not have given prophets some obvious miracles to substantiate their claims "to have [had] that special authority which was due to their special revelation" (Evans 118). We and Muslims can accept revelation in a reasonable manner, yet we are to judge the prophets (Dt.13).

Razi had a good grasp on textual transmission. And he knew that God's investment in literature couldn't fundamentally fail. His position aligns with Sir Frederic Kenyon's, the pre-eminent British authority on New Testament manuscripts at the turn of the twentieth century, though they disagreed over whether the OT witnessed to Jesus or to Muhammad. In discussing the differences between the traditional and the Alexandrian text-types, in the light of God's providential preservation of his word, Kenyon wrote:

> "[God] would not allow his Word to be seriously corrupted, or any part of it essential to man's salvation to be lost or obscured; ...the differences between the rival types of text is not one of doctrine. No fundamental point of doctrine rests upon a disputed reading: and the truths of Christianity are as certainly expressed in the text of Westcott and Hort as in that of Stephanus."[15]

---

[15] www.bible-researcher.com/kutilek1.html (2008)

# Chapter 2  Global Go-Power

History said to John that the Bible had originated among a people who were seldom more than a sideshow in the international ring. John tried to cut History short: the people of the Book were "just one of [the] Pagan peoples—and a peculiarly unattractive one" (Lewis 1978:195). The Bible is tainted with that smear, which arch-heretic Marcion reacted against. Yet it has become the global best seller, numbering perhaps as high as 5 billion. The tiniest seed became the global tree.

The messiah, long prophesied, came in order to go global, and established a base of twelve apostles. And after his resurrection, he inspired *via* the spirit a new body of canonical literature (the New Testament), which was subject to their corporate scrutiny. It focused on the ins and outs of the new covenant. He also gave his community the command to go global, baptising folk with reference to the trinity—one name, three persons (Mt.28:19).[16] Where his community has gone, his Testament in some way, shape, or form, has boldly gone. Our message is to conform to it. The Word's gone global.

The Global Word has gone North and South. Camp Wycliffe (a.k.a. the Wycliffe Bible Translators), the dream child of William Cameron Townsend, began in 1942. Even as Wycliffe had believed that every English reader should have the Bible in English, so Townsend believed that the Bible should be translated into every language. Under 2,000 languages await their global touch, moved by the belief that however good indirect Bible access is, direct access is better. Western missionary activity covers many areas, and all the major languages are served by good translation. But now let's move briefly to the East.

---

[16] In my opinion, water, whether blessed or unblessed, neither gets anyone into eternal life, nor is a must for Christian believers. Behind the command and helpful death/life illustration was a core meaning of public commitment. I became a Christian and was water immersed, but are not true Salvationists, even if they reject water baptism, as Christian as I?

## Eastern Orthodoxy (Greek)

As a young man, I was quite surprised when I discovered that there were Christians in the East, indeed a sizeable Christian network. Perhaps some Christians out there are as surprised as I was. If we live in the West, we're less likely to hear about the East, partly due to a historical blackout between the two sides. There is one global church, one global tree, and one major eastern branch of that tree is known as Orthodoxism.[17] The East contains large church networks, long severed from themselves and from the West (which historically meant Rome). This section introduces something about Eastern Orthodoxism, which is making inroads into the West, and its textual preference. Being aware of the East paints Christian history on a bigger canvass—we Christians have global vision.

Sadly, the Greek Eastern and the Latin Western sections of the church mutually cut off the other long ago.[18] Different ways of thinking contributed to the stress lines. The East tended to be more intellectual, and the West more practical, and over centuries the common bond of faith became strained. One fateful day in Toledo, 589, the filioque clause, "and of the son", was wrongly added by the Western side of the church into the Nicene Creed. To the East, this seemed to both unilaterally assert Western supremacy, and to undermine the idea of the spirit being eternal. The church of the West only meant that God the son co-sent the spirit into NT mission,

---

[17] Lots of *networks* have branded themselves as *churches*, such as the Roman Catholic *Church*, the *Church* of Scotland, the Elim *Church*, *Church* of the Nazarene. Such branding tends to parochialism and unbiblicality. I think it calls for repentance: God has one church, so it is perhaps better to rebrand them as Networks, Fellowships, denoting them as parts of the larger, global church. One tree, many branches. I rejoice in diversity among the branches, yet (the curse of Adam) each branch carries its particular set of abiotic damage, fungi, and mistletoe without the wine. No branch is perfect. We are interconnected, if we are in Christ, so it is not them and us, but us and us.

[18] I neither buy into the idea that only Orthodoxism represents the church in the East, nor into the idea that only Roman Catholicism represents the church in the West, but *East* can be a convenience term for Eastern Christianity and its major network. Indeed, one severed network, Nestorianism, called itself Assyrian Orthodoxy, though by *Orthodoxism* I exclude it.

which indeed he had. The clause hadn't begun as a doctrinal shift, and had tended to get mention in some creedal copies which some assumed to be authentic. When push came to shove, the pope felt he had to affirm it, even though that sent the wrong signals to the East. Signals of a unilateral breach of harmony; of major doctrinal speculation about the eternal relation of the spirit to the son; of papal authority over the East. There should have been an immediate apology and withdrawal of such an ambivalent addition to this common creed. Certainly, under God the pope wished to claim ultimate authority over the East, after the ideas of Apostolic Succession and Papal Primacy had set in. Anyway, after a millennium of relative unity, 1054 saw the Great Schism, the Great Divide, between eastern and western sections of Apostolic Succession type Christianity.[19]

Centuries on, and Rome was blamed for the savage 1204 attack on Constantinople, the centre of eastern Christianity. Pope Innocent the 3rd had told the Venetians (the Fourth Crusade) not to attack this Christian city, but ignoring him, in their greed they also carried out their personal vendetta against Constantinople. He excommunicated them for their disobedience and anti-Christian behaviour. Nevertheless, the treasures mainly went to, and stopped in, Rome.[20] Nowadays, the Great Schism has been eased between Rome and Constantinople, and fellowship flows more freely between East and West. The dark years partly explains why many Western Christians find the idea of Orthodoxism novel, captivating when they meet it.

---

[19] Early on, Christianity assumed that the C1 apostles had laid the foundations and then handed their authority to a continuum of bishops. Thus began a hierarchical authority structure based on tracing back in theory at least to the general apostolic group, this 'anointing'. It was believed that bishops could anoint others as bishops, continuing the so-called 'Apostolic Succession'. Some in important cities became 'archbishops', 'patriarchs', etc. Later, it became a bonus point to 'trace' back to Peter—Rome was not the only centre of Christianity that claimed his particular 'succession'. Arguably only the big Christian networks of Roman Catholicism and East Orthodoxism divided themselves, although other Christian networks were mainly deemed unchristian by the big players, and so out of fellowship.

[20] http://orthodoxwiki.org/Filioque

Interaction between East and West isn't great, and the rifts are slow to heal, but for a fuller picture of global translation let's briefly look at Bible translation in the eastern part of the church. Much fragmentation has occurred. There are many groups not belonging to Orthodoxism which are rightly or wrongly called heretics. And in Rome, Luther was called a heretic, but today many Roman Catholics would welcome him as a reformer. But I shan't consider translation ideas from all the different parts of Eastern Christianity—a taster must suffice.[21]

Let's look a little at Christianity in Russia. A mission to Moravia became the basis of the oldest Christian Slavic culture. Two C9 brothers (Methodius and Constantine (renamed Cyril)) were named "Apostles to the Slavs", and Slavic Christianity expanded through persecution. The brothers began Bible translation into Slavic, for which purpose they created an alphabet, later replaced by Cyrillic. This work eventually led to Slavic Rus (Russians)[22] being drawn into Christianisation in 988 by Vladimir the Great, the Rus leader who had opted to adopt a new religion and was won over by joyful Orthodoxism. Vladimir even destroyed the statue of *Perun*, hitherto his and his people's chief god (in Scandinavia a lesser but still mighty god known as Thor, second only to Odin). Some film makers have *converted* Thor into a long-life, technologically advanced super being: may they be cast into Ginnungagap! But blame the Christians not for killing off the gods, but only for raising our sights above the gods to God, if blame them you must.

## Eastern Orthodox Bible

By and large, Orthodoxism, which was adopted in Russia (a.k.a. Russian Orthodox network), has used the NT Greek text that it had inherited from

---

[21] Orthodoxism would doubt that some other Eastern groups are Christian. One might consider the Protestant/Catholic divide, when each denied the other was Christian. What of the Baptist/Mormon divide? Some divides are true divides. Not all who claim the name of Christ are Christians, but sectarianism too easily denies others the title.

[22] Some guesswork is needed in defining the Rus. They were perhaps dominant incomers who were dissolving into the resident Slavic people, thus redefining the name *Rus*.

the Byzantine Empire. For its English-speaking congregations, there has been the KJV, and in the C20 an ecumenical RSV. One of Orthodoxism's official versions is the Orthodox Study Bible, which uses the NKJV for the NT, and a translation of the OT from the Septuagint heavily styled on the NKJV. Some Orthodox complain of an Evangelical takeover! More independently, it now has an English version project, called the Eastern Orthodox Bible (EOB), aimed at English speakers.

> "Until the publication of the EOB, the King James and New King James versions have been the preferred translations, partly because they are based on the Textus Receptus (TR) which is a Byzantine text that is close to the normative ecclesiastical text of the Greek-speaking Orthodox Churches. Several versions of the King James Version (KJV) currently exist, but all suffer from the imperfections of the Textus Receptus prepared by Erasmus (1522, third edition) from a small number of manuscripts and revised by Stephanus (1550). Moreover, the Old Testament of the KJV is based on the Masoretic text and fails to include significant Septuagintal variants. Also, even though the original 1611 edition of the KJV included the so-called 'apocryphal' books, these were removed in subsequent editions, thus preventing proper ecclesiastical use in an Orthodox context."[23]

In short, the EOB accepts that the older TR text is not the oldest text. Through a number of visual aids within the text, it has sought to give readers a clearer picture of what the Byzantine text—largely followed by the KJV—has been, and what current scholarship usually teaches. It also has an eye—sometimes both eyes—on the Septuagint text. When significant differences of text occur, it footnotes their Patriarchal 1904 Greek text (PT), the so-called Textus Receptus (TR), the NT Majority Text (MT),[24] the OT Masoretic Text, and/or the 'critical texts' (CT)[25] which most biblical scholars use. The preferred

---

[23] See www.orthodoxanswers.org/eob/download/eobntpublic.pdf.

[24] For convenience I have only used MT to abbreviate *Majority Text*—sometimes the unicode 1D510 (𝔐) is used. For Masoretic Text, I have not abbreviated.

[25] The Nestle-Aland/UBS text, also known as the NU.

OT text is the Greek Septuagint tradition, and for the Greek NT the 1904 Patriarchal Text.

In the EOB, square brackets [ ] indicate words added for clarity and accuracy but perhaps not in the Greek text: read aloud if you wish—for example "Then he will [be able to] plunder his house" (Mt.12:29). Curly brackets { } indicate words added for theological clarity and accuracy: best not read aloud—for example "This man can only cast out demons by {the authority of} Beelzebul, the prince of the demons!" (Mt.12:24).[26] Pointed brackets < > indicate words that may have been added in the Byzantine textual tradition for the purpose of clarification, harmonization, or liturgical use, and which are present in PT—for example "<Two will be in the field: one will be taken, and the other left.>" (Lk.17:36). Like the CEB, most versions might put such alternatives as footnotes, or ignore them.

Footnotes range in quality, and indicate theological stance. For example, for Jhn.1:18: "No one has seen God at any time! The uniquely loved[a] Son[b] who is in the bosom of the Father[c], he has explained him."

- Their footnote 'a' allows the questionable translation "only-begotten" (which it prefers in v16), but I think that their text is etymologically better;
- Their footnote 'b' notes that some manuscripts read 'unique God' instead of "uniquely loved Son". Since Orthodoxism stresses the primacy of the Father and is uneasy about calling God's Son *God*, one can understand their preference. However, here I think that their footnote reflects better manuscripts.
- Their footnote 'c' allows "close to the Father's heart". Here I prefer their footnote as being better English.

## **Western Roman Catholicism (Latin)**

We now move to the more familiar stream, Western Christianity. In the C- BC, many Jews didn't know Hebrew. In Alexandria, Egypt, Jews translated the Hebrew into Greek, for Greek was the common language they spoke there. In Palestine and further east, Jews

---

[26] Compare the CEB: functional equivalence versions add such [ ] and { } details without setting them off from the main text: less precise, perhaps, but less cluttered.

translated the Hebrew into Aramaic, for Aramaic was perhaps the main language there. Of these two traditions of translation, the Alexandrian Jews keep nearer to the text. By the C1, the Greek OT had become the common version in Palestine, and was much used by the Primitive Church.

In Rome, the Greek OT and NT text was used until the mid C-, but some places translated the Greek into Old Latin. Many Christians, untrained in translation, followed this trend. In the late C4, Pope Damasus commissioned Jerome to produce a standard official Latin text, though Jerome had known that any new version would be condemned by many who didn't like change. Jerome was an outstanding scholar with a good command of Greek, and even went to Palestine to learn Hebrew. But to most Latin speaking Christians the idea of translating the OT from Hebrew seemed a silly, almost blasphemous idea: why fix the unbroken Latin by the Christ-rejecting Jews' language, they asked?

## The Vulgate

Because Jerome's Vulgate was not what people were used to, it received much criticism. He would have left out the traditional Apocrypha, and that might have been the end of the Apocrypha. However, Pope Damasus 1 insisted that the Apocrypha should be written in, affirming that tradition into which Roman Catholicism and Eastern Orthodoxy have tapped into.[27] Western Protestantism can cite Early Church Fathers such as Origen, Cyril of Jerusalem, Athanasius, and Jerome, as having deemed the Apocrypha as being sub-canonical.

---

[27] Jesus did not dispute the canonical OT with his people. The NT also shows itself at home with it, "but not once [does it] cite any statement from the..Apocrypha or any other writings as having divine authority. [Quotations from] Enoch 60:8 and 1:9, and..Ac.17:28; Tts.1:12..are used more for purposes of illustration than proof" (Grudem 57).

Bishop Melito of Sardis, c.170, listed the OT as what we have today, less *Esther*; Origen agreed but added in *Esther*, which was probably disputed because the Hebrew text showed no obvious mention of God: both excluded the Apocrypha. Certainly, the deuterocanon has a rich dollop of goodness which we may learn from and teach.

In the C19, Orthodox Metropolitan Philaret's Longer Catechism, contrary to the disputed Synod of Jerusalem (1672), said that unlike the Hebrew canon, the Apocrypha was not protocanonical. But almost uniformly, Roman Catholicism and Orthodoxism sides with Damasus, and challenges the Protestant's interpretation of the Fathers above. One pro-Damasus argument suggests that Protestants foolishly base their biblical canon on the apocrypha-free version sourced from anti-Christian Jews in Palestine, rather than from the apocrypha-rich version sourced from Christian Jews in Egypt.

Mud flinging? Sure. The issue of Christ-rejection remains sensitive. However, this line of argument ignores Jerome's reasons for discounting the Apocrypha. OK, the NT has a few references to Apocryphal and pagan works. This does not validate those writings as canonical (a.k.a. protocanonical). Although it is enjoyable, has devotional value, and helps show the background culture that Jesus lived in, the Apocrypha/Deuterocanon has historical, chronological, and geographical errors. In line with the Alexandrian Jews' biblical naivety, unlike the more savvy Palestinian Jews living closer to their Hebrew base (both Christian and non-Christian), Alexandrian Jewish Christians were predisposed to use the Apocrypha. Moreover, in early days the church hadn't critically weighed the Apocrypha, though it did accept that the core OT was God-inspired, as Yeshua had taught.

It may be that in 1546, Rome finally declared it to be on equal footing with the canonical OT because it had long happily accepted it *via* Jerome and when push came to shove it alone seemed to offer texts to back certain ideas disputed by Martin Luther (Grudem 59). Jerome's version, named the *Vulgate* (which meant the Common version), became the standard Bible version in England. Being a Latin version, therefore unreadable by the average English reader, was later thought an added blessing: it protected laity from misinterpreting the text, and the clergy from having to publicly conform to the text.

Unsurprisingly variations developed as copies were made, and since the printing press a few attempts have been made to standardise the text. The main ones are...

- the 1592 (later revised) Clementine Vulgate (begun under a previous pope and officially issued under Pope Clement 8). It can be identified by Heva in Gen.3:20;

- the 1969 Stuttgart Vulgate (fifth edit. 2007), by the German Bible Society, to critically go back to Jerome. It can be identified by Hava in Gen.3:20;
- the 1979 *Nova Vulgata* (produced under popes Paul 6 through John Paul 2): it sought to revisit, revise, and supersede Jerome in the light of current textual scholarship. It can be identified by Eva in Gen.3:20.

# Chapter 3      Bibles for the Masses?

"And did Those feet in ancient time, walk upon England's mountains green?" Highly unlikely, is the short answer. Ah, sweet England. England (I use the term loosely) has a multilayered culture, and English (I use the term even more loosely) is a multilayered language. Early English versions usually were secondary translation, that is, translation from a translation, English from Latin. Christianity came fairly early to England.[28] How early we don't know, but Tertullian (C-) certainly knew of Celtic Christianity, and there were some bishops from England at the Council of Nicea in 325 (Metzger 55). Perhaps the earliest use of Old English for Scripture was in the C7 (Lindisfarne Gospels). With the Norman conquest of 1066, Old English gave way to French, and Bible translation in England more or less stopped.

The Norman-French occupation also produced a new kind of English called Middle English, deemed suitable for the lower social classes—the more sophisticated preferred the Anglo-French language. Indeed, keeping the Bible out of Middle English would help keep it away from peasants, lest they see that the ruling class was unbiblical and revolt. Church clergy generally wished to keep their monopoly of Scripture, partly from fear that if the laity should read it, they would realise that clergy was spiritually corrupt. Even the private reading of unauthorised English Bible versions was banned (The Constitutions of Oxford, 1408). John Wycliffe was out of favour.

## Wycliffe

Who was John Wycliffe? He was a C14 Oxford theologian, the Morning Star of the Reformation. Deserving high praise, he inspired the translation of the whole Bible into Middle English, though friends and colleagues, Nicholas of Hereford and John Purvey were the major players. He believed that neither people nor pope had equal or higher authority than Scripture, which he believed even peasants should have in down to earth language, heaven on earth. He was eventually

---

[28]     One idea is that the centurion (Longinus?) who saw Jesus die, became a missionary to England. Biblically, all he probably said was that Jesus was a demigod, a son of a god, and whether he investigated further and became a Christian we don't know.

condemned for heresy.[29] Perhaps his real offence was giving access to what the Bible taught, access that could then challenge what Rome taught. The first Wycliffite version (1382 Early Version) was what some have called a *literal* translation, or better, *formal equivalence*.

The term *literal* is misleading, not least because some use it to mean accuracy, unaware that *literal* translation can be inaccurate (page 152). A basic idea of formal equivalence, is to use the same common meaning of the foreign word, wherever it is encountered, regardless of its context or its range of meaning. The un-English style of the Wycliffe EV was perhaps due to a deliberate policy to match the Latin Vulgate as a law book. An example of this foreign structure is Gen.1:3: "And God seide, Be maad liȝt; and maad is liȝt".[30] The King James Version would prefer using this formal equivalence version, though it would make a better job of it.

The Later Version (1388-95), produced after Wycliffe had died, was more *functional equivalence*, better translating the Vulgate's Latin style into rough English style. This version helped develop the English language by being a national book for the church in England. This outcome shows that it made a deep impression on the country. However, Middle English was snubbed by the snobs as being a low language, and this limited the market from a financial perspective. In truth it had been a work of love and self-sacrifice, used by the Lollards, Christians who were keen to evangelise according to the insights of Wycliffe. A neglected language for a neglected people, the common people.

---

[29] There was however a justified fear that homogeneity was safe, but heterogeneity socially dangerous, somewhat akin to today's Values Clarification, where values as toyed with as merely subjective (itself an *indoctrination*), each person becoming a law unto themselves. Roman Catholicism today seems to accept that Wycliffe did good, both as highlighting abuses and producing common language translation. The Wycliffe prologue attacked various sacerdotal teachings (Celibacy of 'priests', Relics, Purgatory, Mass). But that unwelcome attack aside, Roman Catholicism today broadly welcomes his version, and even in the C14, copies lacking the prologue were happy used by Roman Catholics.

[30] https://www.scribd.com/document/324581901/Wycliffe-Bible-Early-Version. This site makes a decided push to sign you up.

## Bibles for the Masses?

But it's not surprising that some Latinisms made it through, such as the word *Calvary*:[31] Luke (23:33) wrote *kranion* (skull) from which we get our word *cranium*. In line with the Gospel parallels (Mt.27:33/Mk.15:22/Jhn.19:17), it seems better to replace the Latin term *Calvary* by the word *skull*: Matthew (27:33) wrote *golgotha...kraniou*.[32] But it is hard, and sometimes unnecessary, to drop all loan-words.[33] After Wycliffe, it was another 150 years before another such challenge to the clergy power bloc was made. By that time English language, Gutenberg, and Luther, had become forces to reckon with.

### Tyndale

With the movable type printing press invented by Johannes Gutenberg in 1456, Hebrew and Greek parts of Scripture began to circulate in 1488 and 1516 respectively. A scholar named Erasmus had called attention to misrepresentations in the Latin Vulgate, such as the command to *do penance* when what John had said was *repent* (Mt.3:2), and Mary being *full of grace*,[34] rather than *favoured* or had

---

[31] With spelling variations, the *Vulgate's Calvariae* became *Caluerie* (Wycliffe), *Calvary* (Tyndale/Douay/KJV), *Caluery* (Coverdale), *Caluarye* (Matthew), *Caluary* (Great), *Caluarie* (Geneva/Bishops).

[32] With spelling variations, the Vulgate's *Golgotha quod est Calvariae locus*, roughly retained by Wycliffe (Golgatha...place of Caluarie) and Douay (Golgotha, which is the place of Calvary), became *Golgotha* (Tyndale/Matthew/Great/Geneva/Bishops/KJV) or *Golgatha* (Coverdale); *deed mens* (Tyndale/Coverdale) or *dead mens* (Matthew/Great/Geneva/Bishops)—KJV dropped this expansion. And, significantly, *sculles* (Tyndale/Coverdale/Matthew/Great), *skulls* (Geneva/Bishops), or *skull* (KJV).

[33] Yep, some KJVO folk lambaste the 'modern versions' for removing *Calvary*, as if that means removing salvation. The facts are that Luke never had *Calvary*, that if they insist that Luke had had then they must lambaste Matthew for dropping Calvary, or if he had had it they must lambaste the KJV for dropping it from Wycliffe, and they find themselves siding with the Roman Catholic Douay and the Vulgate against Luther and Wesley.

[34] In English versions, the phrase *full of grace* was first challenged by the Geneva. The Douay-Rheims-Challoner kept both; Msgr. Knox corrected *Matthew* but not *Luke*; the modern Roman Catholic translations NABRE and NJB, following Pope Pius 12's call back to Greek (his *Divino Afflante Spiritu*, 1943), correct both. The Vulgate of *Luke* is enshrined in the *Hail Mary*, and it has the driving

*found grace* (Lk.1:28). These were theological ideas at the expense of proper translation (McGrath 2002:57-8). The literary giant William Tyndale yearned to give England a simple English version, which would also cut through Latin corruptions. He tested the waters in 1523.[35]

But England being too unsafe a workplace, he ensconced safely in Europe. From there, copies of his work were smuggled into England. His was a very bold and free translation, simple and direct: "tush, ye shall not die" (Gen.3:4); "the Lorde was with Joseph, and he was a luckie felowe" (Gen.39:2); "the Lord thy surgeon" (Ex.15:26).[36] Tyndale's momentous English innovations included translating from the original Greek NT and Hebrew OT (rather than from Latin), and highlighting God's name. Eventually Tyndale was conned out of his safe haven and condemned for heresy. Even Thomas Cromwell, King Henry 8's chief advisor, was unable to save Tyndale from execution in 1536. But by then he had managed to translate most of the Bible into English, and his work became the backbone and paradigm for English translation through the centuries—for this we remain highly in Tyndale's debt.

Roman Catholicism condemned his work, not so much as shoddy work, but as Lutheran work. To restore biblical meaning, he had shied away from priestly terms: for example, *priest* became *elder*, and *church* became *congregation*. His translation thus helped the church to rethink some of its set ideas. In particular, his footnotes vigorously undermined Roman Catholic authority, and reopened questions of Christian leadership and salvation. He had, to a fair extent, followed the example of Erasmus, soon followed by Luther, in removing Roman tints from the biblical canvas.

## Coverdale

In C16, English history moved into a state of flux, Rome's authority began to wobble, and relationships between European monarchs and

---

force of tradition, as has the idea of Jesus' body being broken (KJV: 1 Cor.11:24), though both ideas are now deemed noncanonical.

[35] www.biblicalstudies.org.uk/pdf/kjv_lewis.pdf

[36] For a slightly updated version, go to www.pcministry.com/TyNT.

## Bibles for the Masses?

Rome, began to change. Academically, Miles Coverdale, once an Augustinian friar from York, was like a rowing boat among battleships, but he had a real flair for literary style. He built on the work of Tyndale, who had not yet been executed. Citing Jerome, he introduced the idea of downgrading the noncanonical Apocrypha into its own section, an appendix to the OT. This potentially weakened its public status, asking us to re-examine canonicity. Coverdale generally kept his head down, not pointedly attacking Roman Catholicism. He introduced the micro-commentary idea of chapter summaries. His was the first complete English Bible. This he later updated as *The Great Bible*, called *Great* because of its size. It was "a judicious blend of Tyndale and Coverdale, with the offending words of Matthew's [1537] Bible removed" (McGrath 2002:95). In Robert Louis Stevenson's *Kidnapped*, David Balfour's Bible could be carried in a *plaidneuk,* but Great Bibles were church sized.

### Matthew

What about the offensive *Matthew's Bible*? This version was actually the work of a Cambridge scholar named John Rogers. He used a pen name to protect his work both from his name and from Tyndale's, both demonised by the press. Tyndale had been executed a year earlier; Rogers would be burnt to death about 20 years later (the French ambassador marvelled that Rogers died cheerfully). Wycliffe's bones were burnt; Tyndale's body and his translation were burnt; Rogers was burnt to death. Working for the pope, Jerome got off nicely! Rogers was able to use both Tyndale's published and unpublished translation, as well as using Coverdale's Bible. And Cromwell was able to steer King Henry 8, whom he had kept in the dark about its true Tyndale-Rogers roots, into approving it. Ignorance can be bliss. However, the Thomas Matthew Bible contained footnotes offensive to Rome, and too Protestant for English comfort. With bad reviews, Cromwell soon looked about for a replacement, which led to the Great Bible authorised in 1539—the first Authorised Version!

### Geneva

However, Protestantism would soon challenge the Great Bible. During another wave of persecution, many Protestant scholars moved to Geneva, Switzerland, and in 1560 produced a new version—

the Geneva Bible (a.k.a. Breeches, Place-Makers, or Pilgrims'). The main player was William Whittingham (Oxford). Miles Coverdale played a minor part. Both had escaped from Mary Tudor's neither so sweet nor green England. The Geneva used English chapter divisions, probably incorporated by C13 Stephen Langton (who would be "the...Archbishop who signed the Magna Carta") into Jerome's *Vulgate* (Chadwick 208).[37] The 1560 Geneva Bible first divided chapters into versification, and turned sentences into paragraphs.[38]

Controversially, it was peppered with comments critical of papacy and monarchy. When he became the king of England, King James 1 was not amused. Yet the Geneva became "the Bible of Shakespeare, John Bunyan, Cromwell's army, [and] the Puritan pilgrims to the New World" (Metzger 66). The popularity of the Geneva over the Great Bible, annoyed many people, including James. Their initial solution to this annoyance was to upgrade Coverdale's Great Bible.[39] Enter the Bishops Bible (1568), a much more user-friendly, Rome-friendly, version. This became the second authorised version. In many ways, it was not as good as the Great Bible, and it did not banish the Geneva Bible either. The third [debatably] authorised version, though

---

[37] While this, along with versification, can help groups to read together the same sections, it has its downside, such as breaking down the literary nature into propositional statements—"give me chapter and verse". See Christopher R Smith's *The Beauty Behind the Mask*, for a fuller argument against the chapter/verse system.

[38] One curiosity is the last verse of 2 Cor.13. The Geneva and the Bishops Bible combined the greetings from God's people with v12. However, the KJV— perhaps in error—numbered it as v13. All three agree that the next part was a verse, so numbered as v13 in Geneva and Bishops Bible, and v14 in KJV. All three had extra wording after 'Amen' about Titus and Lucas. The KJV of 1769 has deleted from the KJV of 1611, the words "..the second Epistle to the Corinthians, was written from Philippos a citie of Macedonia, by Titus and Lucas." Another curiosity is why what made one verse in Lk.6:42, made two verses in Mt.7:4-5.

OT versification goes back at least to Rabbi Isaac Nathan, c.1440. The history of chapter divisions is older and less clear.

[39] This response is similar to the TNIV having annoyed some Evangelicals into updating the RSV into the ESV.

## Bibles for the Masses?

officially to be based on the Bishops, would use only about 4% of it (Metzger 67n). Canterbury's versions weren't Rome delight, but the point had been made that Rome should have an English voice.

### Douay-Rheims

Turbulent days followed the children of Henry 8. In the days of Elizabeth Tudor's England, it was then Roman Catholic scholars who felt the need to flee. One side sought to redeem folk from Roman Catholicism; the other tried to redeem folk back into Roman Catholicism. In those days, civil law and muscle were too often thought to be fair means for Faith Fights. The fight mattered. Some believed conversion into Roman Catholicism was the only way to heaven; some thought that Roman Catholicism was only a sure way to hell: God can be lord to both parties (Rm.14:23).

Monarchs felt insecure unless all their subjects were also subjects of their religious brand—Constantine had felt the same way. The true split was perhaps autocracy and spirituality: "the reformers, although we may now label them [Roman] Catholic and Protestant, were on one side, and the politiques and the traditionalists on the other. Henry 8, the pope, and Charles 5, against More, Loyola, and Luther" (Ives 108). Sadly, as is more common nowadays under Communism, Islam, and the West, the persuasive word was backed by the persuasive hand, for the good of the faithful and the wayward. Turbulent days indeed.

William Allen, a Roman Catholic academic, became an Oxford scholar in exile, and established an English training centre in Douay (now in north France). Perhaps to establish absolute religious freedom for Roman Catholics, Allen convinced the pope to go against the English queen, to undermine her position, and to threaten her life. He would later incite Spain's invasion of England. The gloves came off. The queen moved from religious tolerance to religious cleansing. Roman Catholic opponents came under official persecution.

Government agents and political rebels sought to assassinate Allen. In response, his college moved about 100 miles south-east to Rheims in 1578, where Richard Bristow, another Oxford scholar, took charge.[40] There, a few top scholars under Englishman Gregory Martin,

---

[40] The French spellings are Douai, and Riems.

another Oxford scholar, sought to counter Protestant English versions by producing an English pro-Catholic NT in 1582.[41] It would play a significant part in wording the 1611 KJV. The Rheims NT was translated from the Vulgate, but with a discreet eye on the Greek NT. Its patchy style and Latin terms (for example, supersubstantial bread), often sounded too foreign to English ears.[42] Yet it carried much good plain English, including matchless expressions such as, "throttled him" (Mt.18:28: likewise, Geneva).

Martin's OT section could have been published first, but funding wasn't available until the college had resettled in Douay. Together, his work became known as the *Douay-Rheims* version (1610)—often put simply as the Douay (or Douai).[43] After the Douay, the next big step would be the KJV (page 52). Douay was a blessing to English speaking Roman Catholics, in the sense of being able to access the Bible in their native language, and with the sense of papal blessing. It also endorsed the idea of the Bible being adaptable to local languages. For these reasons those who would see the Bible in the hands of everyone, can honour the name of Gregory Martin.

## From Majority Text to Textus Receptus: Check Mate?

What texts have the East and West tended to use? To begin, it helps to know that the Old Testament was mainly written in Hebrew, and that the New Testament was mainly written in Greek. Together they

---

[41] In footnote sniping, the pope was "the angel of the bottomless pit" (Rv.9:11: Geneva); Calvin was Baal (Mt.6:24: Douay).

[42] Even Protestant versions have kept some Latinisms, which can be OK. For example, unlike the Geneva, the Bishops Bible, followed by the KJV, kept *omnipotent* in Rv.19:6: the Vulgate has *Dominus Deus...omnipotens*. Strangely, some older preachers still assert that Rv.19:6 is the only mention of *omnipotent* in the Bible! They mistake a *version* for the *Bible*. The Bible does *not* mention this word, since the Bible was *not* written in Latin. The Bible has *pantokratōr*, which was used in ten places in the NT (for example 2 Cor.6:18; Rv.1:8; 21:22), but which Bishops/KJV *inconsistently* translated by the Latin in this one place.

[43] This was very heavily revised in 1749 by Richard Challoner, a Douai University scholar, effectively making the DRC a new version. So much so, that even today there is Roman Catholic kickback, a Douay Bible Only element that rejects Bishop Challoner as a creeping Protestant (http://realdouayrheims.com).

## Bibles for the Masses?

form the Bible.[44] Some parts of the Bible were written with small amounts of Aramaic, notably an Aramaic section in *Daniel*, and some Latin loan-words. Besides being translated into other languages, especially Aramaic and Greek, the Hebrew text has continued to be copied, though basically only within ethnic-Jewish circles. I won't spend much time on its transmission history: in Christian circles it rarely had one. Suffice to say that Christian translators who have sought the ancient Hebrew text, have found a generally reliable text.

Let's suppose that the early Hebrew text was translated reliably generations ago, into English, Greek, or Latin. The translations would inevitably have imperfections. Even the Greek text that Jesus and his apostles used, had its imperfections: Jesus wasn't born into a perfect world, and used the imperfect tools at his disposal.[45] He even used an imperfect temple to prophesy about the true temple (Jhn.2). But that's simply how translation goes. The United Nations has batteries of translators, who probably drop some nuances in each sentence they translate, but heh, it's not yet led to war, except over words. Better to get a translator's working approximation of what a Russian president says, than for each U.S. senator to become fluent in Russian.

But translation can never improve on the original. Moreover, word meanings change in any living language—people change them. To translate from a primary translation is to translate into a secondary translation, increasing the amount of lost meaning. Even reverse engineering, for instance, getting back to Hebrew from a Greek translation, would have lost meaning on the return journey. As Jerome realised, the Hebrew text has remained the best overall choice for the OT, although not all Hebrew texts are equal. Incidentally, the Greek form of Jerome's name was *Hieronymus*, itself slightly Latinised from *hieron* (temple/holy place), and *onoma* (name), which meant

---

[44] Judaics usually call it the TaNaK or similar, not seeing it as *old* in the sense of *ended* covenant. Roman Catholicism remains officially tied to some deuterocanonical writings (such as the enjoyable *Tobit*) canonised by the Council of Trent (1545-63). Where such are included, Roman Catholics tend to integrate them, and Protestants tend to separate them.

[45] They had limited access to various texts, Hebrew, Aramaic, and Greek, and were led by God's spirit in proper understanding.

something like 'priestly name', but all that gets lost in translation. *Jerome*, put back into Greek as *Ierōmos,* would be pretty meaningless.

For good and sufficient reasons, most Western OT translators use the Hebrew text, unless they think there are very good reasons for doing otherwise. After all, translations lose some nuances of the source language, so secondary translations fall even further away. But it is also true to say that in some places the later Hebrew text has fallen into error, and ancient translations can help restore the original text. The tenacity of the true text is such that even minor points (such as a copyist might be less attentive to), seem to have been preserved aright somewhere in the multitude of manuscripts globally. This allows the original data to be reconstructed back into place, surgical reconstruction. No fundamental uncertainties exist. We are able to trace most texts through the manuscripts back to the original reading. Yet even if we fall short of the ideal, picking at random any combination of copies from any text-type will give us a rough copy of God's written word. Like a photo at different resolutions, any manuscript will at places be a little fuzzy, but better focus and resolution gives us the better picture.

So, what texts did East and West use? Well, focusing now on the NT, in the beginning were the originals, the autographs. After them came copies of the NT portions. Copies of letters and of Gospels travelled around the Roman Empire and beyond. Some places began to translate into their own native languages (for example Arabic, Armenian, Ethiopic, Gothic, Nubian, and Syriac). Probably even initial copies had mistakes: to err is human. In the West, Jerome's NT used mainly what's called the Western [Greek] Text, to check old Latin versions.

The Eastern section of the Roman Empire became the Byzantine Empire. Its capital, Constantinople, covered most of the Mediterranean Sea coast, but became limited to Turkey. It was basically Christian, and basically Greek, so most surviving Greek NT manuscripts come from the form of text which crystallised in Byzantium. Since it clung to Greek, the Byzantine Text became the Majority [Greek] Text (MT). This became the biggest, but not the best, Greek NT text-type family.

Why wasn't biggest, best? Let's put this another way. In one C1 vote, the Yugo GV, produced in the mid-eighties in Yugoslavia, came out

## Bibles for the Masses?

as the worst car of the C20. OK, imagine if Yugoslavia banned car imports, and kept rolling out their Yugo well into the C22, 100 years after all other countries had discontinued car production. Then in the C23, exploring C22 cars, James T Kirk would presumably mainly find Yugos, and indeed if he found a few crushed remains of Jaguars and Porsches, he might conclude that Yugos had been the best, and dismiss the rest. Why? Because unlike other cars, they had proliferated into the C22. Similarly, other countries had discontinued Greek NT production, but Byzantia kept rolling them out. But its text-type incorporated errors that had slowly infected the text-types it had used to build its own.

Once older and better Greek manuscripts had died out elsewhere, Byzantium's lower quality text-type became, by default, the only Greek show in town. Admittedly, some feel that special preservation must have been at work, God 'sending' the best text to 'Egypt', so to speak, until 'Nazareth' became safe—similarly the seed from Galathilion that had been safely secured until the time was ripe. Yes, there was special preservation, but in the sense that those committed to copying the biblical text were especially committed to God, thus giving special care to their task. But being fallible, and mainly being lay copyists, they still made mistakes.

Jerome found mistakes aplenty in the Old Latin Bibles. He starting position was threefold. 1# for the OT, foundation translation should be from the Hebrew, not Greek, not Latin. 2# that for the NT, the Greek text should be foundational, not Latin. 3# that the Apocrypha was merely sub-canonical, unworthy of incorporation. In this threefold approach, he aimed to focus on God's word, not man's words, and to weed out errors introduced by copyists.

Even cautious Bible copyists and translators, make mistakes. When Jesus affirmed that the smallest requirement of Sinai's covenant, was as secure as heaven and earth, unsinkable as it sailed to the port of its destination (Mt.5:17-9)—which was the messianic age—he affirmed that Sinai's commands remained intact, not that ever Hebrew, Aramaic, or Greek, text, was absolutely flawless. Even Jerome's best Hebrew and Greek manuscripts, had errors.

To some, it seems obvious to simply to put together all the Greek copies we now have, and based on what the majority of manuscripts say, reconstruct the text. They must reject the KJV tradition as wrong, since although it drew manuscripts from the Majority text, it only used a few of the samples available. Is the majority always right, or at least right if it's God's majority? Man, God's creation, casts its majority vote against Christ, though its majority vote for deity. Since I vote for both, I obviously don't assume the majority to be necessarily right or wrong.

This goes for counting Bible manuscripts. Come to think of it, most manuscripts are from the part of the world that had extra centuries to develop extra errors. Yet even this late residue of the Greek text, turns out to be more generally reliable than Latin translations from earlier and better Greek text 'families', because translation always loses more than transmission. Yet surviving Greek manuscripts from earlier days, spread around the Roman Empire, have come to light, enabling an even better Greek text to translate from: crushed Jaguars and Porsches, so to speak, have now been examined by Scotty. Why reconstruct a Yugo when you can reconstruct a Jag? More of this later.

As we move to the KJV, it is good to know that the MT, though not the best representation of the original text, was nevertheless substantially correct. It was from this large MT family pool, that C16 scholars, beginning with Erasmus, were able to compare limited amounts of manuscripts, and then work towards getting back to a standard Greek text. Their result is often misleadingly called the Received Text/*Textus Receptus*/TR.

For the record, the *textus receptus* term comes from a 1633 Greek NT produced by the Elzevirs of Leiden, South Holland. It largely followed Greek NTs of Erasmus, Stephanus, and Beza. Beza had been particularly influential for the KJV. Compared to Beza's text, this Dutch *Novum Testamentum Græce* produced by the Elzevirs, had about 50 minor textual differences. They put the words *textum ergo habes, nunc ab omnibus receptum* into their preface. They were saying that their Greek text was received by all. Their *textum...receptum* (text..received) became *textus receptus*. Retrospectively, the term is used to refer to the reconstructed Greek NT text of Erasmus, and the Greek NT family his text sparked off. There is a whole TR family, which flowed from a few mainly Byzantine manuscripts, and as D A Carson's said, "the Byzantine text-type must not be thought to be the precise equivalent of the TR" (Carson 1985:67). Some speak of *Textus Recepti*.

The KJV TR has in our day and age collected militant supporters. They are usually happy to defend its parent body, the MT, but prefer the KJV TR above all before and all since, deeming non-KJVists to be knaves or fools or deceased. Among themselves, some say that in the KJV we have everything exactly as Peter and Moses wrote it (except it's now in English). A few even say that we have a *better* Bible than Peter and Moses gave us, as if God perfected the Bible through King James.

Are these ideas a reaction to the fear of textual insecurity, preferring the reign of James to Insecurity? When a false look-a-like Aslan was shown to be false, the dwarves reacted to make sure they were never 'taken in' again (C S Lewis' *The Last Battle*, ch.13). It was as illogical as those who, discovering they've been taken in by counterfeit money, refuse thereafter to believe in real money. The dwarves closed their minds to any real Aslan, being wise in the self-conceit of their folly.

The apostle encouraged a robust faith (1 Pt.3:16), and that is what we can enjoy: we have the text *in its essentials* and in almost impeccable accuracy. The TR has been an honest member of the same family, neither the real McCoy nor a false Aslan, and the same goes for what until around the C9, had been the *majority* text, namely the Alexandrian Text. As good and faithful servants, both have played a humble part, and received a "well done".

Unsurprisingly, the TR's history has been quite like the Vulgate's before it, and the NU's[46] after it—troubled. Particularly for the NT, objections that were raised against the 'new version' *Vulgate*, were later raised against the 'new version' KJV, and are nowadays raised against new versions willy-nilly. This is partly because we have an aversion to change (conservatism), and partly because we sincerely respect the biblical witness. Some bitterly attack major new versions simply because their tipple has been long established: Moses we know but who is this fellow? Some join them because they prefer

---

[46] NU means the joint Nestles-Aland and the United Bible Society's, Greek NT text.

antidisestablishmentarianism, protestors at heart, or really fear that God's wrath is on the new and all who sail in her.

The faithful Jiang Wei fought valiantly for the Han Dynasty, even though its last emperor Liu Shan was no longer a good representative of the Hans, and heaven had moved on. In the U.S. American civil war, many good folk on both sides, shot each other to preserve their flags. Such conflict between the good is grief. Yet perhaps even foolish attacks help establish good versions (Heb.12:27): "but test them all; hold on to what is good" (NIV: 1 Ths.5:21). Tests can be good. But those disturbers of the peace, if they are dishonest knaves rather than honest fools, will have God to answer to. History shows that a century or so on, common welcome replaces bitterness, and the church is united, ready again to divide and attack the next major 'new version'. Such is life. Such is the human story.

Like the Vulgate, the KJV has been exalted by historical factors. The British Empire has been among the largest empires in traced history. It might well have had the most turf ever (23%), though for percentage of global population, it had a mere a snippet at 20% (about 14$^{th}$ place), compared to the C5 BC Achaemenid Empire's 45%. But then the KJV wasn't around in C5 BC. Since 1611, only the Mughal (turf 3%), and Qing (turf 10%), empires, have had a higher percentage of the global population. A vast empire Britain had bent, its Bible it did show, and everywhere that Britain went, King James was sure to go. Therefore, inevitably the KJV was a big player in evangelising the British Empire.[47]

But could such evangelism have been done with any other English version? Yes! The Geneva version did well among the Mayflower Pilgrims (1620) and Winthrop Puritans (1630). Did the King James' version make the Christians, or did the Christians make the version? Well, no Christians before 1611 were made by the KJV, although they did make many versions in many languages. Could not an equal or better job have been done had Britain used a different text-type?

---

[47] Many downsides are obvious, as gun and gospel, and cultural insensitivity, has often gone hand in hand, along with the idea that church makes Christians. But let this not blind us to what virtue there has been through evangelism and, often alongside, colonialism.

As said, some believe that divine providence preserved the Majority Text (MT), as if witnessing that this text-type alone was to be used. Some don't like the KJV when it doesn't conform to the MT, and some don't like the MT when it doesn't conform to the KJV. Providence is a funny thing, even preserving the minority text-types. That the KJV was an MT-class English version, gave it equal footing with the Geneva or Bishops. It superseded them because of some factors in its favour, such as establishmentarianism.

## The Terrific, Terrible, or Tentative, TR?

"The textual basis of the TR is a small number of haphazardly collected and relatively late minuscule manuscripts. In about a dozen places its reading is attested by no known Greek manuscript witness" (Carson 1985:36). This history is largely the history of Europeans who helped establish a Greek NT text, thereby moving us away from the Latin text. Since Greek was the original language of the NT, other things being equal, Greek will be the more authentic. But how authentic is authentic, when to some extent the Greek text of the TR was translated from Latin, and by and large was based on Greek manuscripts which had suffered varied corruption over centuries? However, a TR was likely to offer a more authentic text than the prevailing Latin, and the ideal goal would have been to get hold of the originals, penned by such as James and John, Paul and Peter, alas almost certainly long gone. But working back in that direction, we have the mighty pen of Erasmus.

### Erasmus

This big search for the Greek autographs, at least the *ipsissima verba* (actual words), was born in a C16 swing back to original texts—why be satisfied with mere copies of copies of copies? C16 Puritans were those who "wished to abolish episcopacy and remodel [Anglicanism[48]] on the lines which Calvin had laid down for Geneva", and Humanists were those who "taught, or learned, or at least strongly favoured, Greek

---

[48] Christian denominations have churches, but I reject any talk of denominations being churches. Whether or not Anglicanism is an anachronism here (yet see www.meetthepuritans.com/blog/puritans-anglicans), I prefer it throughout.

and the new kind of Latin" (Lewis 1954:17-8). Christian Humanists were Christian scholars who dug back to language source.

One such was the brilliant Desiderius Erasmus (d.1536). He was friendlier with Roman hierarchicalism, than with Reformation fracturalism, but he acted like a Baptist dressed as a Roman Catholic.[49] Following a friends' request, in 6 months he produced a Greek NT, rushing to publish before the rival *Complutensian* came out. Since only the Byzantines had been well stocked with Greek manuscripts, obviously their copies were the easiest to get hold of to produce a Greek text for subsequent translation work. An underlying and unavoidable problem was that the Byzantine text-type had picked up and perpetuated many errors. Lots of copying, lots of copies, and lots of errors. It came with the territory. He drank from a polluted pool.

He produced 5 editions (1516,19,22,27,35). His 1519 edition was used by one-time friend, Martin Luther. Erasmus asked for some help from the ancient codex Vaticanus, possibly evacuated from Constantinople before the Muslims invaded, and safe in its new home at the Vatican library. However, it had too many differences for his liking, and he quickly assumed it must have come from the Latin Vulgate, not realising that it was more parent than child.

His material was actually quite small, but what he had he used well, considering his then common idea (*viz* that scholars improve) that what was most *recent*, was most *reliable*. A friend did him a not too clever copy of a very early Greek manuscript of *Revelation*, which in fact lacked the last six verses: Erasmus turned Latin text into Greek. Some MT advocates claim that he had access to hundreds of manuscripts, shortlisting only the Byzantine best. Well, why then did he have to reverse engineer the Latin into Greek for those missing verses?

Erasmus pioneered the TR, raising objection from JVO (Jerome's Vulgate Only) folk. Ironically, in his days Jerome had himself been shouted down by the Old-Latin-Only folk over changing the text. Yet Jerome's

---

[49] He argued that believers, whether or not sprinkled/baptised as infants, should be baptised as believers. If only receivers of Christ are Christians, this ultimately undermines the whole idea of territorial religion, and perhaps the idea of there being Christian culture.

had become the traditional text, and so Erasmus faced the shouts of protest—"Erasmus prefers the Greek, but the Latin Vulgate is God's inspired text"! So knaves and fools said.

Some likewise would have us throw out the Greek and Hebrew and all the standard texts before the KJV. That's like the 1611 KJV was as big a birth as Christ's, as if before 1611 God's people had like Israel of old been kept in the dark by God until its Birth, as if non-English speakers don't have access to God's Written Word. It's like Catholics saying that mass should only be said in Latin—good enough for Paul.

Erasmus' approach was a cut down version of today's textual critics. Few today match his genius, but they can begin with better insight and with better resources. We now have a vast library of manuscripts, an updated knowledge of Greek—especially Koine Greek (flourished from 300 BC to 300 AD)—and an improved modelling of text-types. Eat your heart out, Erasmus! He clearly saw that the manuscript record had many variants (copyists make mistakes), that there were ways to weed out these variants, and that if he was going to reconstruct the Latin, he first needed to reconstruct the Greek.

For instance, he established the order of words in Rm.4:1, not by the majority vote of Greek texts, but by going back to the early Fathers' quotes of the verse. Even choosing between different words wasn't always clear. For Rm.10:17 he had to guess—did Paul write *God*, or *Christ*? The Vulgate read *Christ*, and indeed Paul's point wasn't about the wider issue of the Bible, but rather about the message (*word*) about Christ being needed for Christian conversion. Not knowing that $p^{46}$, ℵ, and B, confirmed the Vulgate's Western Text, he opted for the higher and wider term, *God*. That choice carried into the KJV. He knew that some mistakes had happened over similarly written or sounding words.

Let's pick up on four things from his encounter with Rm.12:11. One, we see that similar looking words—*kurios* and *kairos* (lord and time)—could confuse the manuscript witness: they could look even more alike when scribes used various forms of shorthand, and the words were in Greek capitals (uncials), and sentences didn't use spacing between words. Two, we see that Erasmus was open to change: he initially opted for *lord*, but he *switched* in his subsequent editions, to *time*. Three, we see that Erasmus opted for the *minority* witness: *time* was the *minority* witness. To affirm that the minority can be right, is not affirm that it is always right. In this case, the majority was right. Four, we can see that Erasmus was fallible. Sadly, Stephanus went along his switch, as did Tyndale/Coverdale/Matthew/Great. Happily, Beza didn't, and, affirming the Vulgate and Wycliffe, the KJV (and the NIV) rightly went with Beza, using *lord*. Weighing the evidence is not always straightforward, but it should be done.

Erasmus also knew that familiarity with a phrase (for example, *Jesus Christ*) could cause additions to the text: copyists sometimes wrote "not what they found in the manuscripts, but what was fixed in their memory" (White 1995:59). Once in a supermarket, a suited shopper mildly imprecated, *Jesus*! Aloud I added, "is lord", completing 1 Cor.12:3: *Jesus is lord*. Politely abashed, the guy responded, "what do you say to that?" We both smiled, and wandered off with our cogitations and carrier bags.

How many copyists have heard the manuscript reader say *Jesus*, and then written *Jesus Christ*, or heard *Jesus Christ*, and written *Lord Jesus Christ*, unintentionally duplicating expressions? Even larger chunks could transfer. Erasmus suspected that "baptism that I am baptised with", in Mk.10:38, had been accidentally duplicated into Mt.20:22, but for the time being felt it should remain pending future judgement. With better texts in play, we can now see that his suspicion was right: the phrase only belongs in *Mark*.

Judging God's Word is one thing, but judging what God's Word *is* is a process every biblical textual critic must do so, so that others may read what God's Word says, not what it does not say. Erasmus' work, somewhat akin to Origen's work on the OT text, set the ball rolling for rediscovering the authentic NT text, on which translations should be based. That job would be carried out by two more outstanding names, before hitting something of a pause.

## Stephanus

In 1528 Robert Estienne, hereafter referred to by his Latinised form as Robert(us) *Stephanus*, had made a critical edition of the Vulgate, based on variants of it. He was a Parisian of humanist (that is, classicist) father, had his own printing press, was converted from Roman Catholicism to Huguenotism, and moved to Geneva to avoid flak.

Later, from Erasmus' 1522 edition. Stephanus produced four Greek NT editions, and his 3rd, in 1550, which also weighed Rome's *Complutensian* (1522),[50] became British standard, and is loosely called the TR (Scorgie, Strauss, and Voth 183).[51] In some places, the Erasmus-Stephanus text translated the Latin Vulgate into Greek, such as 1 Jhn.5:7, nowadays called the Johannine Comma, which we'll look at later. But Stephanus was not the last word before the KJV.

## Beza

Stephanus was modified by Theodore Beza, John Calvin's successor. On many texts they differed, although Stephanus' 3rd and 4th editions, and Beza's editions, were extremely similar. Beza used textual variants which Stephanus had listed, and with some good manuscripts he had access to, added some more, besides modifying Stephanus 1550, at times using 'conjectural emendations' (that is, "it's got to be something like this though I haven't got a manuscript to prove it").

One such piece of educated guesswork, was replacing the correct *hosios* (*pure*), with *esomenos* (*shall be*), in Rv.16:5's "is...was...shall be". Unhappily, disaffirming the Vulgate and Wycliffe, the KJV affirmed Beza, using *shall be*. "And I heard the Angel of the waters say, Thou art righteous, O Lord, which art, and wast, and shalt be, because thou hast judged thus" (KJV 1611). Happily, John Wesley (and the NIV) reverted to the MT, the Vulgate/Wycliffe–Bishops: "And I heard the angel of the waters saying, Righteous art thou, who art, and who wast, the Gracious one, because thou hast judged thus".[52] Beza's main editions were 1588, 1589, and especially 1598.

---

[50] Sometimes dated 1514, printing the *Complutensian* was delayed until it got papal approval.

[51] It is the first Greek Testament that has a critical apparatus—that is, footnotes indicating alternative textual readings. His next edition, in 1551, was almost exactly the same as the 1550, but was the first Greek NT to have verse divisions, and lacked the 1550 critical apparatus. About 25 years earlier, Santes Pagnino had unsuccessfully versified the Latin NT.

[52] The term *lord* is neither in the MT nor in the original Vulgate, but creeped into later Latin editions, passing thus through Wycliffe into English, and was rightly removed by Wesley. Wesley's *gracious* could be put as *pure/holy*.

## Elzevirs

The KJV wasn't a primary translation, but it was a great revision within a translation family.[53] Its aim was to remodel the Bishops Bible, consulting other versions and the Greek NT line produced by Erasmus 1516—Beza. Thus, its own unique text drew on the early stages of producing a standard [Greek NT] text. The art of textual criticism[54] was a relatively new art, and in the age before the motorcar, access to surviving Greek texts around the world was very very limited. The scholars who pioneered the art of building a Greek NT text for translations into English, were never fully happy with their efforts—hence they kept plugging away at revisions. Later scholars continued the trend, although the ecclesiastical authority of the KJV, along with ignorance of a better textual type, reduced a sense of urgency and increased the risk of resistance to change.

As mention above (page 39), the Elzevir Printers of Leiden (a Dutch town about 200 miles east of Nottingham castle) produced a 1633 'TR' edition: neither their first nor their last. Daniel Heinsius' *Textus Receptus*, has become a flag that some attack, and some defend, but the publisher's blurb wasn't meant as a dogmatic title. It didn't mean that their text was exactly the *ipsissima verba* of the NT writers, and in fact their TR differed slightly from the KJV NT. It did mean that the publishers had kept very reliably to the textual stream of Erasmus–Beza: it is almost identical to Beza 1565. Some KJVO folk actually dismiss the TR as misleading us away from the KJV.

A basic TR family flowed from Erasmus. In a popular sense of first mention, we may trace the TR to the Elzevir $2^{nd}$ edit, practically similar to Theodore Beza's text, itself practically similar to Robertus Stephanus' $4^{th}$ edit, as "corrected in about one hundred and fifty

---

[53] Strictly speaking the KJV was simply an excellent *revision*, made by top class translators using existing versions of Scripture (Metzger 76). It was a happy mix of the vocabulary and idiom of Tyndale, the melody and harmony of Coverdale, and the scholarship and accuracy of the Genevan version.

[54] *Textual Criticism* could, if the term were not so widespread, be better called *Textual Analysis*, and textual *critics*, textual *analysts*. In biblical studies it is not criticising God's written word, only critiquing its human transmission, so honours God.

passages according to the readings of the Codex Claromontanus, the Codex Cantabrigiensis, the Latin, Syriac, and Arabic, versions, and certain critical notes of Henry Stephanus." And Stephanus' 4<sup>th</sup> edit was roughly the same as Erasmus' 5<sup>th</sup> edit, which was based on "five rather [then] recent manuscripts corrected in about a hundred passages according to the reading of the Complutensian Polyglot." The smallness of changes should not surprise, since those after Erasmus tried to remain close to him, though factoring in some different manuscripts. We may say that textual critics sometimes followed "a tradition of timidity", even as Daniel Wallace said about translators.[55] They were all examples of a wider family that may be traced at least to the C4. "For about a century the Received Text held undisputed sway; its editions numbered about one hundred and seventy."[56]

## The Trinitarian Bible Society and the Great Chicken

As they looked into various texts, evangelicals such as John Wesley haven't always agreed with the TRs. For example, Edward Hills noted that in 5 alternatives noted by Erasmus, John Calvin chose 3 as being better than the TR, and even added 18 other texts he preferred to the TR (White 1995:69-70). The Reformers were happy both to use and improve the TR. Ah, ah, the TR.

The Elzevirs sparked off the TR term, but not the text that the Trinitarian Bible Society (TBS) favours. How did it form? In 1804 the British and Foreign Bible Society, seeking Bible accessibility for all, began. Mary Jones, a Welsh girl, had been its inspiration. It did not buy into any one version. When ethical objections arose against supplying on demand Roman Catholic versions and the Apocrypha, and about being in bed with anti-trinitarians (Socinians), a split was all but inevitable. Both sides wished to be Christian servants, but some wished to be Protestant servant-leaders.

In a key speech, J E Gordon argued that "no person rejecting the doctrine of a triune Jehovah can be considered a member of a Christian Institution". I'd certainly say that trinitarianism should be the core of the city of God, even if its outskirts aren't trinitarian. Yahweh (a.k.a.

---

[55] https://danielbwallace.com/2014/03/24/can-we-still-believe-the-bible

[56] Main quotes here are from www.newadvent.org/cathen/05286a.htm.

Jehovah) is three persons, and trinitarianism is a key messianic revelation. We do well to heed Gordon. The TBS was formed in 1831. It has never been unconditionally committed to the KJV, since affirming that translation is always by fallible people. Or, in its parlance, *men*, conservatively tending to sageism. But it sought to fly its flag over an existing version, excluding a Roman Catholic version. It asked itself, Should I adopt the KJV?

As noted, the KJV was basically a mixture of TR and earlier English versions. When a fourth Authorised Version was commissioned, F H A Scrivener was asked to construct a TR, based as far as possible on the original KJV. He concluded that the KJV hadn't always used a Greek TR which he could identify. As he had worked through the KJV, whenever it did not match a pre-existing TR member—for example if based on the Latin—he substituted Beza's 1598 text.

His, *The Authorised Edition of the English Bible (1611): Its Subsequent Reprints and Modern Representatives*, of 1884, lists what he called the "wrong readings of the Bible of 1611 amended in later editions"—see its pages 147-202. Another appendix lists actual differences between the two 1611 editions. He was in fact an advocate not of the TR, but of the MT, and has the honour of having been the first academic to publicly differentiate between them. On the *English Revised Version* committee, he locked horns with Westcott and Hort in strong opposition to the Alexandrian text, but largely lost the argument.

Rejecting Westcott and Hort's challenge to the existing sense of security, Scrivener's TR became the convenient standard for the TBS, which decided that the KJV's *basis* was the best among acceptable TRs. The TBS retains the flexibility to dismiss KJV texts in favour of the Geneva, or the Geneva in favour of Tyndale, or Tyndale in favour of the KJV, and all in favour of any modern version which commits to the Erasmus–Elzevirs' TR family, in which it holds that the autographic text is fully contained.

Some knock the TBS, because if its Scrivener text was based purely on the KJV, does that not make the KJV the chicken to the Scrivener egg, so to speak? However, I don't think that the TBS holds the KJV to be the authentic chicken, simply a good egg. What Scrivener sought was simply the chicken (text) that laid the KJV egg (translation). The TBS deems that chicken to be best in the Erasmus–Elzevirs coop on C16/ C17 chickens. The TBS knows that given that hypothetical text, the KJV translators still had to make translation choices within the scope allowed them, and that any translator is, if not a *traitor* to the host language, at least *traduttore transpositore,* a *transformer* of a text "from one linguistic-cultural context to another" (Scorgie, Strauss, and Voth 47).

In short, the TBS sees that the KJV translators unavoidably both lost linguistic content and used words nowadays readily misunderstood. It also sees that by getting back to the KJV's TR base through Scrivener, we can repackage that TR for today's readers. Is that needed? Knowing their own limitations, the KJV translators might well have been saddened that their work has lasted as long as it has. Their wood once enlivened our hearts in worship; have their ashes buried our hearts in idolatry?[57] As their Preface says, "the Kings Speech which hee uttered in Parliament, being translated into French, Dutch, Italian, and Latine, is still the Kings Speech, though it be not interpreted by every Translator with the like grace." They gloried in the Kings Speech, not in their translation.

Did the TBS fixate on the wrong chicken coop. The TR chicken was once a Byzantine egg, which itself was once an egg from birds hatched by the great chicken, the originally God-breathed text. Why *only* give the Erasmus–Elzevirs' TR the benefit of the doubt? Even as James Ryder followed the wrong bird in Sherlock Holmes' *The Blue Carbuncle,* so I'd ask the TBS—are you following the wrong bird?

An interesting aside. On their site, to knock the NKJV (which has He/ Shulammite captions), Rev G Hamstra presented the idea that *Song of Songs* was an allegory about Christ.[58] Here the issue is neither one of text nor of translation, but one of micro-commentary, added features to holy writ. Interestingly, having concluded that the NKJV is not Christ-honouring here, Hamstra concluded by finding fault with the KJV reading of 8:10, saying that *peace,* not *favour,* is the correct translation, citing the 1560 Geneva version which reads *peace.* This confirms that the KJV itself isn't the TBS' chicken. Fine, but going the

---

[57] Is.44 ridiculed the folly of the Babylonians who initially were blessed by the wood they then transformed into an item of worship.

[58] www.tbsbibles.org/pdf_information/151-1.pdf

extra mile, fairness might have led Hamstra to mention that the NKJV *also* reads *peace* here. But fairness did not so lead: the Geneva had his favour; the NKJV had not! The TBS deems the NKJV as somewhat unsatisfactory, particularly because of its generous footnoting of the NU text—how dare the NKJV look beyond the TR-Only coop!

## Summary

The TR should have been a minor yet beneficial sideshow in the restoration of the biblical text, blessing its own generation and empowering the next generation of textual scholars. And it would have been, but for human tradition. Debate about the TR is only about the NT textual basis. The issue of the OT textual basis, is generally much smaller and quieter. The TR was created by a few key players, to whom our thanks is due. Sadly, as with Moses' Snake (2 Kg.18:4), what started out as a blessing, has become a snare that stumbles us. Let's move on to a burning issue, KJV supremacy.

## Part 2     King James: A New Hope?
## Prologue

A new peak arose in the hills of Bible translation, which by the power and the glory of the British Empire's Crown and Clergy, put an English Bible version on the global map. It gained monopoly status, to the extent that some today can praise the 'novel' reading from another version with an, "It's good, but it isn't the Bible". Some, reluctant to praise any other version, prefer to say "It's bad, since it isn't the KJV Bible." That perspective asserts many reasons why only the King James Version will do. We'll look at some of these reasons, and see if they are more heat than light. We'll even look at some counter charges that the KJV is not good enough.

# Chapter 4   A New Fight
## King's Champion

The House of Tudor is dead. Long live the bonny House of Stuart. After King Henry 8's last legitimate heir died, Scotland's King James 6, double great-great grandson to King Henry 7 (and through whom came Queen Elizabeth 2), became England's King James 1 in 1603. In Scotland, the pragmatic James had been a Presbyterian king. In England, he more naturally fitted into the idea of an Episcopalian king overseeing a national church network. He was a canny king, and no Puritan ally.

Did those pestilent Puritans have issues with the Bishops Bible? Tough, but King James had issues with their Geneva.[59] Most bishops were happy with the Bishops. Political tactic: Let the Puritans think they've won at least one major concession by dumping the Bishops Bible, but give them a Bishops' update, not the Geneva update of their dreams, quoth he.

Following his directives, translators (including a few token Puritans) worked in Cambridge, Oxford, and Westminster, consulting both the Hebrew/Greek texts and some earlier versions. In particular, they were to stay as close to the Bishops as they could justify. It was fine to pay or promote them, so long as the king's purse wasn't touched. Established church words, *prelatical* words, were to be preferred: for

---

[59]   Denying that monarchs were semi-divine, even calling some tyrants, it undermined his security of tenure, so was dubbed the worst version (Bruce 1986:97; Scorgie, Strauss, and Voth 205). Likewise Voth signalled that King James wished the Bishops Bible to be the foundational English version, rather than the Geneva, because the Bishops Bible never brought out the social justice meaning behind the Hebrew theme of ṣedaq (which might have focused attention on monarchical injustice) while the Geneva "made a genuine effort to express the wider range of meaning" (Scorgie, Strauss, and Voth 332)— Puritans held to inner righteousness and social justice. Karl Marx' complaint about religion being the people's opiate was partly based on the idea that social justice was often relegated in favour of individual relationship with God. Many today argue that politics and religion don't mix, yet true religion can marshal politics towards looking after the socially needy (Jas.1:27).

## A New Fight

example, *church*, not *congregation*, *baptise*, not *wash*.[60] And nothing written to undermine the king.

Somewhat loosely, the translators spoke of their work as being newly *translated* from the original languages, though adding that they had done so with a close eye on previous versions. Their foundation document had been the authorised version of 1568 (Bishops Bible), though because of KJV eclecticism, only a small bit of the Bishops made its way through. In today's terms, the King James' Version was a revision, an upgrade, a semi-translation. It was a successful attempt "to make a good [version] better, or [put another way,] out of many good ones, one principal good one", as its *Translators to the Readers* put it. The Bishops Bible was dead; the Geneva would soon wither.

The bishop of London (later Archbishop), Richard Bancroft, didn't want a KJV. But he was told it was either that, or a Puritan version. Alarmed, he made sure that the KJV would be in his image, not a puritan's. He determined the methodology, the translators, and even smuggled himself in as a final and secret editor, undermining the tiny puritans' input. They, poor bunnies, could take their precious Geneva Bible, leave the Old World, and seek elsewhere to worship without state bullying.

Nowadays, Christian escape to the New World is no longer an option: the Mayflower and Arbella are no more, and the Last Ship has sailed from Mithlond. Unless space flight ever becomes a Christian option, we must await the good ship Eschaton, while shining our light in our darkening world. Interestingly, the KJV would soon overshadow the Geneva in the Colonies. One reason was that, rightly or wrongly, it better allowed talk about the New World as in a national covenant

---

[60] One might wish that *immersion* had been used, undermining the idea of infant *sprinkling* which had become known as 'baptism'. The Greek *baptizō*, after all, carries the idea of immersion, not of sprinkling. Likewise, *congregation*, rather than *church*, would have more focus on rank-and-file believers, focusing on the ecclesia being the people rather than the buildings or leaders. With good grammatical grounds Orthodoxism holds to full immersion, though with debateable exegetical ground immersion as regenerational (www.bible.ca/cr-Orthodox.htm). Likewise *overseer*, rather than *bishop*, would have loosened the knot of ecclesiastical hierarchy.

with God: the Geneva "stressed the individual covenant of grace" (Noll 64).

Another reason was that the English Crown dominated much of the Colonies until the American Revolution (1776-83). Besides, England printed cheap KJVs. Publisher Robert Aitken (Dalkeith Scotland, to Philadelphia) made the KJV the Congress Authorised Version for the USA (1782). In England, many still preferred the Geneva to the KJV, but King James could bide his time.

Did it become the third Authorised Version in England? Officially, we don't know. Sure, the king planted the seed, but did he or parliament authorise the fruit? Probably the king, but documentary evidence was probably burnt in the 1618 fire in Whitehall, along with other official documents dating 1600-13 (Scorgie, Strauss, and Voth 206). In itself, "appointed to be read in churches" doesn't prove much. Words change. In those days *appointed* simply meant that its layout (format/design) and features were designed to facilitate church use. Probably the king would have blest his baby, and I doubt that parliament would have naysaid him. Considering its kingly inception, I doubt that Anglicanism alone would have forced it upon his subjects. So, although documentary authorisation can be neither proved, nor disproved, parliament's authorisation was almost surely *de facto*, and most likely *de jure*.

## **Church Shenanigans**

The church in England was divided into two basic factions, the Anglican establishment, and the Puritans, some of whom were Anglicans. Establishment and monarchy favoured the unloved KJV, because they disfavoured the Geneva. Or rather, the Geneva Package: the translation wasn't a problem, but the anti-tyranny notes were. On the other hand, the Puritans felt that even the common people should judge monarchs for tyranny, and so enjoyed the way the Geneva justified people-power over princes and popes.

In line with king and clergy, British printing of the Geneva was squeezed out in 1616, and English printing given monopoly power, of which the king took royalties. James 1 probably had slow death, not sudden death, in mind for the hated Geneva. The establishment was sufficiently strong to plant the KJV in English churches, though the

## A New Fight

Geneva was usually preferred elsewhere, particularly for its empowering notes. The KJV gained power top-down, as the Geneva was discouraged by crown and Anglican hierarchy.

Before a Puritan parliament was empowered to muzzle the monarchy as the supreme government, Charles 1, James' heir, had empowered a new archbishop, William Laud, who happily muzzled the Geneva. It was unpatriotic, he said, to buy in Genevas, since this threatened the livelihoods of British printers, and thus the British printing base. His was a Buy British platform. He kept quiet about the exorbitant profits the royal printer was making from overcharging. But all's fair in love and war, it is said. Without good English orders for the English Geneva, European publishing of it ended in 1644: two years after the English Civil War began; three years after Laud was gaoled.

At last, a Puritan parliament was in power. It seems that it aimed to replace the KJV by producing a better version, not by kick starting the aging Geneva. However, in 1660, King Charles 2 was again in office, and the Puritans' chance for change had come and gone. The Geneva, and Puritan drive to upgrade the KJV, then became part of a lost cause. Monarchy was deemed biblical; the Geneva seditious. Let the KJV live; let wounds heal: *vox populi.* Put 50 candles on the KJV's birthday cake. Put over 2,000 Anglican Puritan heads on the block. Gleefully Archbishop Gilbert Sheldon chopped 'em off, ecclesiastically speaking, that is. The Act of Uniformity 1662, called for ecclesiastical surrenders (Latitudinarianism, a.k.a. Low Church), or resignations (Dissenters, Non-conformists) by Black Bartholomew's Day. Religious intolerance sought to squeeze all into the one socio-religious mould.

The KJV had survived the battle, unscathed, unchanged. Over time, initial disquiet would quieten, and it would become seen as a monumental work of English literature, unifying language, thus the people, in line with the 1662 Act of Uniformity. Missionary work sent it around the world as the Best of British, and it may have played a significant part in helping the USA, awash with many language groups, to opt for English as its main language. Through its privileged position, the KJV had gone global. It helped unify an English-speaking Empire. But they do err who assume that its style came *de nova*. For, as Mark A Pike noted, when assessing the literary influence of the KJV in particular, many of the earlier versions contained the same expressions (Pike 83).

## **Eclectic Emergence**

Many don't know that, like many other versions, the KJV NT was created by taking bits from a previous version here, a previous version there, and checking them to a number of Greek NT texts, choosing which bits to use, to modify, or to replace. Unless one has the actual papyri or whatever penned by John or Jude, one has to look at what copies remain, and then make eclectic decisions, a skilled patchwork.

The so-called Textus Receptus, didn't exist as a manuscript. What did exist was an emerging family of a Textus Receptus type NT. Within this family, E F Hills said that the KJV used a mixture of sources, so, while mainly TR, it was also an independent variety of it. The phrase *TR* first came out after the KJV, but may be used retrospectively for the small family of texts.

Since then, a few attempts have been made to create a TR based on the KJV, and before then were some Greek NTs that sought to become the standard received text. The KJV NT was an eclectic text, based on weighing a number of Greek NTs, as well as other versions. As all families, the TR family disagrees among itself, and also with the Majority/Byzantine Text. Much KJVO argument is loaded onto versions that came out after the KJV, almost as if only after the KJV did heretical versions really began. Let's take some examples.

**Lk.2:22**: It may be *meet* (KJV for worthwhile) to note that here Tyndale put *their*, without apparently thinking that that implied that the baby Jesus was a sinner. The Pentateuch makes clear that the purification rite didn't focus on moral sin. For example, if a layperson had enjoyed a special time of holiness (Nazarene Vow), purification, the 'sin' offering, would desacralise them, returning them to their *normal* state of religious cleanness. Similarly, mothers didn't sin by giving birth, but they weren't exactly in their *normal* get up and go state immediately after childbirth!

Similarly, the baby Jesus hadn't sinned. It's possible that *their*, meant Mary and Joseph, if as likely Joseph helped with childbirth, but I think a typical situation would have been meant. There was a whole raft of symbolism about blood being normal inside a body, but abnormal outside a body—too much loss and you'll die. Levitical rites taught a lot through the concepts of the supranorm, the norm, and the subnorm. Nobuyoshi Kiuchi looked back to birth reminding Israelites of the fall, man's distanciation from Yahweh, and the rite of purification as reminding them of how the relational norm should be: "it is not only the mother but also the child who is alienated from Yahweh's presence" (Kiuchi 219).

Accusing others of the *wrong* text, KJVO-ists[61] tend to overlook Tyndale's acceptance of *their*, and the fact that the 'Catholic' Douay Rheims was followed by the KJV here. In line with the evangelist John Wesley, the NIV now simply avoids specifying whether *her* or *they*.

| KJV | Agree | Disagree |
|---|---|---|
| Lk.2:22 | Beza | Erasmus; Stephanus; MT, NU, Tyndale |

**Lk.17:36**: With this, KJV Onlyism tends to accuse later versions of *deleting* text. In alliance with Wycliffe and Rome, it added text to Tyndale and to the original Authorised Version, namely the Great Bible. Though John Wesley bought into this addition, John Nelson Darby did not. The NIV, siding with the majority of Greek manuscripts, excludes it too, noting that it was probably copied late in history, from *Matthew* to Luke: let *Matthew* be Matthew and *Luke* be *Luke*.

| KJV | Agree | Disagree |
|---|---|---|
| Lk.17:36 | Stephanus 4; Beza; John Wesley | Erasmus; Stephanus 1-3; MT, NU, Tyndale, Great, John Darby, NIV |

**Jhn.1:28**: Here, it seems that some tried to correct the text from Bethany, to Bethabara (Origen?), or to Betharaba. But no correction was needed, except in understanding. Probably, *Bēthania* (Anglicised as Bethany, a town near Jerusalem), was an alternative way to spell *Batanaia* (Anglicised as *Batanea*, a region east of Galilee). Place names were less fixed in those days, with varient spelling reflecting varient pronunciations. In John's account, Jesus' way led from one Bethany to another Bethany,

---

[61] Christians to whom "modern versions", is a dirty and/or diabolical term.

the so-to-speak of semantic wordplay.[62] We can see the original Bethany text both in the C10 West Saxon Gospels (*Bethaniä*), in the Vulgate (*Bethania*), and in Wycliffe (*Bethanye*). Tyndale introduced Bethabara into the English. R Riesner located the oldest manuscript (*Bēthania*) to be p66, dating around the second quarter of C.

| KJV | Agree | Disagree |
|---|---|---|
| Jhn.1:28 | Erasmus; Stephanus 3-4; Beza, Tyndale | Stephanus 1-2; MT, NU, Wycliffe |

**Heb.9:1**: For this, the KJV accepted Wycliffe/Bishops, over Tyndale, and most NU versions agree with its choice. The text only says *first*, but *first covenant* is a safe expansion that the NIV happily endorses. Some might accuse both the KJV and the NIV of *deleting* text, then *adding* to it. The NIV is happy to go with the KJV where the NIV believes the KJV to be correct.

| KJV | Agree[63] | Disagree |
|---|---|---|
| Heb.9:1 | Erasmus; Beza, NU, Wycliffe, NIV | Stephanus; MT (first tent), Tyndale |

"The KJV translators...drew from a variety of sources, but mainly from Erasmus, Stephanus, and Beza. When these sources diverged, the decision lay with the KJV translators themselves. Edward F Hills, a staunch defender of the KJV, listed a number of instances where the KJV translators had to decide between competing readings" (White 1995:67). I have used some of these above. All those have the KJV siding with Beza, but note that Hills noted that according to Scrivener (1884), in 252 passages of disagreement, the KJV agreed with Stephanus against Beza 59 times. Obviously the KJV translators didn't believe that there was a perfect TR within the textual family they visited. This discordance shows, not that God didn't divinely guide the KJV into the right textual choices, but that if he did he did not always guide those the KJV used, into the right textual choices, even allowing them

---

[62]    www.tyndalehouse.com/tynbul/library/TynBull_1987_38_02_Riesner_BethanyBeyondJn1.pdf

[63]    All agree the text isn't *skēnē* (tent); all versions supply the implied *diathēkē*.

# A New Fight

to chop and change their texts. Indeed, if the text needed not to be flawless in 1211, why does it need to be flawless 2011? I think of a quip where, having been told that God had waited until 1611 to breathe the only authorised version, the other guy asked, "wow, did he really hold his breath that long?"

Neither the KJV nor the NIV should be condemned as being eclectic, though their particular judgements, as too their policies, remain open to disagreement. Since even the KJV 1611 editions varied from each other, and the KJV 1769 is the general form now (though with several minor variations), *which* KJV is Only to be used?[64] "The KJV that is carried by the average KJV Only advocate today looks very different than the edition that came off the press of Robert Barker in 1611" (White 1995:78), though the great majority of changes are of typography[65] and spelling. Even without using other than MT manuscripts, it might seem that access to more manuscripts than the KJV had, would improve the textual basis. Indeed, some scholars *both* reject other text-types, *and* argue for the MT, since the TR only tapped into so few manuscripts within the Majority "God preserved" family.

## **KJV Transmission**

In England, Bible printing was a royal monopoly, and monarchy didn't always choose the best printers. In the early years, the King's Printer (Robert Barker, London) made numerous gaffes in the KJV text. When Oxford and Cambridge came into play, they made more accurate texts, but even today, their KJVs differ in certain places, to

---

[64] There is now *The New Cambridge Paragraph Bible, with the Apocrypha* (as the original KJV had), edited by David Norton, which has restored as well as it could the 1611 text to a pre-printer stage, but given modern spellings and presentation to make studying easier. Arguably, for consistency, KJVO should embrace this and repent of its adoption of the 1769 edition, minute though the textual changes may be. Incidentally, Norton estimated that Blayney's standard text has about 11,000 departures from the 1611 text, excluding spelling/punctuation changes (Norton's *A Textual History of the King James Bible*, 2005:117).

[65] www.lamblion.com/articles/articles_bible7.php. For example its Gothic v, u, and i, which in Roman script look like u, v, and j. Our double-u looks like a double-v. Another is the long s—ſ. I have sometimes updated quotes.

some extent based on the variations before they came on stream. One example is of Jr.34:16: "...whom ye had set at liberty..." (Cambridge); "whom he had set at liberty..." (Oxford).⁶⁶ As a leap of faith, you can say that the original KJV was God's perfect text.

A problem is that God has allowed variations within the KJV tradition to exist. Did he inspire the text, only to allow printers to introduce errors? If he allowed printers to make errors, can we not allow that he who inspired the authentic text allowed scribes to make errors, and translators likewise? Versions, like manuscripts, are all imperfect and secure carriers of God's word. Even the Wicked Bible (a KJV edition, see below), telling Sinaitic Israelites to commit adultery, is corrected within the context of Scripture. Is there a great problem if we go with Oxford? As a matter of interest, is Cambridge, or Oxford, exactly as the original KJV delivered to Barker? How can you know since we don't have the original KJV Bible?

For Jr.34:16, if you accept that the Hebrew and Greek texts are the key to authenticity, you can check your particular KJV. They will decisively show that Cambridge, not Oxford, got it right. In the same way, C20-1 translators, using this method (*ad fontes*: going back to source), are able to trace back and correct the KJV tradition on numerous texts. It's the same Bible, but they carry on the aim of the KJV translators to make good versions better. Anyway, since we can see that the Cambridge got Jr.34:16 right, why not footstool Oxford, and enthrone Cambridge? Hold on. The Cambridge KJV 1769 says "she went into the city", while the earliest 1611 KJV, the Great He edition, has "he went into the citie" (*Ruth* 3:15).⁶⁷

---

66  The KJ21/KJV side with the Oxford; AKJV/EJB/MEV side with Cambridge.

67  Examples from Jr.34:16 and Ruth 3:15 are from White 1995:80. White's book continually points out reasons to reject the radical KJVO position that the KJV is, or was, infallible and that all other English versions (and presumably other language versions if not at least based on the KJV text) are corruptions away from God's word. His argument here is both about textual preservation—would God allow his only inspired English version to become altered?—and that to base all decisions on the KJV original, sometimes leaves questions unanswered, since we cannot always be absolutely justified about what the original text was. KJVO prefers to use the KJV text (which it assumes it has) as the divine baseline, and tends to avoid the earlier non-English manuscripts. The other

## A New Fight

Editions of the KJV have not always been as good as intended, nor fortunately has the text of the KJV remained exactly at the 1611 stage. One gaffe built into the KJV, which transmission has retained, has been "strain <u>at</u> a gnat", which should have been "strain <u>out</u> a gnat" (Mt.23:24). Earlier versions, such Tyndale, Geneva, and Douay, all had "strayne/straine/strain out a gnat"—was the KJV a blynde gyde? Or was John Wesley, who had "strain out a gnat"? But quite a few gaffes *were* soon strained out. "There is no <u>man</u> good, but one, that is God" (Mk.10:18) which implied that God is a man, but the masculine singular, "no man", was soon corrected to "none". "Then cometh <u>Judas</u>", was corrected to "then cometh <u>Jesus</u>" (Mt.26:36). "And he spake unto his sons, saying, Saddle me the ass. And they saddled <u>him</u>" (thou art the ass?), was corrected to "And they saddled <u>it</u>" (1 Kg.13:27).

Errors later made include the 1612 revelation, "<u>printers</u> have persecuted mee without a cause" (Ps.119:161), the 1631 Wicked Bible's "thou <u>shalt</u> commit adultery", and the 1795 Murderers Bible's "let the children first be <u>killed</u>" (Mk.7:27). Gaffes belong to the human arena of fallibility. One might recall a 1979 NIV advising us to kill off sexual *immortality* (Col.3:5)—shades of Charles Wesley's doctrinally dubious, "the immortal dies"! Strange.

---

two 1611 editions (with over 200 hundred variations in the biblical text) were the Great She editions (Metzger 75), which Cambridge reflects.

# Chapter 5   Neomisian Flames

Build a bonfire, build a bonfire, put the teachers on the top, put the prefects in the middle and burn the jolly lot. So we used to sing. In the seventies, I was a devotee of J T Chick publications, which issued comic literature useful for evangelism. Chick's *Demon's Nightmare* can still evoke daydreams of when, as an office boy in Hull's Old Town, I delivered mail to related businesses in the area, handing out Chick tracts to fellow office juniors (some attractive;)), reception staff, and to bank tellers. A number were eager for new ones—or was it my charms? If memory serves, it was some time before I came across more dubious Chick tracts, which made 'historical', or perhaps 'hysterical', claims, slating 'modern' versions.

Please understand. In those days I literally walked into a lamppost while reading my KJV—a dent perhaps remains in that lamppost in Silver Street, just left of The Land of Green Ginger. Nice names. On the one hand I was never convinced by Chick,[68] and on the other hand I maintain a high regard for the outstanding achievement of the King James Version. History teaches that change is often opposed. Perhaps that's a safety thing, even if it's not a fair thing. Psychologists speak of an inbuilt bias for conservatism, but it can do us disserve. We have had pyromania over almost two millennia. At one time, it was the Roman Empire burning Christian writings, even Christian people, unhappy with Christian change. Since then, much incineration has been within the church. Let's review.

## C4 Jerome

He was well aware that many "learned or unlearned...would...when they took the volume into their hands, and perceived that what they read did not suit their settled tastes, break out immediately into violent language, and call [him] a profane person for having the audacity to add anything to the ancient books, or to make any changes or corrections therein" (Jerome: Frend 183). His version, the Vulgate, got it in the neck.

---

[68]   www.catholic.com/documents/the-nightmare-world-of-jack-t-chick well argues that Jack was too easily and dogmatically mislead by false witnesses. IMO its promotion of pro-RC arguments are weak dressed up as strong.

## C14 Wycliffe

A millennium later, Wycliffe's version was burnt in 1415, and his former bones in 1428—he wasn't using them so didn't object.

## C15-6 Erasmus

He was likewise condemned for bucking the traditional text—*Jerome's*. Did he partly motivate the Reformation? Denying that against praise or censure, he said that Luther's bird hadn't hatched from an Erasmian egg. Erasmus sailed the angry sea between Rome and Reformation, but didn't drown. Yet soon after his death, the Council of Trent officially established a Vulgate Only position, and banned his works.

## C15-6 Tyndale

He sparked Bible Rage. London's irenic bishop, Cuthbert Tunstall, and Sir Thomas More of Utopian fame, were mutual friends of Erasmus and mutual enemies of Tyndale. Ironically, both Erasmus and Tyndale reformed key ecclesiology terms: in Latin, Erasmus put *ekklēsia* as *congregatio* (congregation, not *ecclesia*, church), and *presbutēros* as *senior/presbyter* (older person, not *sacerdos*, priestly person). Perhaps Tyndale's comments made him seem to many a heretic and a Bible counterfeiter, inspired by Antichrist (Bruce 1986:40). Most was content to badmouth Tyndale. Tunstall's policy of buying up, in order to burn, Tyndale's version, backfired, unintentionally funding further publications. But Tyndale's executed body would be burnt too.

## C16-7 Bancroft

Bancroft desperately tried to quell Genevan flames, yet had his own version, the KJV, attacked. Like an angry Eris, Hugh Broughton, a top-notch biblical scholar, hadn't been invited to the KJV party. Understandable, perhaps: he wasn't a team player, hated the Bishops Bible (which was to be the KJV's foundation), and loved the Geneva which Bancroft and King James hated. When the KJV was published, Broughton said, "I require it to be burnt" (Bruce 1986:107)! Was Broughton's itch to burn the new, partly based on neomisia, the hatred of newness?

A hundred years on, fire raising evangelist, perhaps apostle, John Wesley, was also far from the KJV's greatest fan. His own NT version (1755) was not even based on the TR, and "was a marvellous anticipation of the Revised Version of a hundred and thirty years later" (Bett 80). Wesley made over 12,000 alterations to the KJV text, knowing that some would say "too many" and some "too few". Wesley made enemies by changing the KJV. The pyromania which led Bancroft to metaphorically burn the Geneva, and Broughton to metaphorically burn the KJV, would soon ignite a C19 scholar.

## C19 Burgon

In human terms, Dr. John William Burgon (Dean of Chichester) was the archenemy of the late C19 English Revised Version, hereafter simply called the Revised Version (RV). When the RV kicked in, so once more did neomisia and pyrophilia. Burgon agreed that the TR needed correction at times,[69] though usually about matters of name spelling or word order. In short, he supported the KJV as at that date being our best imperfect text, infinitely to be preferred by anyone of sense and taste to such a version as the RV. The RV was indeed tasteless, unlovely, harsh, and unidiomatic, but his attack on its Westcott and Hort NT text went too far.

Burgon said that Sinaiticus and Vaticanus were most ancient because, no one wanting to use them, they didn't wear out. He seemed to be saying that the older the manuscript, the worse it was (Bruce 1986:148-9). Among other things, he argued that Mk.16:9-20 was by Mark (canonical), so why drop it? Bruce noted that discoveries since Burgon's time have further shown that it was not by Mark (noncanonical), so why keep it? Does Mk.16:12-3 really fit with Lk.24:33-5? For a number of good reasons, the debate seems more about whether Mark intentionally ended with v8, rather than whether any of the endings were his. Burgon leaves believers needlessly vulnerable, for if an atheist or agnostic persuades believers who believe that Mk.16:9-20 is canonical that it isn't, the believers might give up the canon and fall

---

[69] In his *Revised Revision* (1883:108), he actually told off the RV for sticking with the TR's *nekrous egeirete* (Mt.10:8) simply because the earlier uncial texts backed the TR against his opinion! Isolated, the EOB/WEB agree with Burgon though footnote the TR.

into atheism or agnosticism. Better by far for a biblical scholar to show that the canonical garden has had some interesting weeds sown by errant scribes.

Without rejecting their Christian sincerity, Burgon condemned the translators for dropping canonical text from every page. They replied that they only dropped *noncanonical* text, and that there was plenty to drop. But even William Sanday, with whom the verdict of most subsequent biblical scholars has agreed, was not heeded by Burgon. The RV had high cringe, but textually it headed in the right direction, though giving the Alexandrian text-type more room at the table than it deserved. It was an ugly parent of some handsome children. More discoveries have provided even better tools for establishing the authentic text, and for translating it. Its children are alive and kicking, but so too are many Blowtorch Burgons carrying on the feud.

## C20 Revised Standard Version

The RV was eventually upgraded to become the Revised Standard Version (RSV), which an American preacher blowtorched in his church, saying that, like the devil, it was difficult to burn. "Anything more certainly calculated to make every family in the congregation acquire a copy for itself is hard to imagine; one could almost believe that the whole incident was an ingenious publicity stunt engineered by the sponsors of the new version!" (Bruce 1986:196). Many who 'blowtorch' every English version since the KJV, either don't know or don't want to know, that the KJV...

- included the Apocrypha;
- pointed out that it could only guess what some ancient words meant—thus some marginal notes: the KJV translators lived with uncertainty, though their original textual notes, along with their preface, are usually suppressed in its modern versions;
- the KJV's Bancroft, like the RV's Westcott and Hort, was an Anglican, supporting the idea, rhantismal regeneration (a.k.a. infant 'baptism');
- intentionally didn't use one set word for each and every Hebrew or Greek word, but built in variety, understanding that words can mean different things in different settings;
- had thousands of footnotes.

# Chapter 6     James Immortal, Others Immoral?

The KJV was a very good revision of other versions then available, and probably even in its early days had a quaint elegance. McGrath praised it as being unintentionally eloquent (2002:254). W W Wessel preferred to praise it as being intentionally eloquent. After all, Wessel said, the translators had intentionally rejected a wooden, mechanical approach, and had intentionally voice tested it before approving it, thus indicating a "conscious concern for English style" (Scorgie, Strauss, and Voth 210). Well, however it came about, let it be said that the KJV was a good work of literature. In fact, it became more popular as its antique literary style gained the wistfulness of the seeming safety of a bygone age. It had always been, along with the other early English versions, a solid contender, and a blessing even in its earlier years.

Sadly, to defend the KJV, some treat its friends as fiends. The KJV needs no defence, only a thank you for its help in days gone by. To list every written attack on every other English version since 1611, would make for a tiring book. For convenience, I shall focus on one target, the NIV, and when justified use its 2011 edition, which leaves the 1984 for dead. Personally, I would cremate with honour the C20 NIV editions. Yet I would keep the KJV, not for those who want to read the Bible, but for those who delight in literature, who may rejoice in it insofar as they can stomach its spiritual challenge—it still reflects the underlying and undying Bible.

Yet those who deem its fate far above the ghost-life of the museum and the specialist's study, are far from dead. Let us sample their arguments, sometimes humorously wrapped in gibes such *Serpent's Scribes*, and *Lucifer's Lexicons*. The songwriter Isaac Watts got similar treatment, such as *Watts' Whims*, for allegedly cutting off his congregations from the spirit, and thrusting him "utterly out of the church" (Mouw and Noll 366/3767). Really, rubbishy rhymes readily reduce reason.

## Greedy Graspers?

"If I am a proud man, then, so long as there is one man in the whole world more powerful, or richer, or cleverer than I, he is my rival and my enemy" (Lewis 2002:123). About to buy some carrots, I'm warned that they're irradiated. Wow, I don't want my hands strangely warmed.

## James Immortal, Others Immoral?

About to buy a NIV, I'm warned that it's irradiated by greed. Wow, I don't want my spirit strangely warmed, or my feet burning in hell. I ask, how is the NIV contaminated? I'm told that it's contaminated by greed, putting money before God, but that the KJV put God before money: "the love of money is the root of all evil" (KJV: 1 Tm.6:10).

Is it? A reluctant prostitute may be such because they love money,[70] but their clients put sexual kicks, domination, and sheer naughtiness, above the money they hand over: and what of rape, which is nothing to do with the love of money? Did Cain have a love of money that caused him to murder Abel? Where's the love of money in my sheer bad temper? If you were cut off from money, would you be cut off from sin? Does commitment to poverty make a nun pure? Was Satan's sin his love for money?

It seems to me that either Paul misunderstood evil (which I don't buy), or that the KJV misunderstood what Paul meant. The Greek text does not say 'the' root; 'a' root is better. The Greek text says *evils*. The KJV guessed that meant "all evil", but Paul's point to Timothy was simply that even among Christians, many kinds of evil came from this warped love—"a root of all kinds of evil" (NIV).[71] Having noted in passing that some use a lesser translation of Paul's words to knock a better translation, we must ask why they claim that the KJV was produced untainted by the love of money, and that the NIV was produced tainted by the love of money. "Unchastity, anger, greed,

---

[70] More often they're not greedy, simply forced into feeding a drug habit and/or children. Some are first duped into drug addiction, or trafficked.

[71] Even this might be too broad, though short of an explicit "root of all *the* kinds of evil". Is the emphasis on 'all', or 'all kinds'? If 'all', it implies that somewhere behind every kind of exciting evil, love for money figures. If 'all kinds', it's a figure of speech implying that behind many different sorts of evil, is love for money. It's a text that might have applied to some who 'peddled' God's message, doctoring it to make it more sellable. It might have applied to those who, rather than lose their cushy jobs, denied Christ. One can think of televangelists today, using God's name in vain to improve their audience ratings and income, or businesswomen dropping the 'Christian' thing in order to climb the social ladder rather than Jacob's. The love for money is a root of many kinds of evil, but not the root of all evil.

drunkenness, and all that, are mere fleabites in comparison [to pride]" (Lewis 2002:122).

Peter Ruckman's, *The Bible Babel* (1964), seems to have started a copyright-free idea rolling. Twenty years later, Gail was saying that the KJV is the only version not bound by a [human] copyright, because, she claimed, God is the author (Riplinger 171). She claimed the same authorship for her *New Age Versions*, so I guess royalties go to God's bank, not to her bank. She conveniently overlooked that the KJV had its early form of copyright (*cum privilegio*, doubling as royal censorship and income), that some other versions are post-copyright (for example ASV), and that those producing the KJV rightly expected financial and/or promotional gain. If "the labourer is worthy of his hire" (KJV: Lk.10:7), getting paid for services was, and is, fair. Likewise, publishing houses need to recover their expenses and prevent unauthorised changes to the text. Making a reasonable profit is fine—why should Bible production alone be exempt from profit? Profit can be ploughed into evangelism. Profit can be ploughed into good scholarship, as has been the case with Cambridge and Oxford. The KJV has copyright in Britain.

World-class committee translation, costs in time and expenses. The KJV translators knew that. As an author of confusion, Gail ignored the context about the USA fighting for USA translation control in order to prevent unauthorised changes to the text. Wishing to imply that the RV committee were greedy graspers who contaminated the version's family line, she did a creative cut and paste job from an account about Philip Schaff's role in the ASV (Riplinger 172). As if uninterested in truth, or unable to understand it, she called it both his autobiography (it was in fact a biography written by his son David), and *The Life of Schaff* (in fact it was *The Life of Philip Schaff*, 1987).

This brings to mind C S Lewis, speaking of Rudolf Bultmann—and not doubting that he "wanted to believe—and no doubt did believe" (Lewis 1981:195)—wondered why that learned German had become so blind to the obvious. Yet whether blind or knave, Gail would make us blind. Alas, many genuinely come to believe the folly they wish to believe. One thing Philip Schaff *did* say was that "it is impossible that a work to which a hundred scholars of various denominations of England and America have unselfishly devoted so much time and strength, can

## James Immortal, Others Immoral?

be lost. Whether the Revised Version may or may not replace the King James' Version, it will remain a noble monument of Christian scholarship and cooperation, which in its single devotion to Christ and to truth rises above the dividing-lines of schools and sects" (Schaff 387).[72] My analysis of Gail's interior redesign 'quote'? About 10% by Philip Schaff, about 15% by Hort, about 45% by David Schaff, and about 30% (that focus on the contention theme) I found only in Gail's book. The order of these various voices—is one Gail's?—is, where traced in Schaff's book and simplified, C/A/B/D. The tone has been highly redesigned.

Gail, whose academic expertise, I think, is in interior design, has been rather creative in her 'quotes'. Her redesigns easily mislead readers, whether for her love of money I don't know. Now, we ask and we will have our answer, what has she confessed in her, *New Age Versions*?

"This book is written...to trap souls...so...'Buddha', 'Krishna', and Lucifer become 'The Lord'... [It] made its way to the bestseller's list... [because] [t]he serpent still swings from the tree of knowledge...obscuring God's definition of evil and good.... Buddha says, 'no origin can be perceived'...[T]he world doesn't end...Hell's presentation in the bible can...be extinguished. It has been the purpose of this book...characteristic of the coming antichrist-Big Brother era...[to] break the seed of Israel."[73]

In short, don't let her 'quotes' about financial greed behind English version publishing, pass the eye gate unless you have checked the source she's 'quoted' from, carefully reading its wider context. And to some extent the issue is not motivation but result. As to the KJV, a few senior translators were paid £1.50[74] weekly for 9 months—"no

---

[72] https://archive.org/stream/lifeofphilipscha00scha#page/374/mode/2up.

[73] Riplinger 3,10,12,254,284,291,59-2,3. This copy and paste, prefixed by the aha words 'confessed' and 'we ask', deliberately misrepresents Gail's book in order to show how one can pick up bits here and there, throw in gap marks (ellipses), and mislead readers. "New Age Bible Versions contains a plethora of out-of-context citations and edited quotation, frequently misrepresenting the positions of the authors it attacks" (White 1995:97). It is wise not to take any quotes from Gail's works at face value—if you can chase them down, check for their context, for even the KJV says curse God and die! Even her citations from Bible versions need careful checking.

[74] Riches, in 1609.

## King James: A New Hope?

previous financial payments had been made to translators" (Metzger 72). Generally, those who weren't in church-paid posts were later rewarded by posts, career enhancements. Were they mercenaries, or simply entitled to fair pay and recognition? Printing the KJV was "funded by venture capitalists" (Scorgie, Strauss, and Voth 207), but without some such financing we would not have had the KJV.

The question is, was it worth paying for? And what about the publishers? Until 1695, the Stationers' Company, controlling the English book trade, allowed only London, Oxford, Cambridge, and York, to print books. Official Bible printing was a monopoly under the monarch, who received royalties from the royal printer. The Barker family (London) held this post from 1577, and were therefore printers for the KJV. The final draft that Robert Barker bought for £3,500 was, sadly, lost in the Great Fire of London of 1666—some Puritans of the day might have argued that God's wrath was on the KJV. Before Cambridge and Oxford were permitted to print KJVs, Barker had the printing monopoly, and buying a KJV was well beyond the common person. Many lawsuits were generated, as printers sued and countersued for the profits: Barker didn't have it all his way. Prices only came down though competition. The greed was with the KJV; the generosity was with the Geneva.

Background radiation is part of life. We buy food, knowing greed and goodness are built in between production and shelf. Unless we know that the better fruit and veg come from exceptionally unethical sources, are we not wise to select the better of what's available? We buy a Bible, whether KJV or NIV, knowing both greed and goodness are built in between production and shelf.

### A Bloody Nose for a Bloodless Bible?

The term 'bloodless Bible' is sometimes used of C20-2 versions that do not have "through his blood" (*dia tou haimatos autou*) in Col.1:14.[75] The charge should not be mere conspiracy, but shoddy conspiracy, since they have not 'deleted' "through his blood" in Eph.1:7. Their explanation is that 1# Paul's letter to the Colossians lacked the phrase,

---

[75] It was also derision for the GNB's arguably justified (Rm.5:9f.) approach of translating *haima* as *death* instead of *blood*.

2# his similar letter to the Ephesus region had it, and 3# they didn't wish to conspire against Paul by adding it to *Colossians* or deleting it from *Ephesians*. Was C14 John Wycliffe, who produced the first English version, also a conspirator since *he* left it out?

What excuse did the KJV have for adding to the text? While Paul did not have to repeat every phrase in every context, copyists familiar with both sometimes, from ingrained memories, imported words and phrases from one when copying the other—harmonisation. In fact, even the great majority of manuscripts within the Byzantium text-type—the MT—don't have "through his blood" in Col.1:14. From his *small* sample of the MT, Erasmus thought this phrase authentic, and the KJV translators followed his judgement on this. Additions to the Bible are noncanonical, and it is wrong to treat them as God's word.

## **Sneaking in Sin?**

Castigating C20-1 versions as bowing to Rome, Gail said Jas.5:16 is "confess your faults (All Greek texts have the word for faults here,–not sins.)" (Riplinger 145). Hers is the fault, if not sin. And twice wrong, for not all Greek texts are the same—the TR has *paraptōmata* (faults) the NU has *hamartias* (sins)—and it is not a Roman Catholic change supporting specialist priests.[76] Wycliffe translated as *sins*.[77]

Did she uncritically follow Peter Ruckman on this? Ruckman[78] looked at the Nestle-Aland[25] footnote system, but comprehended it not, apparently thinking that it didn't mention ℵ, B, and A *because they didn't* support its *tas hamartias* text. In fact, it didn't mention them *because they did* support—along with K, P, 048$^{vid}$, 33, 81,614, 630, 1241, 1505, 1739, and others—*tas hamartias*. Likewise, his former student, Samuel Gipp, showing by misspelling the Greek a very basic ignorance of Greek, wrote "Nestle's text inserts 'sins' (tax amarties) with NO manuscript authority".[79] Do they face the double truth that "...they

---

[76] The Douay-Rheims has *priests* (14), but commendably more current versions have *presbyters* (NABRE) or *elders* (NJB). Even if the reference of v16 is to v14, the Greek is not about confessing sins to priests.

[77] http://wesley.nnu.edu/fileadmin/imported_site/biblical_studies/wycliffe

[78] Ruckman's *The Christian's Handbook of Manuscript Evidence*, 1970:101.

[79] www.seawaves.us/na/web4/biblehistory.html—2014

be blind leaders of the blind. And if the blind lead the blind, both shall fall into the ditch" (KJV Mt.15:14)? The simple point James made was that wandering from the truth was sin (Jas.5:19), and frankly admitting it to fellow believers would remove a barrier to mortal healing. The text itself rules out the idea that only some believers were priests (sacerdotally laity confesses to priests, but not priests to laity), along with RC ideas of purgatory. In small study groups, C18 Methodism practiced mutual confession of sins (Moo 182).

## **Sslipery Ssnake?**

"Glory to God in the highest, and on earth peace, good will toward men" (KJV: Lk.2:14).

"Glory to God in the highest heaven, and on earth peace to those on whom his favour rests" (NIV: Lk.2:14).

Is the NIV irradiated by the serpent's spit; has Gail the serpent's tooth? Here that question is, did the angel (Lk.2:14) speak in the nominative case (which has an 's'), meaning God's peace and goodwill *on* (all?) people (TR)? Or did he speak in the genitive case (which hasn't an 's'), meaning God's peace for those who were people *of* goodwill (for example the faithful of Israel such as Simeon (Lk.2:25,29))? If the latter, then has Gail accused God's angel of having spoken with Satan's hiss? If we believe that heaven has a gate patrolled by angels, we might well be concerned lest Gail rolls up when this angel's on duty!

Some funny things have been said about how some words are put in English. Gail has been happy to wrongly gender change the Greek *eudokias* to *eudokios* (feminine to masculine). She has not been happy to rightly change *eudokia* to *eudokias* (nominative to genitive). Departing from the Greek is fine, but not it seems from the KJV! It sseems she was sserious when she sspoke of the "hiss of the serpent" being in the words "sin, Satan, Sodom, Saul (had to be changed to Paul)" (Riplinger 232): her ssatanic *s* of hisstrionics?[80]

---

[80] Enjoying wordplay, she also made the cheeky claim that "daily during the six years needed for this investigation, the Lord miraculously brought the needed materials..so much so that I hesitated to put my name on the book. Consequently, I used G.A. Riplinger, which signifies to me, God and Riplinger— God as author and Riplinger as secretary" (White 1995:99). Or did she mean Satan, the god of the world and New Ageism? After all, using her method of

- Sigma is a perfectly good letter in Greek. Elsewhere Gail argued for final sigmas, stigmas, which look rather like our 's'—χριστος/Christ ends in a stigma.
- 'Sin', in Greek, starts with an 'h', not with an 's'. The genitive form *hamartias* is no more satanically hissful than its nominative form, *hamartia*.
- In English and Greek, 'saviour/*sōtēr*' begins with the same 'hiss' she's knocked on the head—is she a secret Luciferian? But ah, she might say, I didn't say *every* s word was a serpent word, to which I might respond, well, why brush *eudokias* with that tar? God inspired Paul to use *hamartias* in Php.2:13: of "good wyll" (Bishops).
- While among Gentiles, Saul identified by using his Gentile name (as apostle to the Gentiles), and the Holy Spirit was happy to use the name Saul (Ac.13:2); Peter's Jewish name was still spoken as 'Simeon/Simon' (for example Ac.15:14 by James) and indeed it had been by his *Petros/Kephas* name that he had been rebuked as Satan (Mt.16:23). At what of SStephen?
- Gail, theology should never be based on ssuperficial sounds, even to rally ssupport for your pet theories and to ssell your books. Why be on guard against certain sounds; why issue an alert from coincidences?

Erasmus chose *eudokia*. Beza also bowed to strong MT witness, but seriously suspected it should be *eudokias*. E F Hills quoted Beza's hunch that Origen, Chrysostom, Jerome, and Luke's context, backed *eudokias* rather than Erasmus, Stephanus, and the MT (White 1995:170). The earliest copies were in uncials, and *eudokias* could have looked like $EYΔOKIA^C/EUDOKIA^S$.[81] Had he had Aleph, Beza might well have

---

quoting she did say that "Satan..an accessory in the death of millions...provided me access to documents...which burst at the slightest touch of analysis" (Riplinger 53-4). One might liken her 'moral high ground' assertion to Herbert W Armstrong who founded the once heretical Worldwide Church of God: "self-glorifying sentiments were not uncommon to Armstrong. He had..announced in January 1979 that his book..had Jesus Christ as the author and Mr. Armstrong as the stenographer", and another book by himself, in 1985, as perhaps the most important book since the Bible (Martin 519).

[81] The earlier uncial end-sigma was like an English 'C', and at the end of a line would be smaller like a superscript—in short, easily missed. Along with

followed his hunch and corrected Erasmus, much to Gail's displeasure—only she would then have ssniped at the alternative 'non-KJV' reading since the TR would have read *eudokias! Eudokias* highlights the salvation history stage when those in his special favour, seeking messiah, were typified by Ssimeon—"you may now dismiss your servant in peace. For my eyes have seen your salvation" (NIV: Lk.2:29-30). "Watch out for the letter 's'".[82] You gotta ssmile—and weep.

## **Witch Westcott; Heretic Hort?**

Perhaps we wouldn't accuse John Wesley, who made his own RV, of irradiating Scripture, but what about two who especially influenced the RV's New Testament text? Have all versions following them, been fatally contaminated—with heresy? Would we, who would not buy irradiated food, buy irradiated versions? Westcott and Hort have gotten it in the neck for bucking the traditional text. Sadly, being human, they shared some doctrinal failings.

For some, that's a handy excuse to call down curses on Westcott and Hort's heads. Some declaim them as 'baby sprinklers', rhantisers, and that is what they were. Yet that is but to call Westcott and Hort, *Anglicans*, which is what the KJV translators were! No one is perfect save God alone. And all the Anglicans said, *Amen*. Some would say a more damning charge is what may be called *mediumship*.

King James Version Only (KJVO) people often use the 'Mulligan stew' approach: throw in quotes and misquotes from all real enemies, mix in quotes and misquotes from those you wish to condemn, and serve them up as one of the crowd. Bad taste transfers. This is guilt by association, which Jesus, who dined with prostitutes and 'traitors', probably suffered from too. Cover truth in mud! Those who generally denounce homo-eroticism, or any kind of interpersonal sex (IPS)

---

*eudokias* being the harder text (*lectio difficilior*), this highlights that it was easier to drop the 's' (genitive) form to *eudokia*, than an original *eudokia* to have had a 's' added.

[82] Watch out for the letters A (Abyss), B (Baal), C (Covetousness) and so on, and in Greek A (Apollyon), B (Blasphemy), Γ (Gehenna). All letters in all languages probably have some bad names—why should the 's' sound of a goose be singled out, as if it carries any real implication of wrongness? Even the son of man was lifted up like a snake (Jhn.3:14).

outside of truly wedded marriage, are often dismissed by homophiles as 'bigots' and 'homophobes'—as if diseased in mind and not worth further notice. Fine them, sack them, stick 'em in a stew, says our more tolerant society, crucify Christians.

This is semantic warfare and social engineering at work, sadly all too common in today's relativistic Westernism.[83] But the same dismissive don't-want-to-know attitude surfaces among KJVOphiles too. Those arguing for the KJV's honourable burial are often called Nicolaitane Priests,[84] and Alexandrian Cultists, Servants of Satan, Idiots, and/or the like. Smear terms—like 'bigot'—are substituted for proper debate and discussion.

As regards demonic Spiritualism, did Gail use "false or, at best, implausible speculation", confusing B F Westcott (b.1825) with W W Westcott (b.1848)?[85] Pulled up on this, she suggested that B F

---

[83] *Westernism* has been defined as "perhaps by implication, Christian" (Parrinder 237).

[84] See Rv.2:6 (practice) and v15 (teaching). It's spelt as Nicolaitanes in the Geneva and Darby versions. Some KJVs read Nicolaitanes; some KJVs read Nicolaitans. This term has been used for different purposes by various groups. KJVO-ists liken them to those teaching the NU rather than the TR text. They link those thus branded as heretics, to Roman Catholic 'priesthood', so-called academic Nicolaitan 'priests'. They explain this 'priesthood' as saying that instead of every believer a priest with their own KJV, the 'Nicolaitane Priesthood' says it must mediate between believers and God, interpreting the original text to them. This overlooks the obvious that most believer-priests would have difficulty reading the original Hebrew, Aramaic, Greek, and smattering of Latin, texts, unless translators *such as the KJV translators* had actually weighed many varying manuscripts then translated them into workable English or other native language. *If* the NIV translators are Nicolaitane Priests, *so* were the KJV translators: both groups 1# selected a reading from alternatives, 2# put it into English, and 3# provided footnotes (see http://kjt.biblecommenter.com) of alternative readings. Mulligan's Stew—throw in various nasty terms—Nicolaitane, Romanism—and serve it up to the unwary.

[85] www.jashow.org/wiki/index.php?title=The_Conflict_Over_Different_Bible_Versions/Part_5.

wrote in favour of Spiritualism, under the initials W W. B F's son documented that his father had looked into, but wisely never bought into, Spiritualism. "Westcott believed that 'the way to combat error was to seek the element of good in it, and show that its real explanation and satisfaction were included in the Bible', (*Westcott, Life and Letters*, 1.19)".[86]

At a time when Spiritualism was resurfacing in the West, many looked into it, and some like social activist Bishop James Albert Pike (1913-69) sadly accepted it.[87] For about a year, B F Westcott was a member of the Ghostlie Guild, set up by E W Benson, a future Archbishop of Canterbury, to investigate, not to participate in, Spiritualism (White 1995:245). B F Westcott seems to have been basically trinitarian and his commentaries do not, unlike 'Christian Spiritualism', proclaim that after death all spirits normally rise from death onto a higher spiritual plane, that Jesus' was simply an outstanding spirit.[88] Indeed, B F Westcott seems to have said that Spiritualism hadn't of any real value to the Christian community—he was a fully committed member—and indeed, that parapsychology was biblically unlawful and perilous.

## Edwin Palmer—Anonymous Arian?

In one of her infamous misquotes, Gail linked Edwin Palmer (Executive Secretary of the NIV) to the Mormon, Brigham Young: "The Holy Spirit did

---

Lamentably this site subscribes to Ms ideology, nowadays common through morally deconstructionalism. Gail is Mrs. Riplinger—www.avpublications.org—indeed her third marriage after two divorces: Miss Ludwig to Mrs. Latessa (1969) to Mrs. Kaleda (1976) to Mrs. Riplinger (1984). The website cited considers her divorces as unbiblical, unacknowledged, and unrepented. I lack the data to judge: not all divorces are sinful; not all remarriages are sinful.

[86] www.kjvonly.org/james/may_westcott_deity.htm

[87] Not all who seek both find and remain. Raphael Gasson (*The Challenging Counterfeit*) was an ethnic Jew and long serving 'Christian' Spiritualist medium in the UK. He later denounced real Spiritualism as a deception, simply generated by demon spirits impersonating humans who had died, who counterfeited phenomena only lawfully done by God. Its harm has been in sidetracking from the supreme issue of knowing God.

[88] Believing hauntings to be by *human* spirits not knowing they've died, Spiritualism touts rescue mediumship to educate these spirits to release them.

not beget the Son" (Riplinger 344). Young had the idea that the Father came down and begat him, the same as we do now, a virgin conception in that it wasn't by mortal man. Young even joked, totally misunderstanding reception of the spirit, that otherwise human females had better not be baptised/confirmed, since giving them the spirit could lead to more virgin births! If we think of the incarnation, the NIV is clear that the Holy Spirit came upon Mary so that the holy one born from her would be called the "Son of God" (Lk.1:35).[89]

Again her misquote was out of context, for in the eternal relationship of the trinity "the Holy Spirit did not beget the Son, only the Father did" (White 1995:103). Ontologically, "The Holy Spirit did not beget the Son" is standard, historical, and orthodox. Incarnationally, Palmer specifically said that "the Second Person of the Trinity, remaining God, 'became flesh and lived for a while among us' (Jhn.1:14). This was an act effected by the Holy Spirit...The Holy Spirit is the cause of the conception of Jesus" (White 1995:104).[90]

On Jhn.1:18, Palmer said that looking back to the Greek text "inspired by the Holy Spirit, [it] is one of those few clear and decisive texts that declare that Jesus is God. But, without fault of its own, the KJV, following inferior manuscripts, altered what the Holy Spirit said through John, calling Jesus 'Son'". Gail turned it into a chilling "[there are] few and decisive texts that declare Jesus is God". But heh, if Palmer has said there is even one decisive text, he's said that the Bible teaches that Jesus is God, so what was Gail's beef?[91]

---

[89] I think it important to prefer "[God the son]/[son of God] incarnate", to "God incarnate", in line with the with/is distinction of Jhn.1:1. The Logos (God the son) was *with* God [the father], and *was* God [in *being*]; I am *with* humanity, and *am* human, but I am not humanity. As Tertullian taught, God [the father] was not crucified, but God [the son] was.

[90] White referred back to *The Person and Ministry of the Holy Spirit* (Edwin Palmer: Baker Book House, 1958, 1974), pp15 and 65.

[91] Proper systematic theology notes that *Jesus* can be shorthand for *God's son*, and notes that the few "Jesus is God" texts each have a context that qualifies their meaning in deference to the father, the one usually called *God*: "Jesus is God" is misleadingly simplistic. Sometimes *God* means the eternal society. The Bible thus always denies that Jesus *alone* is God. The biblical revelation is that

White's earlier edition, when citing Gail's misquotation, added an extra 'and' to Palmer's sentence—"one of those few and clear and decisive texts". Easily done, and no big deal. Aha, replied Gail, I didn't say that Palmer said "one of those few <u>and</u> clear and decisive texts", only that he said "one of those few clear and decisive texts". By citing White's insubstantial misquote of her substantial misquote of Palmer, she's ducked the real issue, which is her citing Palmer's pro-trinitarian statement as a chillingly anti-trinitarian (Arian) one.[92] Is her "let's forget White's point that Palmer's a trinitarian, because White's unreliable enough to ridicule away", not a face-keeping act of deception? Later she's said her beef was not that Palmer has denied the son's deity, but that the NIV has whittled down clear and decisive texts to so few.[93]

It's quite a good twist, but even that misses the NIV's stronger witness to that deity, so you could say it's the KJV which did the whittling. In this interchange, it is useless quoting to her "why beholdest thou the mote that is in thy brother's eye, but considerest not the beam that is in thine own eye?" (KJV: Mt.7:3), if she is unlikely to admit either that White's a Christian 'brother', or that his error was simply an insubstantial mote compared to her substantial beam. For my money, slating Westcott, Hort, and Palmer, has shown an irradiation of her bitterness, not of heresy by them.

## **Homosexual Homily?**

OK, another claim of irradiation, this time claiming sexual malpractice. UK Statistics seem to indicate under 2% of the population being homosexual in orientation,[94] though correctivism

---

God's son, beyond creation, is *with* God [the father], and *is* God [as a societal member] (Jhn.1:1). I am *with* humans and *am* human.

[92] Presumably she misspelt *Arian* as *Aryan*, unless she somehow meant *Aryan* as the idea that proto-Indo-Europeans had racial superiority, an idea Hitler highlighted, rather than meaning a theological controversy as to whether God's son was created within time (Arianism).

[93] www.av1611.org/kjv/omadman.html.

[94] www.theguardian.com/world/2010/sep/23/gay-bisexual-population-uk. In context, I take their use of the word 'gay' to be correctivist code for *homosexual*, whether male or female. Teenage phases of same sex attraction

may increase the percentage, even as positive discrimination and celebrating smoking or paedophilia would very likely increase those who follow such as fashion. One might expect that unless a policy filtered them out, homosexuals would work with the NIV, as on many good projects. And homosexualism was not a defining issue in those days, indeed little presumed to exist within Evangelicalism. Who forbids Polar Bears in the Middle East? This drip-through has become hunting grounds for damning the NIV—irradiation by perversion.

Virginia Mollenkott, deemed a committed evangelical, was consulted on matters of the NIV's English style. Incidentally, it seems she wasn't happy with the NIV term *homosexual*. There appears dispute between recollections, and either she has inflated her NIV involvement, the NIV's Kenneth Barker has deflated her part, or truth lies somewhere between: genuine perspectives can vary. What seems clear is that she did not significantly influence the translators or editors in their final decision, but would it matter if she had had a big part in general readability of English as English? Anyway, her homosexualism, a thing much more secretive in the 60s, had been unknown to the NIV committee. Had they known, Barker said, they would never have consulted her. His statement, in times when the more pro-homosexualism the politicians, the more gay their parties are, is bravely un-pc.

Marten H Woudstra was a key committee player. The charges seem to me to say that he was homosexual in orientation, perhaps in practice, and believed that homosex was biblically justified. To argue a distinction between homosexual texts in the OT, and monanthropic (*monogamous* would imply that marriage is possible)[95] relationships, can find a

---

can also be stabilised by the correctivist indoctrination of celebration, so boosting lifestyle homosexuality, and 'orientation' need not define one as homosexual (Dr John White's *Eros Defiled*, 1977.105) but will boost the figures. For more recent USA estimations, see http://culturecampaign.blogspot.com/2011/04/american-homosexual-population-tiny.html.

[95] If the concept, *same sex marriage*, has objective reality, then the concept, *God*, has not; if the concept, God, has objective reality, then the concept, ssm, has not. That is because biblically only God is linked as able and authoritative to define marriage, and he only defined it heterosexually. If the concept God is

sincere range of positions within heterosexual evangelicalism. That the godly assume they can disagree among themselves means that the godly assume they can be in sincere error, though there is an objective right (Php.3:15). Who is to say that Woudstra's position was or wasn't, at least at the end-stage, sincere (Rm.14:23)? One hopes he stood before God. Perhaps within his OT expertise, Woudstra prioritised the meaning of the texts above his own wishes, as a good academic should. The issue here is not that you prove I am the devil's brother, but that you convincingly refute what I have said, as one wit put it.

Ethically, homosexuality should be more generally discussed, if only to block the road to nihilism. For instance, assuming that Dt.23:17 was about pagan temple homosexualism, did Lv.18:22 and 20:13 fit into that tight domain? If not, are they no longer operative? As an aside, James White has taken flak for not denouncing Woudstra before the issue was public domain. How many a mistaken spouse has genuinely believed their spouse not to be an adulterer? Were they *lying* when they mistakenly claimed them faithful? Hindsight is a great teacher.

The boot on the other foot, there is suggestive evidence that King James was secretly a practicing homosexual! For my part, I think it possible that in his childhood James was seduced into homosexuality, later reorientating even as did psychiatrist John White.[96] "But, of course, James' sexual behavior had nothing to do with the translation of the KJV, just as Virginia Mollenkott's views had no impact upon the NIV" (White 1995:246). Of course, James 1, to whom the KJV was dedicated, and who commissioned the KJV, had more *de facto* influence on it than Virginia had on the NIV that consulted her and other stylists. And if Westcott is damned as pro-Spiritist because he investigated demonic 'Spiritualism', then James 1 may be dammed

---

irrelevant, then humanity can define marriage as it will and I could affirm ssm as real, ie transcending legislation yet created by legislation. But I would lack any moral justification to undergird or undermine ssm, having undermined ethics as objective. I would also lack any moral reason to undergird justice, since the only refuge from God is the moral void (Lewis 1981:68-70). As it stands, don't ask if I favour or disfavour same sex marriage, for I reply that the concept is void: I cannot disfavour what cannot exist.

[96] See White's *Eros Defiled*, and *Eros Redeemed*, about his personal reorientation.

as pro-witchcraft because he wrote (negatively) about it in his 1597 book on demonology. Thank God for James and Westcott, in spite of their imperfections. To err is human.

Let's test this claim of irradiation, briefly looking at relevant texts. But first, whether or not you are a homosexual, do you believe that sexual orientation is a 'human right' because it is a human condition? Paedophilia, necrophilia, are human conditions; so is leprosy, so is greed. One psychology professor said that "we are—all of us—disordered. We do not like to think of ourselves as disordered, and this too is a reflection of the fall" (Yarhouse 40-1). Should we, rather than the Bible, be in the dock? Please don't switch off at this sensitive point—we are to turn onto the Bible, not turn off it; to turn towards it, not away from it.

Beware proof-texting, unless it's within sound hermeneutics. The texts don't mean that anyone practicing, let alone resisting their orientation urge, is damned to the burning lake, though the texts don't promise to please us. While homosexual practice is in vice lists, so too is telling lies and habitually getting drunk. Vices are not how people are to live, even if the secular police arrest virtue! Vice lists exemplify the land where those opposing God live, a land neither beneficial nor damning for Christians.

But is doing homosexuality really a vice? If a Christian, your responses are limited. You might say that Scripture is from God, that he outlawed interpersonal sex (IPS) outside of marriage, and that since he never thought up the idea, *homosexual marriage*, homosexual IPS (similarly heterosexual IPS outside marriage) is always sinful no matter what fallen human loves and laws legislate. Well did C S Lewis say that any human love disobedient to dëontological Love is demonic (*The Four Loves*).

You might say that Scripture isn't from God, and is prescientific, outdated, of mainly antiquarian value in the history of religions.[97] Or you might say that within its rightful disdain for pagan temple IPS and homosexual malpractice, being a theanthropic work its human factor unfortunately concealed God's smile on loving homo-

---

[97] Basically, Bishop Spong's position, see Gordon Fee's *Listening to the Spirit in the Text* (2000), ch.7.

sexualism. Indeed, that Scripture is an evolving body of literature, its trajectory of loving monanthropic relationships[98] now rightly interpreted as welcoming what Moses and Paul were right to forbid within their more primitive frameworks.[99]

Some cite slavery and racism as analogies, saying biblical values change. Perhaps they are blind to unchanging values with changing covenants. Or you might say you really don't have and don't want to have, a viewpoint—just trying to live a decent life is hard enough. Whatever your response, this book isn't for deeply engaging in this issue, though hints that we should be. The charge has been put that the NIV fudges the issue, perhaps bent towards homosexualism. Is it, or isn't it?

|  | KJV | Old NIV[100] | TNIV[101] | NIV |
|---|---|---|---|---|
| Lv.18:22; 20:13 | lie with mankind | lies with a man | sexual relations with a man | As TNIV |
| Rm.1:27[102] | men with men working that which is | men committed indecent acts with | men committed shameful acts | As TNIV |

---

[98] Some unwittingly speak of *monogamous* homosexual relationships ('gay marriage'). The 'gamous' part is 'marriage'. If marriage is God instituted, only he defines its meaning, and the fact remains that he has only defined it in heterosexual terms. Thus, for legal fiction to pronounce ceremonialised homosexual unions 'marriage', is akin to pronouncing that Minis have always been Rolls Royces, that red is square, that logic is illogic. Else, it directly attacks the concept, *God*.

[99] The position of Prof. Dan O Via, see Via and Gagnon's *Homosexuality and the Bible: Two Views* (2003).

[100] New International Version (1984). In some contexts, also the 1978 edit.

[101] The Today's New International Version (2005).

[102] A specific mention is made in Rm.1 about homosexualism among women, showing it's not just a guy thing, though more often the issue was biblically spoken about in guy terms. The part text cited is for comparative purpose. The fuller reading of the context clarifies that homosexualism is what's under the microscope.

# James Immortal, Others Immoral?

|  | KJV | Old NIV[100] | TNIV[101] | NIV |
|---|---|---|---|---|
|  | unseemly... error | other men... perversion | with other men...error |  |
| 1 Cor.6:9[103] | effeminate[104]/ abusers of themselves with mankind | male prostitutes/ homosexual offenders | male prostitutes/ practicing homosexuals | men who have sex with men |
| 1 Tm.1:10[105] | defile themselves with mankind | perverts | practicing homosexuality | As TNIV |

The term *sodomite* in the KJV (Dt.23:17; 1 Kg.14:24; 15:12; 22:46; 23:7), was in the ASV, but apart from the Amplified, and the WEB, has dropped out because generally the scientific term *homosexual*, has replaced it in the public psyche. If the former is used, it is likely to conceal the meaning. The NIV reads "male shrine prostitute". As to 'offender', a drug offender is one who breaks human laws about drugs, as well as offending their own body. Are not homosexual offenders they who break God's laws, and perhaps offend their own bodies? Admittedly it also allowed the idea, homosexual non-offenders. Subsequent NIVs corrected that oversight in line with Scripture.

This should be enough to show that the NIV has not fudged the issue and is clearer than the KJV's testimony, at least to C1 western ears. But isn't the NIV soft on non-practicing homosexuals? First, the KJV

---

[103] Others terms include weaklings/abusers of themselves with mankind (Bishops), men who practice homosexuality (ESV), wantons, buggerers (Geneva), homosexual perverts (GNB). The combination is a bit tricky getting into English.

[104] Greek *malakos*, translated 'effeminate' (KJV), is in Mt.11:8 translated as 'soft' [raiment/clothes]' (KJV). Perhaps it was easily understood in 1611, but how is today's KJV reader to know that in 1 Cor.6:9 it was about homoeroticism? The NIV spells it out. It is not a male feeling female (gender dysphoria), but a male sexually interacting with a male.

[105] Other terms include buggerers (Geneva), sexual perverts (GNB), sodomites (Darby), homosexuals (ISV).

also speaks of acts, not desires. Second, as C19 songwriter Horatio Palmer advised, "yield not to temptation, for yielding is sin, each victory will help you, some other to win"—we sin not by being *tempted* (unless we yearned for it) but by *yielding*. It should be clear that the sinfulness being condemned by Scripture has never been homosexual urges, but the practice whether with or without the urge.[106]

Writing as a psychiatrist, Christian, and ex-homosexual, John White concurred: biblically condemned homosexuality is *activity*, not same sex *attraction*.[107] Admittedly many psychiatrists, factoring out Scripture, are intolerant about White's contribution, which lacks the APA's *nihil obstat*. Anyway, whatever we think about *laissez-faire* interpersonal sex, let us let Scripture be Scripture. If it is wrong, it is wrong, but let's at least allow translators to do their job which is to translate its meaning into today's terms. Its claim about sin may seem as offensive as its claim about salvation may seem meaningless, but let us face its claims: bad news, good news, or both? Sufficient to conclude that the NIV seems clearer against homoeroticism than does the KJV, indeed the charge is sometimes made that the NIV translators have factored in their personal dislike for such practice, for such relationships—that is, that we have an unbiblically intolerant NIV!

## Alexandrian Anarchists?

At this stage let's bring in Peter Ruckman, who's fervently lambasted opponents of the KJVO position. Talk of an Alexandrian Cult undermining true faith, puts us into Ruckman's zone. It suggests that heresy was rampant in Alexandria, and that the Alexandrian text-type was a heretical rework. Origen Adamantius of Alexandria (c.185-254), in church history seen as a stern idiosyncratic genius who seemed geared to some rather strange systematic theology (a mix of light and lunacy?), is a name often cited. The 'Alexandrian Cult' is said to be an

---

[106] Scripture does not overlook the sin of formulating sin within the mind, playing with the tasty plans of murder, seduction, dominance, oppression. But the beach on which flows unbidden waves is not cursed, even if it needs a good clean up.

[107] Claims of a gene variation causing homosexuality are at least highly questionable. See White's *Eros Redeemed*.

ill-defined network of KJV rejecters, who seek after the Alexandrian text-type, in short, preferring fallible authority to infallible authority. Its creed, existing at least in Ruckman's imagination, is...

> We believe that God is a spirit, who alone is the final absolute authority, but that a spirit cannot fully communicate final absolute authority materially, specifically in a book. We believe the only exception has been the biblical autographs, long lost. We believe that all transmission is fallible. We prefer to believe that the autographs are *best* preserved through heretics from Alexandria/Egypt (though an ungodly zone), rather than through Antioch (though a godly zone), and that the godly Reformation text is even less accurate. We believe that since there is no final absolute textual authority, we may use whatever we like, even the KJV (White 1995:117-21).[108]

Having defined *Alexandrian* as downgrading to relativism even the 'pure' KJV, yet preferring impure readings, *Alexandrian* becomes a general put down term against any who disagree. Ruckman's position has been something along these lines...

> God suddenly inspired the KJV 100% and perfect, even correcting by inspiration what the TR had wrong, correcting uncertainty with certainty. Hebrew OT and Greek NT manuscripts are at best secondary to the KJV—if they agree, good for them; if they disagree, bad for them, but either way we don't need them. If the actual parchments with Paul's ink are discovered yet different to the KJV, it's Paul we'll ditch. The KJV translators were wrong to call their work imperfect. I know better.

Ruckman's repetitive logic works in reverse. On 2 Cor.2:17 the KJV reads "we...[do not] corrupt the word of God", while the NIV says "we do not peddle the word of God". If Ruckman's right that the NIV allows us to corrupt Scripture as long as we don't *peddle* it, then, sauce for the goose, the KJV allows us to *peddle* Scripture as long as we don't *corrupt* it (White 1995:114).[109] Ruckman didn't ask what the Greek

---

[108] I've rejigged this into Credo format.

[109] This reverse logic makes a fun game. His turn: "the KJV forbids A, the NIV forbids B, therefore the NIV allows A, so must be wrong". My turn: "the NIV

*kapeleuontes* meant—it means dishonest trading. Some 'traded' on the name 'Jesus'—some still do. As a matter of fact, the Geneva version reads "which make marchandise of the woorde of God". Could not Paul make a 'no' point without meaning that all other points are 'yes'? If Ruckman's thinking was logical, then the KJV allows us to *do* evil as long as we don't *appear* evil (1 Ths.5:22), and to *exchange* God's truth for a lie as long as we don't *change* it (Rm.1:25).

Ruckman's position begins and ends with the sheer presumption of the KJV not as a good upgrade, but as the only perfect Bible version. If his 'light' is light, we can justify ignoring the original Hebrew and Greek meanings, but I suggest he's worked in darkness. Commenting on atheist fundamentalism, Alister McGrath made the point that for some "it is the confidence with which something is said that persuades, rather than the evidence offered in its support" (McGrath 2007:64).

## Fire Fighteth Fire?

Can a cloud put out fire? Even colleagues can be demonised. KJV advocate, Dr. D A Waite, eventually issued a severe reprimand to Gail Riplinger,[110] accusing her of severe heresies and a lot of wilful misrepresentation of herself (favourable light) and of the Waites (unfavourable light—liars, traitors, liars). Another fracture line is between

---

forbids A, the KJV forbids B, therefore the KJV allows A, so must be wrong". Sauce for the goose. The deciding authority is not, according to Ruckman, what the original writing meant in its original language, but the KJV, since directly inspired by God the highest authority. After all, the KJVs been well used in the English world for 4 out of 20 centuries!

[110] www.deanburgonsociety.org/PDF/heresy.pdf. Here, Waite claimed certified proof of two divorces of Gail's, and seems to me to have assumed that any divorce is sinful, that Gail is thus an adulteress, and moreover wrong, since a woman, to teach men. He also seemed to have the idea that Pentecostal/Charismatic circles can lead to strange ideas of versions being specially inspired. Admittedly, a tiny minority have claimed canonical inspiration for their 'prophecies'. I wholeheartedly agree with Waite as regards single Bible inspiration, as the original texts alone being inspired—versions are not inspired, however much we might argue that one, in our language, is best.

what one may call a KJVAist,[111] David Cloud, and Peter Ruckman. Cloud noted that the KJVA position was clouded because of Ruckman's "strange ideas, his multiple divorces, his angry spirit, his arrogance, his Alexandrian cult mentality, his extremism regarding the KJV being advanced revelation, and his bizarre private doctrines [that tend] to cause people to reject the entire issue".[112]

Among 'bizarre private doctrines' Cloud rejected the ideas that "angels are thirty-three year old males without wings; and [that] all women in the Church Age will receive thirty-three-year-old male bodies at the Rapture".[113] But Ruckman has disliked moderates, and presumably preferred siding with the gnostic *Gospel of Thomas*: "Simon Peter said to them, 'Let Mary leave us, for women are not worthy of Life.' Jesus said, 'I myself shall lead her in order to make her male, so that she too may become a living spirit resembling you males. For every woman who will make herself male will enter the Kingdom of Heaven'".

Cloud, perhaps close to tears, cited Ruckman's response to him: "... you little lying rascal, you. ... you lying little hypocrite ... Davey, ole son, you need to get you a sail stitcher's needle and puncture your inflated ego. ... you buttery, smook, slick, mush-mouthed sissy ... The wimps all talk alike if you analyze them. ... Correction, Davey! You smooth, slick, little, fluctuating compromiser ... A puffed-up, conceited ass cannot

---

[111] KJV Advocate, the idea of the TR as best textual base, and KJV as best so far translation.

[112] www.wayoflife.org/articles/ruckman.htm. This might sound like an Adolf Hitler type in Christian circles—Hitler's brilliance wasn't always sane.

[113] Presumably based on Jesus' biological sex (male) and presumed age at death (33 y.o.), and the idea that as he is, so, only after death, shall we be: misreading 1 Jhn.3:2. Taken with exact literalness, and overlooking that christification is currently taking place, this would remove all differentiation, transforming us into clones. Some woman, not liking the male bit, ask why we ever assumed that Lk.2:13's angel was male—why not female? Well, maybe female angels do nativity plays better, yet Lk.2:13's Greek is masculine. It isn't a biology thing, but a gender thing. Angels don't come with male/female chromosomes. They are suprasexual, even if male visualisation best represents their masculine highlight: no individual angel is pictured as gender feminine. We shall rise more thoroughly into the genders, transcending the biological sexing as discarded images.

stand to have his balloon punctured".[114] Cloud argued that the KJV was given by *preservation* of the Byzantium manuscripts, particularly the TR thread, not, *contra* Ruckman, by *inspiration*. Ruckman perhaps allowed a secondary level to the best manuscripts, on which God added inspired correction ('special revelation') to the KJV translators, but has strongly opposed any idea that the TR, Byzantine Text, or Alexandrian Text, or even better knowledge of Hebrew/Greek, should alter the KJV.

---

[114] www.wayoflife.org/fbns/ruckman3.htm

# Chapter 7     The KJV Lacketh...

## Justice

There are many factors in translation, not least using current words to faithfully approximate the meaning of the text. Doing this can be influenced by political and public acceptability. Let's look at the Hebrew/Greek ṣedeq/dikaios. You will never read the word 'justice' in the KJV New Testament, and it's about 30 times in the whole KJV, whereas the Spanish RVR (Reina Valera Revisada) translates the Heb/Gk. 370 times as *justice*, and the more recent NVI (*Nueve Versión Internacional*) translates it about 430 times.

In English, the NIV mentions justice about 130 times and the NJB (New Jerusalem Bible) about 250 times. Justice is a big theme: "rebellious sons, stubborn asses, forgetful oxen, and an unrighteous harlot, all four images were used to describe how God saw a people who had forsaken social justice" (White 1979:17). So why was it such a hidden theme in the KJV? Basically, British Anglicanism preferred to translate in the word 'righteousness', even though the evidence presents "a clear indication that the Hebrew term has more of a relational and communal flavor than a moral, individualistic sense" (Scorgie, Strauss, and Voth 328).

This preference can be traced back to King James looking to unite the English people by a version neither tied to the common people (the Geneva Bible: 1560), nor to church leadership (the Bishops Bible: 1568), and which safeguarded monarchy. While the Geneva Bible used 'justice' 40 times for ṣedeq/dikaios, the Bishops Bible never used this word. The Bishops Bible was the basic text for the KJV, though influenced by the Geneva Bible. Those indirectly hired by James were specifically to remove the political threat of the Geneva Bible, such as social disobedience against tyranny.

Thus, the KJV's Mt.5:39 suggests social passivity to evil, whereas the text speaks of accepting wrongful public humiliation, "the backhanded blow", without retaliation (Keener 197). Respect for monarchy and fear of displeasing King James, probably encouraged the KJV translators to spiritualise the social impact of ṣedeq/dikaios. "Powerful words such as justice, just, rights, and communal faithfulness were not in the king's best interests. A religious word such as righteousness, which speaks of a state of being and not of an active, intentional responsibility towards others—especially the poor and the marginalized—is a much safer term" (Scorgie, Strauss, and Voth 333). The Puritans were more theocrats than monarchists. They were involved in the KJV and had an agenda for social justice (challenging to the king) and a strong belief in internal spirituality (not challenging to the king). New versions can only redirect public attention gradually—too much too soon and they will die ignored.

## **Greek**

Missing a page, the Latin *Codex Sangermanensis* for *2 Esdras* (a.k.a. *4 Ezra*) jumped from 7:35 to 7:106. KJVO folk must either reject the Greek 7:35 to 7:106, or admit that *2 Esdras* should not have been in the KJV.

In a number of places, the NT text used by the KJV translators actually came from the Latin, not from any Greek from the MT. Here we look at two particular sections lacking Greek NT witness before Erasmus.

### Rv.22:16-21

In this section, there are 17 textual variants between the KJV and any known Greek text predating Erasmus. Here's one. "God shall take away his part out of the book of life" (KJV: 19), vs "God will take away from that person any share in the tree of life" (NIV: 19). The phrase, *book of life*, is biblical (KJV/NIV: Rv.3:5; 13:8; 17:8; 20:12,15; 21:27). The phrase, *tree of life*, is biblical (KJV/NIV: Rv.2:7; 22:2,14). The disagreement is about whether in this text John wrote *book* or *tree*. One can see how the original Vulgate's *ligno* (tree) could switch to *libro* (book) to fit the more common phrase. It seems that this got into the Latin system early on, and though Jerome avoided it, seems to have transferred around the Empire outside the Greek witness.

Erasmus was strapped for time. He hadn't a Greek text for this final six verse section, but had a Latin text. Quite cleverly, he translated from the Roman Catholic version he was restoring, into his 1516 Greek textbook (*ex nostris Latinis supplevimus Graeca*). Such was his reputation that Stephanus and Beza failed to correct some of his mistakes here.[115]

---

[115] White 1995:86 lists a number of these errors. Herman C Hoskier's (*Concerning the Text of the Apocalypse*, 1929:1.477) suggested that maybe Erasmus used some Greek witnesses—so the horse pulled the cart. White 1995:87 argued that

Following him, the KJV-TR actually stands against the MT. Erasmus' Rv.22:19, followed by the KJV, reads the old Roman way, *book of life*, rather than John's original Greek way, *tree of life*. John Wesley, and later John Nelson Darby, preferred John's way to Jerome's. When Peter Ruckman derided the NU for not even footnoting it, he ignored (perhaps in ignorance) that the NU only footnotes alternatives that have at least *some* Greek support, which this doesn't.[116] The lack of Greek text is a weak spot.

## 1 Jhn.5:7

This text begins...*hoti treis eisin hoi marturountes* (for there are three witnesses). What comes after the comma? This question is called the Johannine Comma, or *Comma Johanneum*.[117] The KJV assumed it was *en tō ouranō, ho patēr, ho logos kai to hagion pneuma. Kai houtoi hoi treis hen eisin* (in heaven, the Father, the Word, and the Holy Ghost: and these three are one). This seems orthodox enough, but adding orthodox statements to the Bible doesn't mean they should be there. Why do some versions treat this as a church insert?

It's simple. Jerome's Vulgate lacked it, so did the MT, as well as testimony from all the big names who would have loved to use it against Arians but didn't because it wasn't in John's text. However, a C4 commentator linked the trinitarian "in heaven" idea to 1 Jhn.5:8—

---

these manuscripts (for example Hoskier's 57, 141, 187) *witnessed* Erasmus' reading because they *copied* Erasmus' text—so the cart before the horse. Perhaps a few pre-Erasmian Greek texts were adjusted to the Latin.

[116] http://av1611.com/kjbp/faq/holland_re22_19.html#_ftn3 (2008) put the case for Greek witness. Whatever the strengths of this site, it is circular to say that "the Greek text copied by Erasmus in Revelation 22:16-21 reflects a consistency that is found elsewhere in the Textus Receptus", since it was Erasmus who produced any 'consistency' the TR has—he founded the TR. Likewise, one should not overplay dissimilarities to the Latin Vulgate, since there were many variations of the Vulgate in circulation. It also overlooks that the MT does not witness to the variations of the TR.

[117] I was recently amused to discover that there is a multicolour edition of the KJV, called the BRG Bible, which flies this distinctive TR flag to show off its colour system, which includes blue for the father, since the sky is blue (what parts of the world and times?), and apparently God's throne is the sky.

spirit, water, and blood. It trickled into later editions of the Vulgate, and had become the norm to Erasmus' audience. At first, Erasmus refused to write it into his Greek NT, simply because it lacked any Greek manuscripts.

He collected flak from the orthodox, and might have been quite relieved when, ink almost still wet, someone bobbed a Greek manuscript (Codex Montfortianus) onto his desk. It was obviously from the Latin text (roughly *et tres sunt, qui testimonium dicunt in caelo, pater verbum et spiritus*), and lacked the definite articles of proper Greek. Yet he may have jumped at the chance to adopt it, keeping his audience happy and avoiding the risk of a heresy trial. Had he known, there was a bilingual C14 Latin/Greek manuscript having it (in Latin to Greek style), Minuscule 629, its witness to the Comma easily overlooked.[118]

Anyway, Erasmus' next edition, his third, included it, though to be fair he noted his uncertainty. It was dropped by Martin Luther since not in the *original* Vulgate, and Tyndale and Coverdale had their doubts. KJVO-ists must assume that God allowed original text to drop completely from the Greek texts for almost 1500 years, and even be missed by Jerome's Latin—did God deliberately hide a trinitarian text about himself? "Even 'liberal' scholars will admit to the...tenacity of [the NT] text" (White 1995:62)—that is that the true text always continues alongside mistaken copies.

Some still argue in its favour. For example, Kevin James (*The Corruption of the Word*, 1990:230-8) argued that grammar favours the KJV, since 'three' is masculine, and therefore relates to the masculine trio of father, son, and spirit, rather than the feminine trio of 'spirit, blood, and water'. That's superficially, but not substantially, strong, since "'three' almost always appears in the NT as a masculine when used as a substantive" (White 1995:85). 1 Cor.13:13, where 'three' in the neuter relating to a list of feminines, is the [stylistic?] exception.

James also said that the modern versions don't have much manuscript support for their reading of Jas.4:14 and 2 Cor.5:3, so in fairness they should not reject the Johannine Comma simply because

---

[118] www.csntm.org/tcnotes/archive/TheCommaJohanneumInAnOverlookedManuscript

## The KJV Lacketh...

*it* hasn't much manuscript support. Saying this, he's bypassed a few points. One is that Jas.4:14 and 2 Cor.5:3 are extremely different from the Comma. The section in Jas.4:14 has at least 6 *very similar* ancient Greek readings—each individual reading is thus very small: the UBS4[119] rated their choice as C to indicate the difficulty of the choice (A = certain–virtually certain; D = very uncertain). 2 Cor.5:3's ancient Greek variant is simply between *ekdusamenoi* and *endusamenoi.*

Though he didn't admit it, James accessed Metzger, so his silence on Metzger's justification for *endusamenoi* must have been wilful silence to 'justify' his own side's weakness on the Comma. Metzger said that *endusamenoi* had better external witness, and *ekdusamenoi* was explicable as an intentional change to 'correct' an otherwise tautology.[120] Thus, James' 'sauce for the goose' argument—that the NIV accepts readings as poorly attested as the Johannine Comma, so we can do so too—is weak. In short, James' argument is unwise. The lack of Greek text is a weak spot.

## **Understanding**

Some say that the KJV is an easy read, but their figures don't tell the whole truth. Computers can quickly calculate a Reading Ease figure, but this can simply say how many short words are in sentences, without saying whether the words are difficult or not, or whether a translation is accurate or not. There can also be brownie points for short paragraphs. On the latter, if the KJV paragraph per sentence format is thrown at a computer asked to calculate a Flesch Reading Ease (FRE), since each sentence is formatted like a paragraph, we get an impressive score.

For example, with 1 Jhn.1:1-10, the LEB's format of two paragraphs scored 73.8% FRE (FKGL 10.7).[121] But if put into the KJV style as 10

---

[119] The 4th edition of the UBS Greek NT text.

[120] Bruce Metzger's *A Textual Commentary on the Greek New Testament* (United Bible Societies 1995:580). Incidentally Westcott and Hort went with the TRs of 1550 and 1894/Majority Text, and against the Alexandrian, on this.

[121] Though largely based on the FRE, FKGL grading isn't the same, and aims to show at what US American school grade the average student needs to be to properly read the text.

paragraphs, it would jump to 81.4% and 8.0 respectively: a letter is simpler than a word; a word is simpler than a sentence; a sentence is simpler than a paragraph; a KJV paragraph is simpler than a true paragraph. Once the verses are put into true paragraphs to compare like for like, the KJV result is less impressive, and that's even before we go beyond computer counts into words and style.

Let's take Col.2:23, a difficult chunk of Greek. Which reads easier? "Which things have indeed a shew of wisdom in will worship, and humility, and neglecting of the body: not in any honour to the satisfying of the flesh" (KJV)? Or, "Such regulations indeed have an appearance of wisdom, with their self-imposed worship, their false humility and their harsh treatment of the body, but they lack any value in restraining sensual indulgence"?[122] The FRE test is not a comprehension test.

I have compared the CEB/CEV/ERV/LEB/NABRE/NCV/NIV/NKJV/NLT/NRSV, taking their text from Gen.1:1-25, Jos.1, Ec.1, Is.1:1-17, Mk.1:1-20, Rm.1:1-17, Heb.1, and Rv.1. To give them the same paragraphing, I have given them all one paragraph for each section of Scripture (ie each version has six paragraphs) and then thrown the FRE test at them. For a comparative percentage, I then gave each a percentage to the highest. If the name of the game was readability, rather than accuracy, the NLV would rule the roost.[123]

|      | FRE  | FRE% | FKGL | Words |
|------|------|------|------|-------|
| KJV  | 76.6 | 82   | 7.3  | 3682  |
| LEB  | 77.1 | 83   | 7.0  | 3592  |
| NIV  | 80.3 | 86   | 5.9  | 3468  |
| NKJV | 80.3 | 86   | 6.3  | 3613  |

---

[122] On this, the KJV has a pretty good FRE of almost 70%, and the NIV has a pretty poor FRE of just over 30%. 100% FRE is maximum points for easy reading, and 0% is the hardest. The Douay is only 1% lower than the KJV, and reads "Which things have indeed a shew of wisdom in superstition and humility, and not sparing the body; not in any honour to the filling of the flesh." The Great and Wesley have approximately 50%, and the NLV has just over 90%. In short, easy reading isn't everything, nor does the KJV top the scores.

[123] A previous comparison showed the order from easiest to hardest, and missing out many, to be NLV/CEV/NLT/MSG/NIV/NRSV/ESV/KJ21/NKJV/NWT/LEB.

## The KJV Lacketh...

|     | FRE  | FRE% | FKGL | Words |
|-----|------|------|------|-------|
| NLT | 81.1 | 87   | 5.3  | 3623  |
| NLV | 92.9 | 100  | 3.1  | 3923  |

Readability is important, though I concentrate on accuracy, and how different approaches and textual bases connect to this goal. Bible translation saves us having to read the original languages and texts, and implies ease of reading. Within our language, English, there are easy and difficult levels of writing. C S Lewis once said that many English theologians needed to be translated for English readers, a job he tried to do. For readability, there are no winners or losers here, simply a ranking from easiest to hardest to read, from the position of those who have a rough and ready knowledge of reading English. And that is important: Wycliffe translated not to improve accuracy, but to make it readable for his people. Some find the KJV hard; some find the NLV irksome.

# Chapter 8   Voices in the Wilderness?

Some individuals made versions between 1611 and 1881, such as Dr. Edward Harwood's 1768 version (*A Liberal Translation of the New Testament*).[124] It was pitched in the language of Johnson and Hume, a kind of C18 Living Bible for the Upper Classes and the Not Too Biblically Minded. The first American version was by Charles Thomson in 1808; it was also the first Bible to be printed by a woman (Jane Aitken, eldest daughter of Robert Aitken). It deserved wider reading—many copies were binned.

The first woman to translate the Bible was Julia Evelina Smith (1876), highly talented but lacking genuine understanding of Hebrew and too self-confident to seek help. Her version was a confusing curiosity of errors. More significant was Noah Webster's version of (1833), a great American grammarian who believed the KJV's language needed updating to overcome common misunderstandings—for example 'be not anxious' for 'take no thought', 'food' for 'meat', 'falsehood' for 'leasing', 'button' for 'tache', 'hinder' for 'let', 'Holy Spirit' for 'Holy Ghost'.[125]

---

[124] This only picked up interest in Germany, where it inspired many to recast Scripture as a moral, but not miraculous, handbook of Enlightenment. His way of putting the Paternoster: "O thou great governor and parent of universal nature—who manifestest thy glory to the blessed inhabitants of heaven, may all thy rational creatures in all the parts of thy boundless dominion be happy in the knowledge of thy existence and providence, and celebrate thy perfections in a manner most worthy of thy nature and perfective of their own! May the glory of thy moral development be advanced and the great laws of it be more generally obeyed. May the inhabitants of this world pay as cheerful a submission and as constant an obedience to Thy will, as the happy spirits do in the regions of immortality."

[125] It can confuse folk to say, "I believe in the *Holy* Ghost but *ghosts* don't exist." While on pneumatology, the KJV is somewhat heterodox regarding the spirit's personhood: <u>it</u> abode (Jhn.1:32 KJV/Geneva, *contra* Bishops); <u>itself</u> beareth witness (Rm.8:16, *contra* Bishops/Geneva); <u>itself</u> maketh intercession (Rm.8:26 KJV/Geneva, *contra* Bishops). In these 3 texts, most versions bias grammar towards the doctrine of his personhood. The NWT happily follows the KJV on these; the NJKV does not. Grammatically the Greek for 'spirit' is a neuter noun, and so good grammar might expect its pronoun to be the neuter

Of wider benefit, the "Revised Version took over nearly every one of his changes, although no credit for his previous labors was given" (Metzger 92). Some versions were motivated by the belief that Scripture had to be correct and current, if it was going to speak to voices crying in the spiritual wilderness.

# **Conclusion**

The KJV was created to kill off Evangelicalism and to consolidate the British kingdom against papists and puritans. But it was created well, building on previous versions and on the beginnings of textual criticism (whose growth it stunted). Though it endured a long time of unhappiness, eventually it gave almost universal enjoyment: Exodus became Canaan, or at least Solomon replaced Samuel. "If the first 150 years of its history were encumbered with hints of discontent, criticism, and suspicion, its next 150 were characterized by something at times approaching uncritical adulation" (McGrath 2002:289-90). It has sparked firefights, and many have been burnt. Though I don't approve of dirty fighting, I'm glad it's not gone down without a fight.

With Roman Catholic Hans Küng (*The Church*, 1986:372), I believe that every Christian is a priest.[126] With priesthood comes obligation to check out God's word, not to live a hand-me-down faith. We must do our own thinking, howbeit wise to the facts and strongest interpretations of others current and past. Each of us should make up our own mind based on light, not heat. Silent slippage, either away from or back into the KJV camp, is a shame. Christians should be matured by understanding the reliability of the biblical text; that Bible versions are not of equal weight; that using a range of top-

---

'it': the dog wags the tail. Yet an outstanding feature of *John* was that John actually broke with grammar a number of times by substituting the neuter noun for 'spirit' (*pneuma*) with the masculine pronoun 'he' (*ekeinos*—Jhn.15:26; 16:8), precisely to highlight the personhood, perhaps masculinity, of the Spirit. The KJV more happily than the NWT picked up this lead.

[126] Even if some ecclesiastics are called *priests*. Some are called *deacons* (*diakonoi*), yet every Christian is a deacon (*servant*); some are called *ministers* (the same word *diakonoi!*), yet every Christian is a minister (*servant*). Admittedly *priest* (which came from a word for older) invites the Q, what are they sacrificing and on whose behalf?

quality versions enriches Bible study and understanding. There is that sad story of a Christian man who, asked what he believed, replied that he believed what his church believed and when asked what that was, replied it was what he believed. Asked what he and his church believed, he simply said they believed the same thing. Some real answers are expected of us.

I have looked at some allegations against post-KJV versions. There are more to look at, in which I shall argue in a non-condemnatory way that the KJV addeth and taketh away from God's text. Jesus never condemned godly attempts to translate the scriptures. Let's rise above the fog.

# Part 3 Translating Theology
## Chapter 9 God's ID

"Strictly speaking, Yahweh is the only 'name' of God" (Douglas 572). "A strange scruple has, for the most part, prevented translators...from using the Divine Name" (Motyer 12). "...God's name, 'Yahweh,' is used rather than the traditional term, 'the LORD,' whenever God's name is relevant in the context" (Köstenberger and Croteau loc.3132). I fear that God's ID is lost in lordship, for who is today's focus as lord? Jesus is. God is not Jesus. His name is highly meaningful, predating Moses, but entered a new phase with the Israelites, in the format of a covenant player. Yahweh is God's salvation name of deliverance into covenant (Martens 23). The big thing is to show his personal name as his personal name.

Ethnic Israel still looks back to the exodus from Egypt, celebrating the ancient Passover (Jhn.1:29; 13:1). For them it also functioned as a covenant name, and roughly divided themselves, when they were in special relationship with him, from all other peoples. For Global Israel, Jesus/*Yēsous* is the name that expresses this same idea, though *Yahweh* remains a wider, trinitarian, name. The Hebrew *hôšea'* means salvation. The son of Nun, servant of Moses, once bore this name Hoshea (Nb.13:16). He was renamed *Yehôšua'* (= Yahweh is saviour), usually put as Joshua in English versions. In Aramaic, the language spoken later by ethnic Jews, *Yehoshua* was shortened to *Yešu'* (Neh.3:19 = Yeshua). The Greek (*Yēsous*; Latin = Jesus) says Yahweh is saviour, from the common Aramaic of C1 Palestine (Mt.1:21).

Arguably, 'Jesus is lord' hints that Jesus is Yahweh and Yahweh is lord. Of course, good theology neither confines Yahweh to one person, such as Jesus, nor to lordship. Similarly, 'I am human' does not mean that I alone am human: if we sing "you alone are God, Jesus", we have left the trinitarian path and sung into the unitarian path: may God forgive us and heal us. Yahweh as deliverer and covenant lord, was a great theme.

By the time the Hebrew was translated into the Greek tradition that we now call the Septuagint, or, quote me not, the Greek Seventies Version, ethnic Israel had twice suffered Yahweh's top level rebuke, banishment. Most of the 12 tribes (the Ephraimites/Israelites) had been exiled by Assyria. The few who remained (the Judahites/Jews) had later been exiled into Babylon. Self-confidence had been severely shaken, and the *Jewish* identity was far diminished from ancient Israelite identity. Jews were left with a sense of Yahweh being more distant— as if being too close had been the problem! They had become nervous of even speaking his name, and had developed workarounds to avoid uttering it.

Familiarity had given way to superstitious taboo; a thick curtain was hung as a temple veil between that glorious name (*ha shem*—the name) and themselves. When translating into the Greek, they decided to camouflage God's name as the Greek word, *kurios* (lord). Yet even then, as Jack Lord of Hawaii Five O would be called *Lord* as a name, God's name was often put as [Lord], not [the Lord], an unarticulated/ anarthrous (that is the-less) form (see Wevers: Hiebert, Gentry, and Cox's *The Old Greek Psalter*, 2001:21-35).

Take a clear example. The Septuagint of Gen.39:2-3 translates very formally as "and was lord with Joseph...of the lord the Egyptian. He saw and the lord of him that lord with him". In the KJV 1611 "and the LORD was with Ioseph...of his master the Egyptian. And his master sawe that the LORD was with him". In the LEB, "and Yahweh was with Joseph...of his master, the Egyptian. And his master observed that Yahweh [was] with him." When in Hebrew mode, the people of Sinai continued writing God's name. When reading out aloud, they would substitute the word *'ᵃdōnāy* (lord).

At the early stage in Hebrew writing, vowels weren't written in, so Hebrew left an ever so slight risk of someone speaking YHWH as God's name. However, when folk learned to read, they learned by those who knew the name-avoidance ropes, so mistakes weren't likely. When eventually Hebrew writing developed vowels, the 4 consonants of his name, in English the letters YHWH, were written with the vowels of *'ᵃdōnāy* below them. This visual reminder removed any danger of accidentally speaking God's name.

However, it would mislead non-ethnic Jews. By the Middles Ages the church had long been remiss in not missionising ethnic Jews in the way it did other ethnicities. Jacob Prasch has not been the only voice to lament that not evangelising ethnic Jews is the worst form of anti-Semitism (*The Final Words Of Jesus*, 1999:79). Some even say that any

Christian who hasn't yet evangelised an ethnic Jew shouldn't evangelise any non-Jew. They proof-text "to the Jew first".

Some say that the church should incorporate Levitical customs, and that Christianity is a sub-section of Sinai. They don't tell us to be physically circumcised, but still belong to the wrong circumcision party (Php.3:2-3), since in their minds they subjugate Yeshua to Sinai. I have known several good Christians of this persuasion, and I can see why their policy formed. But to see all is not to excuse all. I have been there. In exploring salvation, my *Israel's Gone Global* deals with this in far more depth. I now believe that the Jewish race is nothing special in spiritual terms, and that it has no ethnic covenant. As nothing special, there is no special reason not to missionise it, nor special reason to missionise it. Mission is global, transcending ethnicities as does the global covenant established by Yeshua. People is people.

So, what's been lost by a policy of not evangelising ethnic Jews? Well, individual ethnic Jews missed out on messianic life, and a passive or negative missioning policy resulted in a dearth of them bringing their insider information into God's kingdom. It would have been win-win, and quite possibly we would have avoided the Middle Ages' blunder about God's name. For ignorant of Hebrew conventions, we saw in Hebrew texts the vowels for *adonay* (ᵃoa, in the then lettering eoa), and simply combined them with the consonants (YHWH, in the then lettering IHUH/JHVH), resulting in the hybrid *IeHoUaH/JeHoVaH*.[127]

Nowadays, the formal meaning of *YHWH* is *generally* taken to require the vowels a and e, and, using English lettering, to be put as *YaHWeH/Yahweh*. Though workarounds such as *ha shem* (the name), and *l'Eternel* may be popular, these hardly come across as a personal name, so miss the very point that God intended. Such evasions of piety are needless except perhaps to make the Jewish race wistful for those days when Israel from which she came had, shall we say, a first name relationship with God.

Jehovah's Witnesses have an investment in rendering YHWH as *Jehovah*, as have KJVO-ists. The Witnesses (benchmark 1931) would like

---

[127] Try doing this with your first and last names: for example, Alexander Boddy can become Abedadey, or Clive Lewis, Liwes (or Celiv), or Susan Pevensie, Puvans.

to see it about 7,000 times in the Bible; KJVO-ists (benchmark 1611) prefer to see it there exactly 7 times.[128] For the OT, the Witnesses have the better case; for the NT, the KJVO-ists. Both sometimes say that if we don't know exactly what it should be in English, then by default we should go back to the medieval form, *Iehouah/Jehovah,* since we're familiar with this form. Others say, go with the balance of probability, let God's name be honoured. Let's bring this into English translation.

## Tyndale

Is.19:4 is an interesting text for this section, since it contains *lord* once for a human and once for God, and also has God's name. Note how below it is lower case *lord* for a human, upper case *Lord* for deity, and either four capitals, *LORD*, or *Yahweh*, for God's name.

KJV: "And the Egyptians will I give over into the hand of a cruel lord; and a fierce king shall rule over them, saith the Lord, the LORD of hosts."

WEB: "'I will give over the Egyptians into the hand of a cruel lord. A fierce king will rule over them,' says the Lord, Yahweh of Armies."

Early English versions generally followed the Latin version, which in turn followed Greek practice. Thus "the lord seide to my lord" (Wycliffe: Ps.109:1).[129] As he pioneered English OT translation from Hebrew, faced with God's name, William Tyndale established a general midway policy for his countrymen, by bucket loads of a simple 'the LORD', alongside a sprinkling of *Jehovahs.* As an endnote to *Genesis,* his 1530 edition says that "Iehovah is God's name...Moreover, as oft as thou seeist LORde in great letters (except there be any error in the printing) it is in Hebrew Iehovah..."[130] He could have added that

---

[128] Perhaps wilfully blind, Gail said that "the KJV is...the only bible (sic) that distinguishes between the Hebrew Adonay and JHVH, using 'Lord' for the former and 'LORD' for the latter" (Riplinger 376).

[129] Again, following the numbering system of the Latin Vulgate, from which Wycliffe translated the Bible. Roman Catholic English versions have improved, thus "Yahweh declared to my Lord" is Ps.110:1 in the NJB. Sadly, IMO, Pope Benedict 16 (28 June 2008) insisted that the Roman network revert to the Septuagint/Vulgate position, perhaps to foster good links with Judaics. I hope that his directive, not infallible in Roman Catholic terms, will be overturned in favour of the original Israelite tradition, too long ignored by the church.

[130] Several versions footnote this point at Ex.3:1-5

numerous times when we see *Lord* it might be *Yahweh*, not *Adonay*, since not infrequently he treated both God's name and lordship as equal (for example Ex.5:22). For rank-and-file Christians, Tyndale bravely translated from the original languages. He toyed with ways to show God's name, but inconsistently.

His Jehovah/LORD/Lord distinction (mostly in *Exodus*) shows he tried out ways to differentiate God's *name* from God's *authority*, perhaps in the face of critics. But at the end of the day, God's name as 1 permille *Jehovah*, and 999 permille *LORD* (as the KJV did it), is diluted, artificial, and undermining. Yet whether by hook or by crook, as had Martin Luther, Tyndale often very helpfully visually (even if not vocally) discriminated between God's *name*, and God's *lordship*, both of which Latin scripture put lowercase as *dominus*: the LORD (LORde) was lord; DOMINUS was *dominus*. Let us praise Tyndale as first to put God's name as a name into mechanically printed English Bible versions.

## **From Tyndale to KJV**

After him, most simply kept but capitalised the Vulgate format. Jerome could have done as much by changing *dominus* to *DOMINUS* where the text had God's name. The Latin Vulgate occasionally used some alternative to *lord* (*dominus*), such as *Omnipotent* (Ex.15:3–Wycliffe/Douay, *Almighty*), or *Adonay* (Ex.6:3–Wycliffe/Douay). But it never used God's name, and generally Roman priests, such as Wycliffe, followed suit. Tyndale was a notable exception.

Friend of Tyndale, and scholar of a lesser rank, Miles Coverdale, was also a Roman Catholic priest. In line with the Vulgate, he did not discriminate between God's name and God's lordship (for example Is.6:1), but put both as *LORD*, though when seeing that *adonay* was about human lords, put *lord* (for example Nb.32:25). Perhaps he assumed that Tyndale had merely flagged up God's special lordship, and wished to follow such piety—piety highlight.

Likewise, some throw capitals at every pronoun directly linked to God, a process the KJV sanely avoided. Coverdale later worked on the Great Bible, and the Geneva, which perhaps thought it needless to write *LORD* instead of *Lord*. Tyndale was the only one, I think, to stand out for God's name, until we reach the KJV.

## Translating Theology

A weakness of the Geneva is that though it ignored the capitalisation method, it accepted the idea of God's name as his personal name but hardly ever used it. A weakness of the KJV is that it kept both options (Jehovah/the LORD), and strongly favoured Latin conservatism, rather than increasing coverage of God's name as his personal name, as Tyndale had possibly hoped—creeping familiarisation. Thus, while the Geneva's "the Lord faid vnto my Lord" (Ps.110:1) is bettered by the KJV 1611's LORD/Lord distinction, it would have been better to read, "Jehovah said unto my Lord" (Darby).

The trouble is, that putting either *LORD* or *lord* when God's name is at stake, easily makes it *sound* like it is Jesus, because Jesus is *lord* and many Christians don't know that *LORD* doubles for God's name. There is a biblical complication: [the] LORD is lord (Ps.68:20). *Lord* (*kurios*) can function as, or in place of, a name, and it can also function as a function, lordship, mastery, sovereignty. And while the father is ultimate lord, his son strategic lord, and the spirit tactical lord, it is strategic lordship which in our covenant is the default setting, while the default setting for *Yahweh/God* is the father, not his son (1 Cor.8:6).

Some begin prayer to the father, then call him lord, then thank him for dying on the cross (patripassianism). Christian songs citing Yahweh-texts, usually end up on OHPs as if they're citing Jesus-texts. Even some theology professors seem to blithely downgrade 'the LORD' to 'the Lord'. This trend ignores the Athanasian Creed, and undermines trinitarianism, by confusing the three persons who are the eternal society, God, and dividing in our minds that one society. How many popular church songs imply that Jesus *alone* is God? Like Muslims, many Christians are poor in biblical theology, whether too busy, too afraid, or simply too lazy. Bible versions should make it clear when we're talking God's name. Like Tyndale, the KJV could have helped us more, but did help us some.

### Wycliffe-KJV Tetragrammaton Chart

### Texts

The texts are A (Gen.15:2); B (Gen.22:14); C (Ex.6:2); D (Ex.6:3); E (Ex.15:3); F (Ex.17:15); G (Ex.23:17); H (Ex.33:19); I (Ex.34:23); J (Dt.3:24); K (Jg.6:24);

# God's ID

L (Ps.83:18); M (Is.12:2); N (Is.26:4). Versions having *Iehoua[h]/Jehovah*,[131] at those days state of the art, have a **Y** for Yes/Yahweh. Those given a **4** (Four Caps) show Tyndale's convention of capitalising God's name, howbeit it still implied a title, not a name. Those merely expressing *Lord/lord*, I have marked **L**. An **o** (other) indicates either *Adonay* (Vulgate), *Almighty* (Vulgate), or *God* [eternal], which includes the practice of compounding *Adonay Yahweh*, or *Yah Yahweh*, into *Lord God* (*Domine Deus*)—KJVs have either Lord GOD or, better indicating a name component, LORD God. A dash (-) is for missing text.

|  | A | B | C | D | E | F | G | H | I | J | K | L | M | N |
|---|---|---|---|---|---|---|---|---|---|---|---|---|---|---|
| 1 Wycliffe LV | o | L | L | o | o | L | o | L | o | o | L | L | L | o |
| 2 Tyndale | Y | 4 | L | Y | Y | Y | Y | Y | Y | - | - | - | - | - |
| 3 Coverdale | 4 | 4 | 4 | 4 | 4 | 4 | 4 | 4 | 4 | 4 | 4 | 4 | 4 | 4 |
| 4 Matthew | Y | L | L | Y | Y | Y | Y | Y | Y | o | Y | Y | o | o |
| 5 Great | o | L | L | Y | L | L | o | L | Y | o | L | L | o | o |
| 6 Geneva | o | Y | L | Y | Y | Y | Y | L | Y | o | Y | Y | o | o |
| 7 Bishops | o | L | Y | Y | L | L | o | Y | Y | o | L | L | o | o |
| 8 Douay | o | L | L | o | o | L | o | L | o | o | L | L | L | o |
| 9 KJV Cambridge | o | Y | 4 | Y | 4 | Y | o | 4 | o | o | Y | Y | Y | Y |

## Comparative Class Grades

Let's not tetragrammatise *adonay* texts, nor detetragrammatise *Yahweh* texts. On this chart, yet aware that sadly Tyndale often reverted to the Latin method of non-*differentiation* by *Lord*, I rate Tyndale no more than average, followed by the KJV. Let us be surprised, however, not that Tyndale didn't go as far as we might have wished, but rather that he went as far as he did. He was the baker expecting execution, whereas the KJV translators were the butler expecting exaltation (Gen.40).

Coverdale seemingly scores well, yet he clueless killed off the lord (*adonay*) by thrashing Tyndale's four cap method to death. God's name was conflated with a title, to a mere reverential TITLE. Upgrading

---

[131] The KJV 1611 had the former; since 1671 it has had the latter.

lordship to God's name, effectively flattened out the distinction. If all little girls become princesses (and all mothers, queens), then all princesses become commoners. If only the right boxes are to be ticked, does it really help to tick all the boxes, right and wrong? Is Equality Law right, when moral and immoral boxes must be treated as equal (eg *partner*, or *Ms*) to avoid the secular blasphemy of discrimination, and morality flatlined?

Thankfully the KJV achieved greater accuracy than Tyndale and Coverdale, though seldom preferring Tyndale's higher method to his lower, and being confused over compound terms such as Yah/Yahweh, or Adonay/Yahweh.[132] The other versions infrequently followed Tyndale's better idea, and failed to follow his lesser one. Best: Geneva/Matthew; middling, Bishops/Great; worst, Douay/Wycliffe—which followed the Vulgate lead.

## From KJV to Today

Most English versions follow the KJV, showing some distinction, whether by [Lord/lord],[133] [LORD/Lord], [Jehovah/Lord], or [Yahweh/Lord]. One NIV translator admitted that it was felt too risky and/or unhelpful to replace *LORD* with *Yahweh*.[134] That fact that some versions don't even bother to explain their LORD/Lord system implies they're simply carrying on a tradition. Radical in some ways, the New English Bible continued the KJV tradition of *LORD* as standard, and *Jehovah* in a token way,[135] perhaps fearing to radically ruffle Christian feathers.

F F Bruce was sad it had missed the opportunity to naturalise God's name into English versions (Bruce 1986:251). On the other hand, Bruce Metzger was glad that the New American Bible did *not* adopt the

---

[132] For example, Ex.4:10 and 5:22 both have *Adonay* and *Yahweh*, which Tyndale put equally as *Lord/Lord*, Coverdale equally as *LORD/LORD*, and the KJV as *Lord/LORD*.

[133] The capitonym method, where a capital changes the meaning—for example we shall *march* in the month of *March*. In reading aloud, the difference can be missed, as in "the *Lord* said to my *lord*".

[134] In personal correspondence, Eugene Rubingh (email: 3/9/04).

[135] Namely Gen.22:14; Ex. 3:15; 6:3; 17:15; Jg.6:24; and Ezk.48:35.

practice of naturalising such an "utterly un-English" name (Metzger 128)![136] In such as the NLT, even better the 2010 HCSB, there is some drip-feed movement towards best practice. In C20/1 versions, approaches to God's name range from ignoring it, to the standard approach of only contrasting his name to his lordship by means of LORD/Lord (preferably at least telling readers what the difference means, as the NIV84 did), to enriching LORD/Lord by the occasional *Yahweh*, to a fully-fledged distinction between *Yahweh* (or Jehovah) and *Lord*.

Most Christians, unaware that most translators have already downgraded *Yahweh* to *LORD*, further downgrade *LORD* to *Lord*, thoughtlessly even misquoting English versions. Many think it's about, and only about, Jesus (Jesus is Lord), verging on, or overflowing into (eg Hillsong), an alternative to trinitarianism—a "God is one person and his name is Jesus" theology called Oneness. *Jesus* is not God's name. *Jesus* is the name for the eternal second person in his incarnate mode. Jesus is *lord*, but not the LORD who gave the Sinaitic covenant. Jesus is not Yahweh, but without personal names to differentiate, how can we expect Christians to instinctively know that the LORD who spoke to David was not the lord who spoke to Saul (Ps.110:1)? Nor is Jesus he who gave the global, Yeshuic, covenant—he became its mediator (1 Tm.1:5; Heb.12:23-4) and basis. Translation theory promoted by Jerome advocated OT translation from the Hebrew, but sadly we hybrid God's name between Hebrew and Greek. Tyndale's gain is often lost.

Most scholars prefer to let the source (donor) languages speak for themselves. The original OT documents (autographs) were mainly Hebrew, so let us establish the original Hebrew text and translate it within that context. Likewise with the NT Greek autographs. If this throws up differences between OT and NT—such as *Yahweh* and *kurios*—let us translate as *Yahweh* (name) in the OT and *lord* in the NT. The inspired NT writers could have used other than Greek if they wished to highlight an important feature. They did that with their *rare* use of Aramaic (for example *abba*, *Kephas*, *maranatha*) to flag up

---

[136] What was his problem? Nebuchadnezzar/*Nebuchadrezzar* is utterly un-English but English folk can get used to it. Probably new converts lacking a Bible background, wouldn't understand why a name has been replaced by a title.

concepts deeply ingrained among the first Jewish Christians—should we be more Hebrew (or Aramaic) than them? I suggest letting both the OT and NT speak for themselves, and then letting loose the commentators to explain, not explain away, the differences.

In the tetragrammaton chart below, I have not factored in the quality of any explanative footnotes. Nor have I penalised what I deem to be the bad practice of messing with the authentic NT.[137] The NT simply used *kurios,* which was to its original audience a useful start to the trinitarian road. We should not throw *Jehovahs* or *LORDs* into the NT, but in the Letters translate *kurios* the same way in referring to Jesus as to his father, not adjusting the text to the OT text. Nor have I penalised the policy of converting *Adonay* text to *Yahweh* text, such as Coverdale in effect did. Nor have I factored in the practice of some versions to transliterate, rather than translate, some of the Yahweh-predicate names (*Yahweh š`ālôm*: Jg.6:24). I think they may be treated as names, so long as functional equivalence is given in text for footnote form. And I have bypassed debated text, where ancient manuscripts divide between God's name, and *lord* (*adonay*). For example, for Is.6:11, 1QIsa$^a$ reads *Yahweh,* but the Masoretic Text reads *Lord*. There are numerous places where I'd expect to read God's name, but find *Lord* printed instead. I suspect that at times name migrated to title. But where no manuscript indicates *Yahweh, lord* must be translated, for example Is.6:1.

In Islamic circles, I can allow that *allah* can function the same way, and is of the same root, as *elohim*. However, it can generate confusion as to whether conceptual baggage of Muslim ideology is nowadays too strongly tied into that word. If we put it as *Allah*, we can use it as a personal noun fixing the Islamic form of monopersonal monotheism. Christians might be happy to say that they worship *Allah* (God), but not *Allah* (Islamic definition of God). The Al-Kitab English

---

[137] www.jw.org/en/publications/bible/nwt/appendix-a/divine-name-christian-greek-scriptures/#p1 argues for justification, partly on the assumption that Jesus acting under his father's name meant saying Yahweh: it meant authority, *not* vocalising his name. Likewise, "I come in the name of Caesar", not "I come in the name of Nero". At the end of the day we should work with what we have, rather than what we do not have but wish to conjecture. That others have itched the same way does not justify the NWT scratch.

Bible translation badly replaces the Hebrew personal, proper name for God, YHWH, with the semantically unrelated *Allah*: "Hear, Israel: Allah is our God, Allah is one: and you shall love Allah your God with all your heart, and with all your soul, and with all your might" (Dt.6:4-5).[138]

## Tetragrammaton Chart C100

### Texts

The more obvious texts for having God's name are those that talk about his name. Is it not more sensible to say that "Yahweh is his name" (WEB), rather than "the LORD is his name" (KJV: Am.5:8) or *"the RULER is his name"*? "I represent the lord" sounds great, unless I live in a land that has many lords. Which lord is yours? I have looked at Ex.3:15; 6:2,3; 15:3a&b; Jg.6:24; Ps.83:18; Jr.33:2; Hos.12:5; Am.5:8, to represent one batch of texts crying out to feature his name. Then I have considered another random batch of text (Gen.2:4; 4:1; Ex.5:2; Jos.2:9; 1 Sam.3:9; Ps.110:1; Pr.30:9; Is.14:1; 26:4; 43:11) less likely to show his name. Less likely, that is, unless the version has a proactive policy to honour God's name.

Here, as we used to say, we separate the men from the boys, adults from children. Any version factoring God's name at this level is more likely to comprehensively restore God's name than fellow versions that simply, though correctly, restore it in the more obvious places. My order of preference has been: Yahweh/Yah; Jehovah/Jah; Eternal [god]; GOD; [the] LORD; Yud-Heh-Vav-Heh/YHVH; Adonay; other conventions being zero rated.

### Comparative Class Grades

| C100 | Grade |
|---|---|
| LEB/LSB/NJB/NOG/WEB | A+ |
| NWT | B |
| HCSB | B- |
| TVB | C |
| ERV/NABRE/NLT | C- |

---

[138] See http://hamilim.netronix.com/2013/07/01/is-allah-the-god-of-the-bible.

| | |
|---|---|
| CEB/CEV/CSB/EEB/EJB/EOB/ESV/GNB/GWT/ISV/ KJ21/KJV/MEV/MSG/NASB20/NASB95/NCB/NCV/ NET/NIV/NKJV/NRSV/NRSVU/REB/RNJB/RSV | D+ |
| CJB/LSV/TLV | U+ |
| FBV/NLV | U- |

## Scribal Downgrading

Some suggest that as society softened, ancient scribes deliberately softened some bits of the harsher texts, for instance using euphemisms. I suspect that in more places, God's name has been softened to lordship. And a good case can be made for adding occasional explanations, and updating names. Scripture was a living word. Scholars can seek a Hebrew text predating the standard Masoretic Text (MT), removing textual dust. But unless we have good grounds for change, we must be based on what we have.

In 1946 a scroll of Isaiah—and later some others Isaianic texts—was discovered at Qumran, predating the MT by about a millennium, and it helps us restore the ancient writings—their need of restoration is not great, but refinement is welcome. Consider God's name, which sometimes got downgraded to 'lord'. Today's songwriters are also infamous for ignoring the significance of his name, as do many biblical scholars who sing their songs.

The only Bible versions I have seen in line with the Great Isaiah scroll, are the CEB/CEV/ISV/NABRE/NWT. Intext the NWT84 (citing Ginsberg) claims that there are 134 scribal changes from YHWH to Adonai, with perhaps 7 Yahweh to Elohim downgrades—the NWT13 lacks such explanation. Downgrading the MT once (*viz* Jg.19:18, upgraded by the NWT13), upgrading it five times, and factoring in its list of 141 alleged MT downgrades, the NWT84 used *Jehovah* 6,973x, compared to the MT's 6,828x, that is just over a 2% increase.

While some increase is IMO justified, I think it was a little too taken up with Ginsberg in overestimating the downgrading of the sopherim (scribes/copyists): on this the NWT13 is little changed. The MEV upgrades, probably accidentally, for Is.28:2—there seems to me no other explanation than unintention and inattention. The CEB/NABRE are probably too cautious but have slightly adjusted in line with the Great Isaiah Scroll. Commendably the ISV has sought to upgrade where the earlier Hebrew texts from Qumran permit (except for 37:24), but seems to me to sometimes follow Ginsberg even without direct ancient text (eg 4:4; 6:8; 7:20), while sometimes rejecting Ginsberg (eg 21:8; 29:13; 49:14). Out of Ginsberg's list of 23, probably 9 are justified by extant text, and the ISV is the most competent in correcting Ginsberg and the MT. This is all a matter of good textual scholarship in establishing the text, not an issue of doctrine, although how to render God's name moves into doctrine. Let's re-enthrone God's name, I say. And for Christians who prefer the [the LORD] workaround, I ask, Would you prefer Jesus to just be called [the lord]?

# Chapter 10    Who's for Huiology?

Huiology is the biblical revelation of God's son (*huios*). Unlike Christology, by definition it exceeds the limits of the incarnation: God's son became the christ (anointed) at a point in space and time. Let's compare a number of versions to see how well they witness to biblical teaching on God's *huios*.

## Deificity of God's Son

From the KJVO market, charges against the theological integrity of the non-Byzantine text-types are many, varied, and often mischievous. They need not all be individually rebutted, so long as they can be seen in principle as misdirected. But is there smoke without fire? Well, behind the smoke bombs is pyromania of enflamed hearts. Fire-breathing KJV advocates either claim that only the MT or the TR is orthodox, and claim that the other text-types used by *eclecticism*—Western, and Alexandrian text-types—are heretical about Christ's deificity and cross.

Is eclecticism a big bogeyman? Well, if so, we must settle for the best bogeyman we can get. The KJV was eclectic (page 57)! All modern versions are rightly based on *eclecticism*. All text-types (including Byzantine) should be compared verse by verse, since they vary in accuracy on any given verse. Then translators should adopt a reading from one or more text-types before translating into English. This can reveal greater witness to such as Christ's deificity (eg Jhn.1:18), as the chart below indicates, though that greater witness mainly comes through better understanding of Greek.

Texts Included

These texts have long histories of dispute. To paraphrase C S Lewis, trinitarianism is too crazy to have come out of any human head. Therefore, it must reflect a transcendent reality we are to get into our heads and get our heads around. But some Christians conclude, it's simply too crazy and too hard. The debate goes way back, building a history of claim, counterclaim, counter-counterclaim, and many "yes-buts". Trench warfare, neither side moving, heavy sniping. I have neither the time nor the space to argue definitively for the definite positions I have taken. But I hope to at least show that, whether or not justified by text or translation, modern versions can be more trinitarian than the KJV.

## Jhn.1:1

This is a fulsome text to begin a fulsome Gospel. It carries ideas of creation (Gen.1:1), and that beyond the beginning of space and time is the Logos, which is *with* (a term implying person with person) God [the father], and is deity [in essence]. The Logos is truly deity in substance (Jhn.1:1), truly with God the father in fellowship (Jhn.1:1), and has become true and unfallenly human (Jhn.1:14).[139]

Step back to *Genesis* and see how the Hebrew term *'adam* doubled as a term for *mankind* and a personal name for the male of the species: Eve (the woman) was *with* Adam (the man) and together they *were 'adam* (mankind: Gen.5:2). So too the term 'God' refers, depending on context, to one person or one society.

John meant *God*, not Godlikeness. Otherwise, he could have used the diminutive form of *Theos* (God), namely *Theios*. Nor could John justify Israelite-Jewish monotheism if the Word was a god: there is only one god, God. I'm happy to accept Witnesses as Christians, but not their antitrinitarianism as Christian. Once they insisted that lacking the article (the) *must* mean 'a' god. Nowadays they accept the Colwell Rule,[140] but tend simply to say that the Bible teaches God's oneness, elsewhere never affirms another person as *God*, so cannot do so *in this context*.[141] Yet "if they agree that context is decisive, but can find nothing in this context that supports their view, they have simply lost the argument" (Grudem 234).

---

[139] Moucarry 118 noted that strictly speaking the Qur'an denies—as Christians should—the heresy of tritheism (3 gods)—*not* the biblical position of trinitarianism (1 god as the eternal society of 3 persons).

[140] It says that "a definite predicate noun will usually drop the definite article when it precedes the verb, but the subject of the sentence, if definite, will retain the definite article" (Grudem 234). Likewise, Carson's *Exegetical Fallacies*, 2002:84: Colwell showed "the Word was God" as grammatically possible, and McGaughy's rule makes it certain.

[141] For more, see Martin 108-110.

## Jhn.1:18

There is internal and external evidence, both very good, to support the Alexandrian reading here, namely that the Logos (Word) of Jhn.1:1 is *monogenēs theos* (unique, God, the earliest manuscripts of John—p66 and p75). This reading was accepted by one of the ancient champions of trinitarianism, C4 Gregory of Nyssa.

*Monogenēs* can carry in itself the idea, *son*, and can stand in apposition to *theos*. This could read, *the unique son, who is God*. This no more limits the concept, God, to the son, than does Jhn.1:1 (...with God). Clearly v18 implies distinction of the son to his father, and the revealer to the revealed. If not in apposition, it would say, as Jhn.1:1, that the Logos shared unique deity, in contrast to pagan *gods*, derivative beings or concepts (...was God). So [the unique [son, himself] deity], yields a better intrinsic deificity claim than does the TR.

It's useful to know that *monogenēs* never meant *begotten*.[142] Basically the Old Latin translations kept to the Greek meaning, but Jerome theologically tweaked son-texts to counter Arian ideas that God's son was created within time and space, by insisting that God's son was generated, birthed, in eternity. Jerome thought that *unigenitus* (begotten/born) better undermined the Arian idea than the standard translation, *unicus* (a one-of-a-kind, a unique genus). I do not say he was the first Latin to take this path. Where creeds in English say 'begotten', they reflect Jerome rather than John. Isaac was Abraham's *one-of-a-kind* loved son, not his *only* begotten son (Heb.11:17).[143]

---

[142] "It was thought that [begotten] came from μονος (*monos*), meaning 'only' and γενναω (*gennaō*), meaning 'begotten'. However, further research has determined that the term is derived not from γενναω but from γενος (*genos*), meaning 'kind' or 'type'. Hence the better translation, 'unique' or 'one-of-a-kind'" (White 1995:259.5). For translation for the Gk. *monogenēs* as one-of-a-kind (as in 1 Clement 25:2), see the NET comment on Jhn.3:16.

[143] The Septuagint use includes a use for only child (Jg.11:34—*kai ēn hautē monogenēs*), though the central meaning could be her *specialness* because she was his one and only [surviving?] child. Ancient use included the idea of an *only surviving* child out of a number of children *begotten*. The Septuagint often treated it as a synonym for *agapētos* (*beloved*) (Köstenberger 4-3).

In fact, to keep *begotten*, and to take the reading, *God*, takes us along the road of polytheism. A bad mix. To avoid implying at any cost that the Logos was intrinsically God, the NWT's "the only begotten god" slants to heresy. *Begotten* is unwarranted. To rubbish non-KJV English versions, D A Waite wished to tar them with the NWT brush, and denounce them for heresy. Not God but a *begotten god*, how dare they sir! They dare sir because they say that *begotten* itself is unwarranted. Or is it? Gail cited Büchsel for support that *monogenēs* means *only begotten/born*. Büchsel's extensive article was in Gerhard Kittel's *Theological Dictionary of the NT*. Gail, elsewhere with some justification, lambasted Kittel as having been a Jew-hating Nazi (for example Riplinger 591).[144] Here, she's wished him as an ally, but all she has shown is that Büchsel represented an older generation of scholars who wrongly assumed this etymology. She also claimed that "all interlinear Greek-English New Testaments translate it as such" (Riplinger 342). Sadly, her list of Interlinears is unsurprisingly missing.[145] *Begotten* is unwarranted.

## Rm.9:5

Here, after, say, "Theirs are the patriarchs, and from them is traced the human ancestry of the Messiah" (NIV), should we put a comma and continue speaking of messiah, or a fullstop and begin speaking of God? Grammar, and the early church fathers, strongly favours the former. Somewhat surprisingly, the NABRE prefers the idea that the praise context isn't about Jesus.[146] And if we feel that the NT nowhere

---

[144] She has been willing to use Kittel's work when it suits her argument, but challenges the work of others for using Kittel. Was he pro-semitic for her, but anti-semitic (and thus always wrong?) for her opponents?

[145] For a lexicon list of a truer story, see www.forananswer.org/John/Jn1_18.htm.

[146] Perhaps overly influenced by C H Dodd's idea that 'Christ is God' would be uncharacteristic of Paul, the NABRE argues that God, over all, planned to use Ethnic Israel globally, and is simply being praised in context. While in a few Pauline contexts a 'Jesus is God' text seems grammatically clear, a note of scarcity is valid: Paul struck a balance between a truth that needed clear words yet if majored in would imbalance truth. At the other side of the spectrum, arguably heretical though idolised, Hillsong's Reuben Morgan has written …1# *Mighty to Save*: "my god…rose and conquered the grave, Jesus conquered the grave". My god is Jesus. 2# *You Alone Are God*: "Sing my soul unto God alone:

else makes the deity link so blunt, we might feel that minor grammatical loopholes must be followed, and blow the fathers. Of course they could have been mistaken, but other things being equal, one would expect those closer in time to C1 huiology to be fairly savvy in it: when they speak in unison, we should have strong biblical grounds before rejecting them. Incidentally, another point towards messiah as deific is the fact that *epi pantōn* might link to the *kurios pantōn* texts (Ac.10:36; Rm.10:12),[147] thus strengthening the idea that 9:5 is about the anointed lord being deific on (said a little tongue in cheek) his paternal side. The contextual point would be that Christ unified Jews with Gentiles in lordship. By the way, there is also a choice between good translation (*praised*) and bad (*blessed*) of *eulogētos*.

### Tts.2:13 and 2 Pt.1:1

Since these, according to the NIV but not the KJV, speak of God's son's deity, KJVO-ists must oppose the NIV. One way is to claim that the NIV affirms the deity of God's son *for the wrong reasons, against* the text and/or grammar, and somehow results in heresy.

Riplinger 370-1 1# asserts that the Greek *text* doesn't render these texts the way the NIV has done. Gail then 2# implied that the NIV is Liberal, because Liberals can happily combine their heresy that Jesus never claimed to be deity incarnate, with their heresy that *Titus* and

---

you alone are God...We declare the glory of your name, reign in all the earth Jesus." Jesus only is God—neither father nor spirit need apply. 3# *Forever Reign*: "You are Lord ...you are God, my heart will sing no other name Jesus"— excludes father and spirit. 4# *Let Us Adore*: "The heavens declare the glory of God, and all he has made will rise up to bless the king of all kings. Let us adore him, Jesus Christ is the Lord, eternity's king is coming again"—pretty clear cut. Other Christian lyricists add that *only Jesus can satisfy your soul, only Jesus brings redemption, only Jesus satisfies, Jesus only is our message, Jesus only will we see, Jesus all in all we sing, Jesus only is our saviour, Jesus only is our healer, only Jesus can our every sorrow know; he alone can truly help us.* Trinitarianism far better utilises the full biblical data and concludes (in short) that God is one eternal society of three persons, and that no reference to any person as God, other than the father, excludes the fuller definition of the society as God in close context. The closed context of Jesus God songs is their heresy.

[147] The immediate context of Rm.10:9 shows that in v12, Jesus is this lord.

## Who's for Huiology?

2 *Peter* were written in the C2. Then 3# she concluded that the NIV elsewhere loves to throw out the idea of the deificity of Christ, chucking in *Jude* 25 as an example. A typical creeping barrage, perhaps to prevent readers weighing up one point at a time. Let's see.

1# this is *not* the point, merely one of Gail's smoke screens to imply that the NIV has departed from all the Greek manuscripts. All who know Greek agree the issue here is about what the text *means*, *not* about what it *is*, and knowing what it *means* depends on knowing Greek grammar. Not Gail's strong point.

2# Gail probably misdirected attention in order to imply heretical motivation; we must direct attention to Greek grammar. The grammar is clear. Around 1790, Granville Sharp discovered a rule with common Greek construction. It is in simple the Greek pattern [*the*/non-proper name/*and*/non-proper name noun], where when one noun describes a *person*, both nouns describe the *same* person.[148]

---

[148] In detail, from Sharp's 1807 edition: "when the copulative connects two nouns of the same a case [viz nouns (either substantive or adjective, or participles) of personal description, respecting office, dignity, affinity, or connection, and attributes, properties, or qualities, good or ill,] if the article, or any of its cases, precedes the first of the said nouns or participles, and is not repeated before the second noun or participle, the latter always relates to the same person that is expressed or described by the first noun or participle: that is, it denotes a further description of the first named person" (White 1995:269). White noted that alleged exceptions to the rule were found only when Sharpe's rule was extended to include plural and proper names.

Compare: "a girlfriend of mine..." (I have at least one girlfriend); "a girl and friend of mine..." (I have a friend who is a girl); "a girl and a friend tells me" (I'm talking of two people)—language rules.

A modern reassessment by Daniel Wallace, shows that sharpening up this rule covers all known exceptions. Thus "In native Greek constructions (that is, not translation Greek), when a single article modifies *two* substantives connected by *kai* (thus, article-substantive-*kai*-substantive), when both substantives are (1) singular (both grammatically and semantically), (2) personal, (3) and common nouns (not proper names or ordinals), they have the same referent. In native Greek constructions (that is, not translation Greek), when a single article modifies *two* substantives connected by *kai* (thus, article-substantive-*kai*-substantive), when both substantives are (1) singular (both grammatically and semantically), (2) personal, (3) and common nouns (not proper names or

## Translating Theology

For example [the/god/and/saviour] describe the same person. Thus, Greek grammar justifies the NIV's translation. Moreover, Tts.2:13 has *epiphaneia* (appearing). Since "every other instance of this word is reserved for Christ and him alone", this would favour it referring here to Christ, and v14, while using a Yahweh (who is God) text, refers it to Christ (White 1995:267).[149] 2 Pt. has 5 Granville Sharp constructions: 1:1,11; 2:20; 3:2,18. Note the same construction between these Granville Sharp verses:

| 2 Pt.1:1  | tou theou hēmōn kai sōtēros Iēsou Christou |
| 2 Pt.1:11 | tou kuriou hēmōn kai sōtēros Iēsou Christou |

If Jesus Christ is put as lord (*kuriou*) *and* saviour in v11, is he put as not deity (*theou*) *and* saviour in v1? Gail's quote of Lewis Foster, if correct, does not affirm—as she perhaps hoped—that the NIV only translated these texts as deity texts because of heretical translators. Two people hear me say "curse God and die". One reports that I'm a heretic, the other that I quoted *Job* 2:9. Foster's 'quote'—reportage—could simply explain *why* Liberals can, seeing grammar implies Christ's deificity, justify such translation. Did the KJV translate Jhn.1:1 the way they did because they were Liberals believing *John* was written in the C2, or because they believed that grammar dictated translation? If she could accept that the NIV translated Jhn.1:1 the same way as the KJV simply *because of Greek grammar*, rather than a Liberal idea that *John* was C2, could she not accept that deeper knowledge of Greek grammar lay behind the NIV's translation of 2 Pt.1:1? Here the Geneva backs the NIV—was Calvin a Liberal? John Chrysostom referred to Tts.2:13 to establish that Christ is indeed called *theos* and not inferior to the Father.[150] Was Chrysostom a Liberal?

3# throwing in *Jude* 25 allowed let her shift the ground and hurriedly move on, goal scored before the referee can cry 'foul'. She said that in *Jude* 25, "God our Saviour" is Jesus, because "our Saviour is Jesus;

---

ordinals), they have the same referent" (https://bible.org/article/sharpi-redivivus-i-reexamination-granville-sharp-rule).

[149] 2 Ths.2:8; 1 Tm.6:14; 2 Tm.1:10; 4:1,8.

[150] Post-Nicene Fathers, 13.207—www.ccel.org/ccel/schaff/npnf113.v.v.v.html; www.tertullian.org/fathers2/NPNF1-13/npnf1-13-116.htm#P3712_2540745

therefore Jesus is God" (Riplinger 371), and since our saviour *is Jesus* the NIV et al are wrong to have added "through Jesus Christ our Lord". Here she was at best foolish, since the term 'saviour' sometimes applies to God the father, sometimes to God the son, and the point is really what Jude actually said. Perhaps more knave than fool, she ignored that the KJV reads "God our Saviour, and Lord Jesus Christ" in 1 Tm.1:1, since Paul showing there that the saviour was *not* Jesus makes it harder to knock "to the only God our Saviour be glory...through Jesus Christ our Lord..." by her flimsy claim that our saviour is *always* Jesus: did the KJV get 1 Tm.1:1 wrong, Gail? Is not her talk of a "100 or so [NIV] verses" denying Christ's deificity, as flimsy?

## Texts Excluded

### Ac.20:28

This might well fit the general pattern of the blood (that is, death) being God's son's, not directly God's. The former "is grammatically possible and fits in with the use of the phrase his own son (Rm.8:31)" (Marshall 334). That is, it could mean either "the blood of his own/his own's blood", meaning, as in Lk.22:20, his own son's blood, not *his own blood*. Versions that indicate this approach include the GNB/LEB/NABREn/NCV/NIVn/NJB/NLTn/NRSV/NWT/TVB.

### 2 Ths.1:12

Of interest to the question of whether non-KJV versions always shy away from the deity link of God's son, we may consider this text. None except the GWT/NABRE/NIV/NLT/NOG/ISV consider it to be a positive witness, including the KJV. Yet their *failure* shows not their slowness to climb the mountain of proper translation, but their general reluctance to obtrude trinitarian translation when it is not demanded by the text. So my chart below also excludes this text. From a trinitarian perspective, those above which seem to grade highly on this text, though following the hunch of good theology, may be over reading the first grammatical rule of Granville Sharp, since the term *lord*, in "Lord Jesus Christ", seems to involve a proper name, which is outside the scope of Sharp's rule.[151]

### 1 Tm.3:16

This *might* favour the KJV text. The Greek in 1 Tm.3:16 in the earliest manuscripts—later the capital sigma changed to Σ—would be ΘΕΟΣ (God) or ΟΣ (he who). In fact ΘΕΟΣ was often abbreviated to ΘΣ (a line above both letters). In a long string of letter without spaces, this could easily be confused (White 1995:207). Some versions read *God*, some *he*: some footnote the alternatives. The fact that this text might indicate the deificity of Christ is not feared so much as doubted by versions which otherwise agree and support the doctrine of the son's deity.

### Heb.1:8-9

Here, linked to Ps.45:6-7, a basic principle of interpretation requires it to have made good sense in its original setting even if it has a fuller meaning (Fee and Stuart 64). In the original setting of the psalmist, covenant kings were functionally as God to his people, and as other leaders, were rightly reminded that they themselves were under God. Whether or not a hidden depth of meaning was coded in—a *sensus plenior* as in Is.7:14 and allowing for trinitarian translation in *Hebrews*—it is sufficiently ambivalent to allow alternate translation by trinitarians.

Even if the traditional reading is most justified,[152] interpretation must ask if the Writer was beginning with God's son as Deity incarnate, or as Davidic. IMO, if the former, the Letter first asks for the camel to be swallowed, and then invites readers to swallow some gnats. I suspect the authorial intent was to start low, then build up fulfilment themes one after another, however likely the readers were to look back and see deity even from the start of the Letter. One distinction to note, however, is that whereas the Israelite king was God-by-adoption, by anointing, Jesus was the permanent temporal mode of God the father's co-eternal uncreated son.

---

[151] See https://bible.org/article/sharpi-redivivus-i-reexamination-granville-sharp-rule.

[152] See Beale and Carson's *Commentary on the NT Use of the OT*, 2009:937.

## Huiology Chart C200: Deificity

### Texts

The texts are A (Jhn.1:1); B (Jhn.1:18); C (Rm.9:5); D (Tts.2:13); E (2 Pt.1:1).[153] For each text a clear text gained 4 marks, a slightly less clear, three marks, a standard footnote indicating the proper text, two marks, if hidden in footnotes and/or misrepresenting the proper text (for example the NU as *begotten god*) 1 mark, and missing without trace, zero marks. There are some small bonuses for outstanding notes. Whether one likes or dislikes the mixing of English and Hebrew (for example "The Word was Elohim": Jhn.1:1), I have not discounted marks for such. The results indicate both academic commitment to textual and grammatical accuracy, on which systematic trinitarianism was based. Had C16/7 translators a better textual model, and better Greek grammar, their scores would have been higher.

### Comparative Class Grades

| C200 | Grade |
|---|---|
| NET | A+ |
| NLT/NRSV | A- |
| CSB/ERV/NASB20/NIV | B+ |
| EEB/GWT/NCB/NCV/NOG/NRSVU/WEB | B |
| CEB/CEV/HCSB/ISV/LEB/LSB/RSV/TLV | B- |
| EOB/MSG/NJB | C+ |
| EJB/ESV/FBV/GNB/MEV/NASB95/TVB | C |
| LSV/NABRE/NKJV/REB/RNJB | C- |
| KJ21/KJV | D+ |
| NLV | D- |
| CJB | U+ |
| NWT | U- |

### Some final observations:

- The Geneva Bible highlights Christ's deificity more than the later KJV;

---

[153] On this last text, the old Geneva, and the Moffatt, score much better than the KJV.

- The earlier versions lacked manuscripts and our improved knowledge of Greek;
- If the low score NWT is because of the Witnesses' denial of God's son being God the son, the CJB's seems to be in spite of Stern's belief;[154]
- KJVO-ists, maintaining the infallibility of the KJV as they have it, will turn fuller witness to God the Son's deificity, into covert anti-trinitarianism, saying that the new versions take more with the left hand than they give with right, even that what they give they give as fifth columnists—heresy in disguise.

## **Christological Terms**

Over centuries, many a scribe has seen the word, *christ*, in a Greek copy, mentally added the familiar term 'the', and copied as 'the christ. Over centuries, many a scribe has seen the words, the lord, in a Greek copy, mentally added the familiar term 'Jesus', and copied as 'the lord Jesus'. Over centuries, many a scribe has seen the words, 'the lord Jesus', in a Greek copy, mentally added the familiar term 'christ', and copied as 'the lord Jesus christ'. The KJV was weak at paring back the many piety expansions to the text. They are best removed, not because of wrongness in principle, but because of wrongness in text. They who honour the idea of Scripture having been inspired by God at the highest, and unique, level, would not wish even good expressions added to the canonical text.

Some turn the tables, and say that whatever the KJV has is the text, the whole text, and nothing but the text—the divine baseline. Thus, to remove as expansion a term from any text, is to remove canonical text. Although no version removes all traces of the words *lord, Jesus*, or *christ*, some say that even one such removal is heterodox, rather than orthodox. But lists by the KJVO folk proclaiming "200 *deletions* from the KJV" or such, could well be put by the NIV folk as "200 *additions* by the KJV"![155] David Daniels has written, *Look What's*

---

[154] http://www.mayimhayim.org/Academic Stuff/David Stern Article.htm.

[155] A handy KJVO site is www.alcorne.free-online.co.uk/jasp_niv.htm. Again, the basic questions are whether these are KJV additions to God's written word, whether they are correct updates of language (that is, KJV terms which needed changing to keep their meaning), and whether the NIV *et al* really play down

*Missing* (about $13). If he repents, he might select the same verses to write, *Look What's Added*. Ah, the folly of our times. Let's look at this general charge that expressions of deificity and lordship are removed from Jesus. The bigger picture is this: as a whole, have true teachings been deleted, or false teachings been added, by either the KJV or NIV, and have they always sought to be true to the autographs?[156]

## *The* christ?

"...And Peter answereth and saith unto him, Thou art **the Christ**" (KJV: Mk.8:29). For KJV to C20-1 versions, Gail charted differences between 'the Christ' and 'Christ' (Riplinger 318). And as usual, she gave one or two out of context quotes from scholars—for example Norman Geisler,[157] who did not support KJVO-ism, and whose context was about phrases which denied that Jesus was/is THE christ, phrases such as 'the Christ spirit', and 'Christ-consciousness'.[158]

Gail rejected the NIV, NASB, et al, for having "**the** Christ" in such places as Mt.22:42; Mk.12:35; Lk.4:41; Ac.5:42, 27 places in fact where the TR has "**the** Christ", but where the KJV, based on the tradition of man, took away from the TR. Yes, the textus receptus often has links the article ('the') with the Greek term christ, Gail, though you kept

---

biblical truth. One should look for keywords elsewhere in English versions; sometimes KJVO folk intentionally overlook them in the surrounding verses.

[156] Both the KJV and NIV have sought to reconstruct how the autographs read. It is circular reasoning to say in one breath that the NIV's goal is misleading *since* we don't have the autographs, and in the next breath to say that the KJV must act as the autograph. This reasoning would presuppose that the KJV perfectly captured the autographs, and that *only* all Greek texts and Bible versions before *it*, were imperfect. The issue is not which English version is imperfect in its textual base, but which is least imperfect, while recognising that all are basically true to the autographs.

[157] Riplinger 318: Possibly she relied on the hope that her 'quotes' would seldom be checked. The big picture she painted includes a global conspiracy of loony and lying leadership remarkably leaking its demonic intentions left, right, and centre, yet hidden from most except her, and of big names apparently supporting her position when in fact they did no such thing. Her picture she has called God's: for all its obvious mistakes we may call it a forgery.

[158] www.iclnet.org/pub/resources/text/cri/cri-jrnl/crj0187a.txt

## Translating Theology

quiet about Jhn.7:41 and 18 other NT verses where the KJV has "**the** Christ", and kept mum about the other 150 times that the Stephanus 1550 'TR' has *ho christos* (in its various NT cases). So, did God not inspire it correctly in the TR? In fact, the TR has it twice in Jhn.7:41, though for stylistic reason and human tradition, the KJV has it only once, whereas the NASB has it twice. One rule for you, one rule for me?

Incidentally, putting the Greek ὁ χριστος as '**the** christ' (small 'c' intended), or 'the messiah', actually takes us back to the C1, when among his ethnic people the expectation was for **the** messiah. Later, among the Gentiles, his title soon functioned as a personal name. Soon Christian tradition so overlooked the Gospel's titular use, that unsurprisingly the KJV simply though sadly followed suit, mindless of the historical ethno-Jewish messianic hope of the text.[159]

Contrary to what she intended, Gail's somewhat choppy chart therefore highlights 27 texts where, in line with the TR, C20-1 versions have improved on the KJV—for which she tells them off. For example, demons (not devils) were silenced because "they knew that He was **the** Christ" (NKJV: Lk.4:41). Would Gail have preferred "Thou art Christ, the Son of the living God", to the KJV's "Thou art **the** Christ, the Son of the living God"? Of course, Gail obliquely noted that the KJV has the phrase—when she says, The less the merrier. One could rightly say something similar about the extra uses of *lord, Jesus,* and *christ,* that the KJV offers, when Gail wrongly says, The more the merrier. What's merriest is what's in line with the authentic C1 text. The Stephanus 1550 'TR' helped us to get back to this text; Gail missed the memo.

Most C20-1 versions feel that the [definite] article should be translated more often to reflect the text and the historical age of the ethno-Jewish people—it's nothing to do with 'New Age' spirituality, except in Gail's vain imagination or her bank account. "Whosoever believeth that Jesus is the Christ is born of God…" (KJV: 1 Jhn.5:1): one

---

[159] I think reminders of the ethnic Jewish setting should be in original ethnic Jewish settings, though not in original ethno-Gentile settings: borderline cases exist. Thus for the Gospels, such as the HCSB/ISV/NABRE/NIV/NLT do well. Of these, for the Letters, the NLT drops out, NABRE/NIV tread far too softly, the HCSB is too eager with a 50:50 policy, and the ISV betrays its ethno-Zionizing itch, almost totally excluding the term *christ*!

## Who's for Huiology?

hopes that Gail believes that Jesus is *the* christ. Some versions opt for historical particularity in reverting to 'messiah', at least when the context was significantly ethno-Jewish.

### Teacher or Master?

Gail charted the KJV translating *didaskalos* as *master*, and attacked C20-1 versions for translating it as *teacher* (Riplinger 322-3). She said New Agers seek a Teacher—did she reject Bible teaching?—and argued that that proves that C20-1 English versions are New Age Bible versions. Again, her Greek, her integrity, or both, show limitation. In 2 Tm.1:11, Paul used the same word to describe himself as "a teacher of the Gentiles" (KJV). And as a verb, *didaskō* is used of Jesus, and the Holy Spirit, *teaching*—if one may believe the KJV (for example Mk.4:1; Jhn.14:26). In earlier days teachers in England were often called 'masters'—school masters—rather than 'teachers'. Thus 'master'—from *didaskalos*—was translated 'master' as a noun, 'teach' as a verb. Nowadays noun and verb translate into English as 'teacher/teach'.

"What New Agers seek, the NIV offers, therefore New Age be the NIV", is faulty reasoning, but perhaps kept Gail happy. Policewomen wear uniforms; he wears a uniform; therefore he is a policewoman? New Agers seek food; I seek food; therefore I am a New Ager! Obviously. By the way I kinda thought that some New Agers sought masters, but what the heck.

This issue does not impact on teaching of lordship. *Ho didaskalos kai ho kurios,* pans out as master and *lord* in the KJV, and teacher and *lord* in the NIV. Riplinger 32-7 has a chart showing that the NIV has changed 'doctrine' to 'teaching'. Again, it's simply a case of how we put the TR/NU word—*didachē* (teaching/doctrine). Gail has lacked, or refused, the knowledge of the Greek TR, and ignored the fact that words vary from one generation to another. Mt.15:9 (TR/NU) reads *didaskontes didaskalias* (literally 'teaching teachings'). The KJV put it as "teaching <u>for</u> doctrines the commandments of men"; the NIV as "their teachings are merely human rules"—the KJV put good Greek into good C17 English; the NIV put good Greek into good C20-1 English—is the New Ageism all in Gail's imagination and her bank account?

## Lord?

Another little chart (Riplinger 331) shows some omissions from the KJV of 'lord' titles, as well as some changes from the KJV's 'lord' to 'master'.[160] The former are omissions *from the KJV* which added them into the canonical text. The NIV is guilty of removing human additions to God's word, additions made in good faith by the KJV. Changes from the KJV's 'lord', to 'master', simply use a synonym to highlight human masters (for example the parable of the bags of gold: Mt.25:14-30).[161] The Greek is *kurios*. The KJV usually translated 'teacher' as 'master', but sometimes translated *kurios* as *master* (for example KJV/ NIV: Rm.14:4; Eph.6:9).

Arguably, the KJV should have translated *kurios* in Mt.25:21 et al as 'master' even as it did with Rm.14:4 et al. As an aside, Gail's chart makes two slips on Mt.25:21: missing out the word 'your' from the NIV's "your master", and changing the KJV's "thy lord" into "thy Lord". She, who has dismissed objections and objectors on the grounds of slight misquotation, would doubtless be happy to be similarly dismissed for her slight misquotations.

But should she be dismissed the way she has tended to dismiss others? Do unto others? No. If a fool claims that Julius Caesar has died, we would be fools to deny it simply because spoken by a fool. We listen and assess. And sometimes we weep, as when Gail cites Gen.28:21 to prove that *lord* is a unique title of deity, seemingly unaware both that *LORD* in the KJV means not *lord* but God's name, and that *lord* (*adonay/kurios*) was biblically used of many non-deities,

---

[160] White 1995:19-5 provides a good one.

[161] Incidentally, synonyms also play a part within any good English version, though this can lead to unintended results. For example, William Kay picked up how often Pentecostals, even in the 1960s, assumed a distinction between demon *oppression* (as possible for Christians) and demon *possession* (as impossible for Christians), based largely on the KJV translating the same Greek word by two different English words. Most English versions seem to likewise render these passages differently, although *daimonizomai* (demonised?) in the Greek "[does] not allow the reader to locate the demon precisely" (Kay 135). Hackers can affect computers remotely; can demons affect us remotely?

such as Moses and Philip: "JEHOVAH, Jesus Christ and the Holy Spirit alone are given this title" (Riplinger 332)—nonsense.[162]

The NIV fully affirms the lordship of Jesus—"he is the Messiah, the Lord" (Lk.2:11); "Jesus Christ is Lord, to the glory of God the Father" (Php.2:11), as does the KJV. Far from being an unbiblical conspiracy, removing titles from various KJV texts is repentance over KJV additions to God's text. Piety expansions can be traced through the history of textual copying. In conversation mode a copyist might often have spoken of 'the Lord Jesus Christ'. In copying mode, they could absentmindedly slip 'the Lord' into a text that simply said 'Jesus Christ' or *vice versa*.[163] The earlier the influence, the more likely the error would become dominant in the Byzantine text-type.

Thus John's 'Jesus Christ' (NIV) became 'the Lord Jesus Christ' in 2 Jhn.1:3 (KJV), though remained as "Jesus Christ" in 1 Jhn.1:3 (KJV/NIV), though was 'the Lord Jesus Christ' in 1 Pt.1:3 (KJV/NIV). The KJV and NIV translators wished to know what the inspired writers wrote. The NIV translators were better placed to do this. Reducing expansions of piety is not reducing the authentic text, simply removing additions to God's written word, a reduction we should commend, not condemn. But whether in or out of any given text, all the key terms are well represented in all the text-types, and all versions. Within the KJV/NIV there are plenty of texts that have the key words—Jesus/Christ/Lord—on their own, in some combinations of two, or all three.

Of interest is Mt.16:20, where the KJV implies that what wasn't known was that Jesus was *Jesus*, as well as being *christ*, whereas the NIV rightly shows that his personal name wasn't doubted, only his

---

[162] She seemed unaware that God's name wasn't simply the father's name as such.

[163] 1 Cor.16:22: are we to love "the Lord Jesus Christ" (KJV) or "the Lord" (NIV)? Is this ideological reductionism by the NIV, as Gail asserted? Ac.10:48: are we to baptise in the name of the "Lord Jesus Christ" (Wycliffe), or "the Lord" (KJV)? Is this ideological reductionism by the KJV? Gail goes quiet on counterevidence, such as the NIV's full agreement with the KJV in the other 8 texts in 1 Cor. in which the KJV has "the Lord Jesus Christ", and that while the NIV only has the fullest title in 60 texts compared to the KJV's 81 texts, Wycliffe's LV has it in 99 texts. Did the KJV drop messiahship from 1 Cor.6:11 for ideological purpose, when both Wycliffe and the NIV read "the Lord Jesus Christ"?

messiahship.[164] But most of the time a piety expansion—even to the KJV platform—doesn't cause any problem.

## Douay Rheims Only-ism?

Linked to the sales of the ancient Douay, some similar challenges have been made against the Douay makeover by Bishop Challoner, and the KJV in general.[165] One site claims to list "more than 100 times...where the various names of our Lord and Saviour, Jesus Christ, are removed" by the KJV. A fine plug for its own sales' pitch, but does it cut the mustard? Did Anglicans remove the name/title, *christ*, from Is.45:1? The Vulgate said *christo*. Wycliffe/Douay followed suit. But Coverdale said *anointed*, and Challoner/NJB/NABRE, followed suit.

So what's wrong with that? After all, the Greek *christō* means an *anointed*, a messiah, a christ. Besides, the context is not even about Jesus, but about the Persian king, Cyrus, anointed by Yahweh for the benefit of Yahweh's people. Why diss Challoner for ditching *christo*? Is there good reason why the rebellious King Saul should be called Yahweh's *christ* (1 Sam.24:6/7), even though the Vulgate has *christus Domini est?* Did Anglicans remove the name *Jesus*, from Hab.3:18? The Vulgate mentioned God as *Jesus*. Wycliffe/Douay/Challoner followed suit: "...I will joy in God my Jesus." The Hebrew/Greek mentioned God as *saviour*. Erasmus/Luther/Coverdale/NJB/NABRE followed suit.

Is it possible that the Vulgate had simply mistranslated his name into the text? Must names be removed from the later Clementine Vulgate's *de libro vitæ* (book of life), or even from the earlier Vulgate's *de ligno vitae* (tree of life), to appease Rv.22:19? Did Anglicans add the name *Jesus*, into Mt.8:5, where the Vulgate didn't name Jesus? The MT/Wycliffe/Douay/Challoner/Darby/NU/NJB/NABRE, followed the Vulgate. Erasmus named Jesus here. Luther/Tyndale/KJV/ Wesley, followed Erasmus. Must the plagues of Rv.22:18 be piled upon Luther's head, simply for saying that *he* who entered Capernaum was *Jesus*, following the later TR's *Iēsou* (*Jesus*) against the earlier Greek

---

[164] "..tell no man that he was Jesus the Christ" (KJV); "not to tell anyone that he was the Messiah" (NIV).

[165] I have used http://drbible.org for rants, and https://sites.google.com/site/aquinasstudybible/home for readings.

reading *outou* (*he*)? It's all too easy to play this add and take game, which is all too often an Onlyist fantasy.

## **The Incarnation**

The early creeds state that Jesus was born by a virgin, highlighting the one-of-a-kind paternity. One of the early heresies, called Docetism, revealed Jesus' deificity by concealing his humanity, teaching that he only *appeared* to have had a human body (like Bree's folly in *The Horse and His Boy*: C S Lewis). The Bible teaches that deity assumed humanity through virgin conception—incarnation, real humanity. Three texts in particular, each with a keyword, are sometimes held to benchmark orthodoxy and to dismiss modern versions as heterodox. These are the words, *virgin* (Is.7:14), *firstborn* (Mt.1:25), and *Joseph* (Lk.2:33), all present in the KJV. Some falsely presuppose their conclusion that the KJV is right, and that therefore disagreement with it is wrong. Let us first chart English versions.

Incarnation Data

**Texts Included**

**Is.7:14**

This issue's about translation. In Matthew's context, all versions rightly translate with the word *virgin* (Mt.1:23)[166]—though the versatile word *maiden* can be a handy compromise. So, should *Isaiah* be translated in Matthew's context, or in Isaiah's?

Most agree that Isaiah's word selection, *almah* (*'almâ*), is able to mean a virgin. But some say that Isaiah would have used *bethulah* (*betûlâ*), the closer word to *virgin*, if that's what he'd meant to say. After all, Matthew's *parthenos* is the "usual [Greek] rendering of [the] Hebrew

---

[166] But the NLV reads "young woman...never [having] had a man": interesting wording. If we compare the RSV to the NRSV for Dt.20:7, we can see how the distinction between *betrothal* (marriage level 1) and wedded *taking* (marriage level 2) has been replaced by the Western contrast of pre-marriage/marriage. Between marriage and wedding, one was to remain a virgin, not 'having' a man or woman until a third party witnessed the covenant commitment.

## Translating Theology

bᵉṭûlâ", not of 'almâ (Bromiley 787).[167] We can also see that *almah* could be translated by other than *parthenos,* for example by *neanis* (Ex.2:8–maid: KJV) and *neotēti* (Pr.30:19–young woman: Bishops) are among others. Wait a minute. Some actually argue that it's the other way around, with *almah* being the closer word to *virgin*, and thus say that Isaiah had virgin conception in mind.[168] I think it's good to recognise that God allowed the biblical authors some flexibility in choosing between similar words. The solution lies in context.

Isaiah, I think, should be taken as having prophesied two conceptions, the first being before Ahab died and perhaps the only one Isaiah had in mind. Yet if there was an initial C8 fulfilment, then *virgin conception* would be the wrong idea.[169] For Isaiah, the status of both mother and son was relatively unimportant: the child would be a countdown clock to deliverance day. Very possibly it was a normal honeymoon conception, whereas the subsequent fulfilment was on a deeper unexpected level of virginal conception (the incarnation) for a deeper, global, perhaps universal, deliverance. You see, if the Hebrew specified non-verifiable *virgin conception*, then it wouldn't have spoken as such to Ahaz. As it was, the keyword is somewhat

---

[167] The *almah* texts are Gen.24:43; Ex.2:8; 1 Chr.15:20; Ps.46:1; 68:25; Pr.30:19; Sg.1:3; 6:8; Is.7:4.

[168] Motyer suggested that in Gen.24, 'almâ (43) *summed up* a girl (na 'ᵃrâ: 14) old enough to marry (bᵉṭûlâ: 16) and, the text adds, a virgin (16). I think Motyer thought that Isaiah prophesied only the incarnation.

[169] On www.roffers.com/home/scott/kjv/weapon.html, a mother foolishly said that a *young woman having a son* would have been no big sign to Ahaz—only a *virgin* having one. Her folly lay in the facts 1# that if Ahaz was a man of the world he would not have known *beyond doubt* that any woman claiming virgin conception was speaking the truth, and 2# that Isaiah's prediction was not about the woman, but about the child being a marker of time. *By the time* a boy soon to be conceived, was old enough to understand right from wrong, the bullyboys Syria and Israel (7:2) would be defeated by Assyria. Judah's cultivation would suffer Yahweh's lesser rebuke for its faithlessness (7:9), so the boy and his people would subsist on goats' milk and wild honey (7:21ff.). God with his people (Immanuel) was God in punishment—only the goats would be blessed (kidding)! So, post-invasion social collapse within a few short years, would signal to Ahaz his sin (2 Chr.28:19). His son Hezekiah read the sign, and renewed the covenant (2 Chr.29:8-11).

academic. What counted there and then was that a recent or imminent conception began a countdown to deliverance. *Immanuel* was a prophetical 'countdown' name, perhaps a nickname. King Ahaz would within a few years see that Yahweh's word was true.

I think that what we have here was Isaiah prophesying a non-virginal conception and child—perhaps Isaiah's son Maher Shalal Chash Baz. That's the *initial*, first level meaning. Translation of *Isaiah* should be true to Isaiah: historical particularity. Moving on, God, who had planned a fuller C1 meaning, might well have nudged Jewish translators to use *parthenos* here, as they had with Gen.24:43. *Parthenos* is the best Greek word for *virgin*, so was divinely convenient for Matthew, who looked back on this greater intervention in world events.[170] That's the later and fuller meaning (*sensus plenior*).

If there was only one fulfilment—the C1 incarnation—then in what way was Jesus' birth a sign to C8 BC Ahaz? If C8 and C1 BC fulfilments were both by virginal conception, who was the father in Ahaz' days? If God, was God's *son* (Jesus?) born in Ahaz' days, and if he were, why, and what became of *that* human body? Let Isaiah be Isaiah. The C8 BC conception was chaste but natural, and translation should be 'young woman' or similar for Is.7:14. Let Matthew be Matthew. Jesus' conception was at the supernatural level, and translation should be 'virgin' for Mt.1:23. A difference in translation highlights this two-level fulfilment/application, a prophetical feature the KJV missed.

## Mt.1:25

This issue's about text. . Did Matthew here say *firstborn* (so the MT) or not (so the NU)? Either way, I'd recommend a footnote. Note that for Lk.2:7, where the text *firstborn* son is secure, the versions translate it in. Thus, while the range of meaning does vary somewhat, all the versions say that Jesus was her first son, some saying her first child,

---

[170] Though the emphasis of the Septuagint *parthenos* is virginity, its range includes other than virgins. After being raped, Dinah remained a *parthenos*, probably in a sense of unmarried and celibate at heart (Gen.34:3). If a counsellor tells a new, previously sexually promiscuous, convert, that they are a virgin in God's sight, it's not totally wrong, though social, psychological, and spiritual, issues might remain.

though this latter idea is true is not true enough since lacking Luke's focus. The NABRE correctly notes that firstborn need not imply other births, as it was a technical term for one's inheritance son, especially dedicated to Yahweh.

## Lk.2:33

This issue's about text. The main options are whether Joseph was (so NU) or was not (so MT) called Jesus' *father* here. Rome might be expected to deny Joseph being Jesus' father, but the Vulgate, followed by Wycliffe, is in line with the NU. Jerome and Wycliffe saw that it was not a case of theology, although some lesser lights seem to think that it is. Thinking genes, some are confused by the idea that both God and Joseph were somehow father to Jesus. Yet the KJV also calls Joseph Jesus' father: "Jesus of Nazareth, the son of Joseph" (KJV: Jhn.1:45). You might say that Philip was mistaken—John Calvin did. And for Lk.2:48, "thy father and I have sought thee sorrowing" (KJV), you might say that Mary was mistaken and corrected by Jesus' reply.

However, since Mary knew full well that Joseph was not biological father to Jesus, her use of *father* (*patēr*) must have been correct within given norms. These norms are reflected in v33. Jesus did not rebut her but he highlighted the deific fatherhood of God, whose house his parents should have searched first. Jesus many times spoke of humans as fathers, yet in another sense God as father. His opponents' claim of both Abraham and ultimately God being their fathers (Jhn.8:39,41), would have seemed fair enough within the given norms.

A related issue is the RC teaching that Mary remained physically a virgin.[171] The KJV/RV/ASV/NABRE et al speak of her womb being opened by birth (Lk.2:23). Most versions do not. Have most bowed to

---

[171] Based on the late C2 *Protoeuangelion of James* 19:3, the idea developed that Jesus never opened the womb, simply materialised out leaving Mary physically virginal. It's one of a number of false Western strands tied around the true insight that Christian life is to be spiritual, and a false dichotomy between physical and spiritual. On the broader issue of church authority and discipline, East and West developed the idea of a priesthood within the church. Rome factored various celibate-is-better ideas into this, and opted for celibate church priesthood. The East didn't factor these in, and opted for chaste church priesthood. Protestantism opts for all Christians as chaste priests.

## Who's for Huiology?

Rome, or faithfully reworded Luke's Semitic wording into current language? Does Ex.13:2 contain an antidote to Rome's perpetual virginity teaching? Its historical setting probably meant, in Semite phrasing, what the West today means by 'firstborn son'. After all, it hardly meant breaking the hymen, nor that if one's first child was a girl, if they then had a boy it was exempt. It also related to domestic cattle: "...every first-born male Israelite and every first-born male animal belongs to me" (GNB). Anyway it is hard to lean towards Rome, when Rome's English versions lean *both ways*: the NABRE uses 'open the womb' (Ex.13:1/Lk.2:23); the NJB uses 'firstborn' (Ex.13:1/Lk.2:23). Both RC versions support officially the idea that Mary remained celibate. Protestants would say she became through chastity, not celibacy, an excellent pattern for believers, parents, and spouses.

### Text Excluded

Mt.1:23 is excluded from the Chart, since all versions agree the point that at Jesus' conception, Mary was a virgin. So, her son Jesus would have to be her *first-born*, whether or not Mt.1:25 specifically says so. Some suggest that *firstborn* is nevertheless needed to deny Rome's idea that Jesus was her *only-born*—yet the Vulgate has *primogenitum* and Matthew wasn't interested in what Rome might come up with. Versions conspiring to remove the first-born theme would have to do more than merely remove 'first-born' from Mt.1:25. It seems that some copyist, with Lk.2:7 in mind ('parallel influence'), slipped in the extra word, which subsequent copyists established as if part of Matthew's text. Any conspiracy to either hide the miracle of Mary's virgin conception, or bow to Roman Catholicism's *only child* thesis, would have to chop out Lk.2:7 as well—versions do not do that.

It is unfair to make conspiracy claims from Mt.1:25, without noting that modern versions properly handle Mt.1:23 and Lk.2:7, and without noting the possibility that somewhere along the line a scribe added into Matthew's text from Luke's, an error that modern versions *undo*. Looking at the versions, I am slightly unhappy with a mere, "the baby" (NCV: Lk.2:7), apart from which all versions charted rightly translate Luke's text as *firstborn*, or at least *first son*. I am also slightly unhappy with a mere, "young woman...never had a man" (NLV: Mt.1:23), apart from which all versions charted rightly translate Matthew's text as *virgin*: the NLV had a different audience in mind. Today's versions, alongside the older versions such as the KJV, affirm Mary as having had a virginal conception resulting in her firstborn, her son Jesus.

## Incarnation Chart C601

### Texts

The texts are Is.7:14; Mt.1:25; and Lk.2:33.

### Comparative Class Grades

| C601 | Grade |
|---|---|
| NET/NRSV | A+ |
| CJB/ERV/NJB/NWT/RSV | A- |
| CEB/CSB/GNB/HCSB/ISV/NABRE/REB | B |
| CEV/FBV/LEB/NCV/NIV/NLT/NRSVU/RNJB | C |
| ESV/GWT/LSB/MSG/NASB20/NASB95/NCB/NLV/NOG/TLV/TVB | D+ |
| EEB | D- |
| EOB/MEV/NKJV | U |
| EJB/KJ21/KJV/LSV/WEB | U- |

### Summary

Together Joseph and Mary were Jesus' father and mother (Lk.2:41) *on the social level*. Joseph was rightly called Jesus' father, even though not his genetic father, as Matthew, Luke, and Paul, made clear. And Jesus' point about calling no-one 'father' (Mt.23:9), which some throw in to confuse, was not about social or genetic fatherhood, but a manner of speech to highlight the spiritual fatherhood of God.

Criticisms might sound serious, but are seriously silly.

- Is.7:14: even were the KJV not the weaker translation, *young woman* is not heterodox.
- Mt.1:25: most C-1 versions are committed to incarnationalism, but not to extrabiblical additions.
- Lk.2:33: biblically Joseph was socially Jesus' father—no big fuss.

## Part 4 Today's English Versions
## Chapter 11 Textual Criticism and You

The KJV has cast a long shadow, and some remain in its light, even if that light is dim compared to better constructed versions. The light is the KJV itself; the shadow is its textual basis, the TR. As said, that text was itself a work of textual criticism, eclecticism. This chapter goes a little more into how eclecticism works.

Some say, let's use the latest manuscripts, since updates are best, or even the majority witness of the texts, regardless of when or where they were written. If you go this route, you might choose to use the TR (*Textus Receptus*), which roughly stands for the Greek NT produced by Erasmus, modified by Stephanus and Beza, and used by the KJV translators.

Some say, let's use the oldest, to cut out the many scribal additions that soon began to build up, but nevertheless try to compare whenever we can each NT verse, from all of the manuscripts that have them, aware that the later they are, and to some extent where they were copied (their provenance), does show a trail of the original text plus variations. We can then strain the variations out of the text to leave the original text. This method has produced what some call the NU text, the base-text of the **Nestles-Aland Greek New Testament** (*Novum Testamentum Graece*), and the **United Bible Society** (*Hē Kainē Diathēkē*).

Both TR and NU were produced using what's called Textual Criticism (TC). Erasmus was a textual critic, as had been Jerome. TC does not criticise the Bible—PC does that. TC only looks critically at the scribal efforts of the past. Both TR and NU have had to make choices between which manuscripts to keep, and which to dismiss. Let's look at how textual criticism is done. The third English Authorised Version (KJV) was based on a few manuscripts, weighted heavily from the old Byzantine Empire. The forth Authorised Version (RV) was based on a mix of Byzantine texts, plus older texts conventionally deemed as from Egypt (thus Alexandrian), and weighed in favour of this

Alexandrian text-type.[172] Nowadays the NU is more critical of that text-type, and has reduced the bias of Westcott and Hort.

The Alexandrian text-type is the *most* reliable text-type, but is neither infallible nor neutral. However, it is called *traitor* by those deem the Byzantium text-type to be *lord*. א has picked up over 20,000 scribal variants over its long use, trying to adjust it to the Byzantine text, but this does not show it to be unreliable. Imagine I wrote in trinitarian reflection, "you alone are God, Yahweh". Years later, a Sabellian scribe amends it to "you alone are God, Jesus". That scribe would no more discredit my text, than Byzantine scribes adjusting the Alexandrian text. The Byzantium text-type can be seen as far more textually corrupt—not morally corrupt, not heretically corrupt. Both text-types followed the inevitable unintentional minor corruption of human transmission, rather than heretical change, and both Alexandrian and Byzantium convey the authentic message truthfully.

Taking all the NT manuscripts available—over 5,000—there are over 200,000 variants, strung out over about 10,000 places. Westcott and Hort held that just 10% of these were worth looking at—the rest were simply spelling errors, a word missed, a word added, but these easily corrected. Philip Schaff noted that about 200 variants importantly affected the sense of their contexts, but none affected "an article of faith or a precept of duty which is not abundantly sustained by other and undoubted passages or by the whole tenor of Scripture teaching" (White 1995:39). We may say that the two most different manuscripts—across the text-types—agree the fundamental biblical message.

Let's say we have some variants of a text from a Chelal of Judah. You can now do a simple exercise in textual work in pencil.

| Beside | the | river | of | babbling | she | spat | up | and | slept | **Carol's copy** |
| By | the | rivers | of | Babylon | I | sat | down | and | slept | **Cathy's copy** |
| By | thy | rivers | O | Babylon | I'd | sat | down | and | wept | **Charlie's copy** |
| By | the | rivers | of | babbling | I | sat | down | and | slipped | **Cheryl's copy** |
| By | the | rivers | of | Babylon | we | sat | up | and | leapt | **Colin's copy** |

---

[172] These main manuscripts are Alexandrinus (A), Vaticanus (B), and Sinaiticus (א). It is moot, though likely, as to whether any were writing in Egypt or by Egyptians. A seems to have sections from difference provenances.

## Textual Criticism and You

There are 13 variants, none I think doctrinal. Get back to Chelal. Fill in the missing words below—this is textual criticism. First, write in the one word **all** the manuscripts have in common.

Put this word in below, then fill in what only **four** of the manuscripts have in common.

Put these words in below, then fill in what only **three** of the manuscripts have in common.

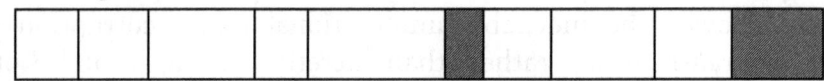

Put these words in below, then fill in what only **two** of the manuscripts have in common.

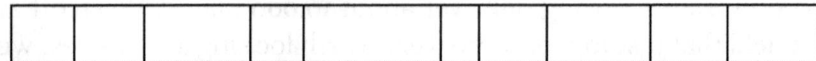

Because of background phrases, some scribes will write 'wept' instead of 'slept', without realising their mistake. As we move from the most agreed to the less agreed, we move from the most secure to the least secure. At this stage one must ask if the reconstructed text makes sense. Assuming Cathy's copy was correct, Cheryl's was next best on a simple count of correct words (8/10). If a number of copies turned up the same as Cathy's, except they read 'slipped' instead of 'slept', we might say that on that point Cheryl *corrects* Cathy.

Most of the variants can be explained simply by the mind suggesting similar sounding words, and we have assumed that most often words were correctly heard. Charlie's 'wept' could have occurred because he remembered Ps.137:1. If we discovered that Babylon had only one river, we might then amend our text from *rivers* to *river*. If we had no manuscript with 'river', this would be a *conjectural amendment*.

This is textual criticism at a simple level, seeing where most witnesses agree and reconstructing what was the original text. We can say that 'and' is secure, while 'slept' is least secure. If we could date the copies,

## Today's English Versions

and if these were sentences from a much longer document they all copied, we could ask whether they showed signs of being copies of each other. We might discover that certain mistakes early on were picked up and continued by a later line of copyists. We might see that sometimes a variant was at some point corrected. For example, imagine someone in the C16 copying a C11 copy. Then, having been handed a C5 copy and comparing it, they realise that the C11 copy had made a mistake. Being a good scribe, they then correct their C16 copy by the C5 copy they had found. So, let us say that Cedric was copying Carol's copy:

| Beside | the | river | of | babbling | she | spat | up | and | slept | Carol's copy |
|---|---|---|---|---|---|---|---|---|---|---|

He then found in an ancient library two much older manuscripts—Cheryl's and Colin's.

| By | the | rivers | of | Babylon | we | sat | up | | and | leapt | Colin's copy |
|---|---|---|---|---|---|---|---|---|---|---|---|
| By | the | rivers | of | babbling | I | sat | down | and | slipped | | Cheryl's copy |

Correcting Carol's copy, Cedric might create this:

| By | the | rivers | of | Babylon | I | sat | down | and | slipped | Cedric's copy |
|---|---|---|---|---|---|---|---|---|---|---|

'The', 'of', and 'and' are undisputed, textually secure. 'By', 'rivers', and 'sat', have united ancient support, so correct Carol.

'Babbling' has ancient and modern support, but Cedric knows that Colin and Cheryl's society hadn't believed that there had been a city named Babylon. Cedric's generation discovered that Babylon existed. He asks himself, which is more likely: that Colin changed 'babbling' to a place name Colin believed was imaginary, or that Carol 'corrected' an earlier witness, to 'babbling' from a name she believed meaningless? He concludes that Colin's copy reads 'Babylon' because Colin simply copied the manuscript that he had had before him, whereas Cheryl had tried to correct it by changing the text to her belief. That is, Cedric is asking about what explains certain changes made to a text—getting into the mindset of scribes along the way.

In opting for 'I', Cedric might point out that the wider context indicates that Chelal had been on a sad journey, but didn't mention any particular woman. Therefore, Cheryl's copy would make more sense than Colin's, and be preferred to Carol's copy because older. Indeed Carol's copy reads strangely from this point on, and feels like an unreliable copy. Putting her to one side, Cedric asks, did I "sit up and leap", or "sit down and slip"? He might wonder whether to toss a coin, put the winner in the main text, and footnote the alternative as "or, ...". If the next sentence in the wider document reads "Getting up I journeyed on", he might decide that Cheryl is right, but footnote Colin as "one ancient manuscript reads...". Indeed, the *mood* of the context (sad journey) would suggest a downward unhappiness, a stumbling, not a perky "Jack in a box" leaping up, so favouring Cheryl's copy even without the following sentence. Colin might still get a footnote vote.

Cedric concludes that Cheryl's is the best copy, though she dropped a clanger by dropping *Babylon*—an understandable mistake in her generation. Colin's is the next best copy, sometimes a better witness than Cheryl. Least good is Carol, though even she might preserve, against the older copies, traces of the original text. As he makes his copy of the account, not simply as a copier of Carol but as a *critical* copier, he sees more and more that Cheryl is usually better than Colin, and both usually better than Carol. He becomes more and more prepared to copy Cheryl word for word, *unless* on points that where she stood without Colin's support, there seemed good reason to prefer Colin's reading. Perhaps occasionally even Carol's wording might have the most merit, since Carol, at times not directly witnessing to Cheryl or Colin, *might* have some traces of a copy nearer to the original that even Cheryl's. Looking again at her text, Cedric asks himself, was "I sat down and <u>slept</u>" the original? Cedric decides to footnote 'slept' as a possible reading.

Years later, as Caroline copies Cedric's copy, she now has Cathy's recently discovered copy, which both vindicates Cedric's textual criticism and justifies her correcting his choice of 'slipped', to Cathy and Carol's 'slept', which he had only footnoted.

| By | the | rivers | of | Babylon | I | sat | down | and | slept | Caroline's copy |

Putting together thousands of copies—manuscripts—factoring in their dates, and tracing variations through, helps build up a picture a bit like the branching out of a tree, except that new copies have often made textual choices based on a number of ancient documents compared with each other—like branches or twigs interconnecting. However, some main 'text-types' come into focus: the Alexandrian, Byzantium, and Western—possibly a Caesarean. Like Cedric, if we do much real textual criticism, we might conclude that a certain text-type is primary, another secondary, and another tertiary in general faithfulness to the original writings. Within each text-type we will find some manuscripts better than others. Most of the early copies were not done by trained scribes, but by devoted Christians simply wishing to churn out copies of the NT, or at least the parts they had. Though our faith in Christ is in measure thanks to them, if we wish to get beyond their errors—none are fatal to the gospel—we need to do serious textual criticism, and, to reuse the KJV Translators' comment, to make a good text better.

Some start with the belief that 'Carol' (let's say the KJV) is right, full stop: they grew up with Carol. They often don't ask why God allowed Bible versions *before* 1611 to be wrong, but made sure that one English version in 1611 was 100% right. Some of them even assert—akin to Islam's idea of the Quran being only fully authoritative in its original Arabic—that the KJV 1611 is 100% unchangeable. If moderate, their position is:

> The text behind the KJV is the *Textus Receptus* (Received Text). The *Textus Receptus* is based on the Byzantine tradition. The *Textus Receptus* is most probably the best text we can have. The good aims to update the KJV translation were corrupted by B F Westcott and F J A Hort, possibly heretics, certainly biased scholars, who persuaded the translators to bring other text-types into the equation, thus abandoning the text of the KJV. And so, they produced the misguided [English] Revised Version (ERV/RV), which most versions blindly have followed.

## Textual Criticism and You

The text-type preferred by the RV, called Alexandrian[173] or Neutral (by Westcott and Hort),[174] had been rejected by the early church as heretical. This text-type often reduced (occasionally increased) the inspired text of the Byzantine tradition, probably began after the Byzantine tradition, and was possibly produced by heretics denying such as the deificity of Christ. They promote heresy. The church accepted the Byzantine tradition, at least from the C4, surely showing God's choice of text.

For this softer position, see David Otis' *Which Bible?*; Jakob van Bruggen's *The Ancient Text of the NT*; and Wilbur N Pickering's[175] *The Identity of the NT Text*.[176] Hardliners can slate all who don't use the

---

[173] The main Alexandrian manuscripts are called the Sinaiticus and Vaticanus.

[174] Nowadays their 'Neutral Text'—based on the Vaticanus and Sinaiticus Manuscripts—are seen as part of the Alexandrian text-type. Westcott and Hort did not use the term 'text-type'. W&H used the term 'Syrian' for what nowadays is called 'Byzantine'—the parent text-type behind the KJV text. Other text-types generally held nowadays are the Western text (a possibly messy and poor tradition) and a Caesarean text (perhaps conflated from Western and Alexandrian traditions).

[175] Pickering preferred the MT. The TR is basically a small sample of the MT, and the NU is a small selection that birthed the MT. Rather than observing that the MT simply became the MT because it was the only Greek type to continue being copied in Greek speaking Byzantia after other areas had moved to their native languages, Pickering suggested that this text-type, since most available over the Middle Ages, must be God's first choice. Yet if God preserved the MT, did he not also preserve א? I find it easier to speak of a special preservation of the church, which in turn did a heck of a lot to preserve the written text. Telling against Pickering has been D A Carson and Gordon Fee. Perhaps more so, because a fellow supporter of a Byzantine Priority theory, Maurice A Robinson, whose doctorate was in Textual Criticism. He lambasted Pickering's work: "I also want to avoid any connection with the utter mess that Wilbur Pickering made out of various scholarly quotes in his 'Identity of the NT Text' book, where he blatantly took passages out of context, misquoted other passages, and misapplied the lot in a poor attempt to discredit the eclectic position" (www.bible-researcher.com/majority.html).

[176] See also Zane C Hodges and Edward F Hills. Some simply favour the Majority Text, of which the range of TRs is a subdivision.

KJV only. They needlessly divide Christ's body, hold back the language clock, and encourage secular humanists to assume that the Bible died with previous generations. As Galatians were bewitched back into old patterns by the Circumcision Party, so the KJVO-ists have by carrot and stick returned some from the Bible fold to the KJV fold (Gal.3:1). The KJV is long overdue honourable retirement.

Most papyri are Alexandrian, as are the longer-lasting uncial codices ℵ and B. The Western/Byzantium text-type, is in Greek and other languages (mainly Latin), and became the majority text-type through extended centuries of Greek (White 1995:43). The majority thinking is that the Byzantium text-type is good, but the Western better, and the Alexandrian text-type best. And that while all branches of the family agree the wording on most texts, sometimes the Western text, and sometimes even the Byzantium text, alone preserves the original text. It is from the Byzantium text-type that we have the KJV's TR. Let's look at a version based on the NU, and that won the evangelical heart.

# Chapter 12     **Genesis of the NIV**

Despite the inbreaking Revised Standard Version, I think it was the NIV by which the NU went viral, at least in the Evangelical world. Howard Long, a Christian who loved to evangelise, had a dream child. He loved the KJV, but found it didn't work well in evangelism. He shared his concerns with his pastor, Peter de Jong, of the Christian Reformed denomination in Seattle, Washington, part of a mainly Dutch immigrant denomination. De Jong asked his regional council to ask the governing council to initiate a new and heavyweight English version. The regional council said No.

In 1956, he asked the governing council directly. He had knocked on an open door, the other side of which a committee was already looking for a recommended version. In 1957 the theology department gave the green light to the governing council. The department had sussed that generally evangelicals 1# were feeling that the KJV should be retired with honour, 2# didn't believe the ASV 1901's style would replace the KJV, and 3# believed that the RSV 1952 was too iffy to replace the KJV. The governing council gave the go ahead in 1958, having had feedback from some other evangelical denominations.

The next few years involved co-operation with the National Association of Evangelicals (NAE)—including Stephen Paine, John Walvoord, and Merrill Tenney. Together they formed a Joint Committee on Bible Translation, though still looking to create a broader base. Examining new English versions and English version projects (for example the then NASB (now NASB20)) confirmed they still needed to produce a new English version. Through various steps, the joint committee maintained continuity and gained wider expertise and credibility. Its 15 members included E Lesley Carlson (Southwestern Baptist Theological Seminary), Ralph Earle (Nazarene Theological Seminary), R Laird Harris (Covenant Theological Seminary), Robert Mounce (Bethel College (St. Paul)), Charles C Ryrie (Dallas Theological Seminary), and John H Stek

(Calvin Theological Seminary). All involved in translation had to subscribe to a high view of biblical inerrancy of the original text.[177]

Rebranded as the Committee on Bible Translation (CBT), it also wished to help missionary agencies save money, though at this stage it itself had no money to move forward. The New York Bible Society (NYBS), not a commercial publisher but devoted to spreading the gospel, offered generous financial support, to be repaid if the English version ever achieved profit: it committed to support yet not shape the translation.

The CBT, having been unsatisfied with current English versions and unable to influence the RSV/NASB, began to produce the NIV, working from such places as the Moody Bible Institute. They had a structure of subcommittees, involving translators and English stylists, and guidelines to establish an agreed text[178] and to translate it. Manuscripts found since the KJV, such as the Dead Sea Scrolls showing a Hebrew text about a 1,000 years earlier than that previously known, along with better knowledge of the ancient languages, were taken into account. Each biblical script went through many different stages of checking and double checking, revising and double revising, with translators, theologians, and English language consultants.

Edwin Palmer became a full-time paid executive secretary, helping to coordinate the work. Translation teams included scholars from many denominations and countries. In 1969 *John* began circulating *via* the NYBS, though the name, NIV, had not become official. The NYBS internationalised its own name (first to NYBSI (I for International), subsequently to IBS), and contracted for Zondervan to be the sole American commercial publisher. In 1973, the NT was ready for publishing, and had been named the NIV. It also required new income to bring the OT up to publishing standard—gifts and bank loans were required, and the NYBSI wondered about scrapping the

---

[177] That is, God inspired a genre inerrant (error free) text, which though human copying introduced errors, could be rediscovered almost perfectly through the surviving manuscripts.

[178] The foundation for the OT was the Leningrad Codex B+9A (*Biblia Hebraica Stuttgartensia*), and for the NT the NU.

project that was bleeding off missional resources. In 1978 the full NIV was available for the public.

The CBT had an ongoing task of revision, which among other things involved considering each suggestion or criticism from readers. A number of updates have been issued. The NIV soon reached top place among evangelicals, although this has been challenged by arguably lesser versions, following division over gender accurate updates. In 2011 a gender update was published, officially supplanting the two-pronged approach of a fixed gender inaccurate NIV edition, alongside a gender accurate 2005 Today's NIV. This version backtracked on some inclusive language, perhaps to win back friends.

# Chapter 13    <u>Attack of the ESV</u>

In 1997 (or stardate 50975.2), DS9, a mixture of harmful vice-based philosophy and some happier themes, had a fun line where the Ferengi Rom nervously asked the captain, "would you marry me, I mean us, I mean, would you perform our wedding ceremony?" (5.26). Rom stuttered out the right words, never realising how right they were. In 2001, some who disliked gender accuracy had also felt that the old NIV had been too functional equivalent, and they wished to swing towards formal equivalence.

From these twin feelings was birthed the ESV, which would generally get the wording of marriage right—some versions don't. Functional equivalence can indeed become too deregulated, unduly free, sloppy. But is a certain amount of foreignness—of otherness—sometimes a virtue of formal equivalence? After all, God is somewhat foreign to us, so shouldn't his Message sound like the Book of Mormon? To begin to answer this we must look both at the strangeness of the *content*, and the strangeness or otherwise of the *language* clothing the content. If God's message was given in stilted *language*, then translate it in stilted *language*. But if it was written in the then normal *language*, then translate it into the now normal *language* and ignore misleading talk about reverential distinction.

As regards the content, we can see initial puzzlement (Jhn.12:34), even violent indignation and retaliation (Mt.21:4-6), and the content can still evoke those responses, not least by police ideology. We must remain true to the authentic content. But we need not remain true to any subsequent translation style. One of the aims of the ESV was to have a slightly more formal equivalence than had the old NIV. On marriage this works well.

## **Engaging?**

The ESV's less functional approach basically avoids squeezing Joseph and Mary neither into a sacerdotal, nor Secular Humanist, framework of marriage. Too often we think that marriage is a contract made at a wedding, and call the stage before, *engagement*: breathing space to renege or ratify one's tentative pledge. I'm not suggesting we break our rules of engagement and convert 'engagement' to till death do we part, but the ethical fallout from the western worldview, and our ignorance interacting with the biblical reality and excusing sin, is saddening. Too easily translators, if so conditioned, misrepresent the cultural distance, preferring foreign terms to biblico-historical particularity. Catering for this alien approach, the NLT straightforwardly says that "Joseph, [Mary's] fiancé", decided to "break the engagement" (Mt.1:19). A one-world-our-world picture.[179] It's pretty consistent—consistently wrong. The NIV complicates it, telling us that no, he was simply "pledged to be married" (v18), but although unmarried *was* "her husband" and "had in mind to divorce her" (v19), sadly mixing 50/50 two mentalities.

Though falling slightly below the RSV standard, the ESV almost flawlessly shows us a society that thought marriage was a covenant begun before the third-party witness of wedlock. A one-world-their-world picture. You didn't 'sleep with' your *betrothed*, yet they were your unwedded spouse making divorce an option.[180] Sadly the ESV/NIV's "take Mary as your wife" (v20) falls below par by allowing the idea that his *already* wife (C1 world) should *become* his wife (C1 world). The Catholic NJB and NABRE, the Orthodox EOB, and some earlier versions, do better for v20. From an African perspective, "the Bemba says Nkobekela: te cupo ['an engagement is not a marriage'], but the

---

[179] Alongside a trend not to see any right at all, the West suffers from a trend to call 'right' 'wrong', and 'wrong' 'right'. A C19 Christian, Josephine Butler, was the prime mover of the 'age of consent' law to protect girls from prostitution. Nowadays, to promote paedophilia and/or to demote God, some fools call Joseph a paedophile. They rightly note that Mary was probably between 12 and 16 y.o., and factor this datum into their westernism. In cultures where life expectancy was lower, social maturity came sooner. In Jewish culture, sexual bonding came in only one format, marriage, avoiding the bond-break-bond-break cycle that weakens bonding and makes 'sex' meaningless, impersonal, and in turn depersonalises society and destroys respect.

[180] Likewise, the married girls of Gen.19:14 were still sexually virgins, marriage stage 1 (8). On Rv.19:7 the ESV is less good, saying that the marriage is future: also HCSB/ISV/NJB/NKJV. Properly saying that it's the wedding, not the marriage, that's future, are the CEV/NABRE/NCV/NIV/NLT. I think that this text is less significant to biblical understanding than those relative to Joseph and Mary, and I haven't let it influence grading.

Israelites would have insisted that Nkobekela: cupo ['betrothal is marriage']" (Adeyemo 1109).

"The equivalence of betrothal and marriage is...reflected in Mt.1:18,20, 24-5, which shows that Mary's betrothal to Joseph made her his wife, even though they did not have sexual relations until after the birth of Jesus" (VanGemeren 527). Let's chart this: Mt.1:18.A must not deny them married (*mnēsteutheisēs*), and Mt.1:18.B should, without rubbing in a denial of being married, indicate that they hadn't, but would, experience marital sex (*sunelthein*).[181] Mt.1:19.A must proclaim Joseph as husband (*anēr*), and Mt.1:19.B his right to divorce (*apolusai*). Mt.1:20 must focus on Mary being already his wife (*gunakai*). She was to share his home (that is, wed), not become his wife. Lk.1:27/2:5 must not deny them married.

## Marriage Chart C300

### Texts

The texts are Mt.1:18-20; Lk.1:27; 2:5.

### **Comparative Class Grades**

| C300 | Grade |
|---|---|
| RSV | A+ |
| EJB/KJ21/KJV/LSV/NABRE/NKJV | A |
| NJB | A- |
| LSB/NASB20/RNJB | B+ |
| ESV | B |
| MEV | B- |
| CSB/LEB/NCB/NWT | C- |
| NASB95 | D+ |
| HCSB/ISV/NET/NIV | D- |
| ERV/NCV/NRSV/NRSVU/TLV/WEB | U+ |
| CEB/EOB/GWT/MSG/NOG | U |
| CEV/CJB/EEB/FBV/GNB/NLT/NLV/REB/TVB | U- |

---

[181] RC English versions are phrased towards the general plot of living together in perpetual virginity, as if they shared *board* but not *bed*, rather than both *mensa et thoro*, but they don't *exactly* say so, so get at least one mark.

## Summary

Before their public statement (wedding), Joseph and Mary were unwedded husband and wife, so wouldn't have shared interpersonal sex. As her loving husband, believing her adulterous, he opted for divorce, until assured that it was ethical to wed her (Mt.1:18-20). Some months later, husband and wife went to Bethlehem, where they would probably have had a family wedding (Lk.1:27/2:5) between Jesus' birth and their escape to Egypt. More formal approaches (for example the ESV) score better than the NIV, though curiously the ESV disimproves the RSV it sought to improve.

## Covenant Chart C602

As said, marriage is a covenant, not a contract, and begun by the couple, not by the church. What the church does is wed the married, playing third party witness to their covenant, proclaiming them husband and wife. The idea of covenant is important to grasp. It also relates to issues such as Sinai. Did Israelites and Judahites break that covenant? At what point, if any, was it broken? These questions use the language of contract, not of covenant.

A covenant where there is a decidedly senior party (suzerain), is called a suzerain covenant. There are also parity covenants/alliances between friendly nations or people (for example David and Jonathan). I have covered this much more in my *Israel's Gone Global*. In brief, Israel violated Sinai, raising the option for Yahweh as suzerain to annul it. Christians who support the State of Israel usually have an idea that Sinai continues for ethnic Israel, and that Christian solidarity is therefore beholden. Consequently, Muslims often feel that injustice against Palestine is the injustice of Christianity. This can increase persecution and limit conversions. Evangelistically and politically, it's quite important to understand covenant, and to discount the idea that some covenants were conditional and some unconditional. And it can be personally important.

# Today's English Versions

Now let's briefly reflect on a sad question some Christians have voiced. What if your spouse[182] betrays you by interpersonal sex with another? Have they *broken* the marriage. No, they could not. Are you obliged to? No, in fact you cannot. Marriage cannot be broken by either party. What the betrayer has done is seriously violate the covenant, the intimate bridge between you both. You, taking the position of suzerain, are not obliged to annul the covenant, but you are permitted to do so. If you do, you and your former spouse would be morally eligible to marry again. And 'suzerain' here, IMO, applies in marriage equally to guys and girls—parity. This too I cover in *Israel's Gone Global*.

## Texts

The texts are Lv.26:15; Dt.31:16; Ezk.17:19; Hos.8:1; Zc.11:10;[183] Mal.2:10. Each has been allowed two plus two marks, a linking of covenant with either suzerain annulment or vassal violation. For terms like contract, promise, treaty, zero marks. For the term covenant, two marks. If the suzerain may annul, two marks. If the vassal may annul, zero marks. If the vassal can despise, violate, reject, profane, dishonour, prostitute, soil, etc, two marks, or simply one if the text doesn't link to the associated term, covenant. Only texts with an exemplar above, showing how it could be done, were used in this chart.

## Comparative Class Grades

| EV | Grade |
|---|---|
| REB | A+ |
| CSB/ESV/HCSB/ISV/LSV/MSG/NWT/TVB | A |
| LSB/NASB20/NASB95/NIV | A- |
| CJB/KJ21/KJV/LEB/MEV/NABRE/NCB/NET/NKJV/NRSV/NRSVU/RSV/TLV | B+ |
| EEB/EJB/NJB/RNJB/WEB | B- |

---

[182] Or *partner*? No, that's Correctivism immorally merging marriage with long/medium/short-term living together! This said, some *partners*, though unwedded, will actually be spouses since effectively in a marriage (covenant), not in a contract. Bureaucracy is blind and corrupt.

[183] A broken stick can symbolise an annulled covenant—the connection is gone, but the covenant was not broken.

| CEB/NLT | C+ |
| EOB/GNB | C |
| GWT/NOG | D |
| CEV/ERV/FBV/NCV/NLV | U- |

## **Literally Literal?**

The ESV claims to be "essentially literal...[, but] every translation is at many points a trade-off between literal precision and readability".[184] *Literal* isn't the magic word. Many major changes in structure have been made. For example, for Heb.7:20-2, where the ESV does not keep to the Greek structure. Commendably, the ESV even *added* items for clarity, so "to call such a rendering literal (let alone word-for-word) is a fantasy" (Scorgie, Strauss, and Voth 40). On 1 Ths.1:3, the ESV's "work of faith, labour of love, and steadfastness of hope", isn't more literal than "work produced by faith...labour prompted by love... endurance inspired by hope", since the TNIV took the genitive construction to literally mean one thing, while the ESV has taken it to literally mean another. Genitive constructions are not always clear, which is one of the reasons for comparing versions to get different slants on what may be meant. Keeping *authorial* ambiguity is fine, but otherwise versions should opt for the most likely meaning, saving readers from instinctive guesswork.

Tony Payne's way of promoting the ESV was perhaps not just wrong, but grievously wrong.[185] I agree with him that the old NIV/TNIV lost some connections between sentences. However, often connectives needed in Greek are needless and distractive in a receptor language. Sometimes this principle is misjudged in practice—either way. Versions with an ongoing committee are able to take on board feedback on such things, as commentators make specific verse by

---

[184] http://about.esvbible.org/about/preface

[185] Payne lamented that Carson attacked his molehill as if it were a mountain, since Payne's article wasn't pitched at a scholarly readership (http://matthiasmedia.com.au/briefing/longing/article/4007). Carson may well have thought that undermining the TNIV in favour of the ESV, both misadvertised and short-changed the general public into not supporting the real hero.

verse suggestions for improvement. For instance, Carson condemned both the old NIV's 'yet' in Jhn.11:6, and the ESV's 'and/and/and' construction in 1 Cor.1:30. For the former, he argued Jesus' delay was not *in spite of* his love ('yet' old NIV), but "motivated by Jesus' love for Martha, Mary, and Lazarus"[186] ('so' TNIV).[187] The latter, he argued, meant that 'wisdom' was *explained by* (wisdom, that is...) righteousness and holiness and redemption, not simply one of a group of four (wisdom and...). Should not translation teams consider such arguments?

## Clever Construction?

Here I'll focus on the genitive case and literalism. One issue is about nuancing, rather than replacing, the [of + noun] genitive. Let's take 1 Jhn.3:2. "God's children" (ESV)[188] is worse than "children of God" (ERV/LEB/MSG/MEV/NASB95/NCV/NIV/NKJV/TNIV/WEB). Why? Well, the ESV's expression, though losing an English word, might imply that the audience were the *only* children of God. Strictly speaking, "we're God's children" isn't the same as "we're *some of* God's children", since only the latter makes it clear that we are representative of a wider reality. Likewise in the first person "I am God's child"[189] is not the same as "I am *a* child of God", and "I am God's son" sounds positively blasphemous.[190] 'A' is the indefinite article, which can highlight that we are not It, yet a part of It, members of one family (1 Cor.12:27).

---

[186] Carson 1991:407

[187] The TNIV thus showed a listening ear. It is right to listen to objections, weigh them up, and heed those that are justified.

[188] The ISV and GNB are far worse than the ESV, but here we are comparing it to the TNIV which is put in opposition on gender reasons. Whether the metaphor issue is a common ESV weakness is moot.

[189] Even Gordon Fee's "..one is to live..as God's loved and redeemed child" (Fee and Stuart 130)!

[190] Unintentionally blasphemous, no doubt. Similarly, the currently popular *Be Thou My Vision* song (http://wikichristian.org/index.php/Be_thou_my_vision), which having a good beat ensures it high votes even if each singer replaces Jesus as God's true Son. Biblically there is always both a *commonalty yet distinction* between Jesus and Christians. Paul used *huios* of both, but the singular *only* for Jesus; John used *huios* only for Jesus, and only *tekna* or *paidia* for Christians. Removing

# Attack of the ESV

One of the great shakers in the Christian world has got to be C16 Martin Luther. Luther had tried to earn heavenly brownie points by living righteously in the sense of good ethical living and vigorous religion. But as McGrath (2002:4-5) put it, Luther couldn't see how the message about God being righteous (*dikaios*) in the sense of rewarding godly lifestyle and damning ungodly folk, could be a good new revelation that came with Christ. Eventually he twigged that *dikaiosunē Theou* in Rm.1:17 meant a legal status *given by* God, which made a powerful difference to how we feel and think. For him it was like being born anew. This is another question about genitives: should good translation clarify their sometimes puzzling [of + noun] construction? Payne preferred Rm.1:17 as "righteousness of God" (ESV), saying that while Paul *might* have meant "righteousness from God," it was safer not to pre-interpret—let the reader decide.

Similarly, Leon Morris noted how that Luther's insight would fit in Rm.3:2-2 and in Php.3:9, but not in Gen.18:25 (*Epistle to the Romans*, 1988:103). Grammar alone cannot decide. That is, the Greek has the word 'God' (*theos*) in the genitive case (*theou*), a case that sometimes translates as descriptive possession—for example "it belongs to God/part of his nature"—and sometimes as a source—for example "it is from God". *Justice from* the judge *of justice*. In fact, the TNIV agreed with the ESV against the old NIV, and few versions have ever tied it down to Luther.

I can agree some particulars, such as Rm.1:17 as "righteousness of God" (righteousness intrinsic to God), without agreeing with Payne in principle. Yet "let's not say what we *think* it means, simply say *what* the text says" is naive, since translation demands interpretation at some level. Indeed, neutrality can be bias, pushing readers into the wrong choice. X of Y, can mislead, and translators should attempt to discern and translate the sense. Take [{circumcision} {of Christ}]: Col.2:11. Was Christ the object/patient of the circumcision (objective genitive)—done unto him— or the subject/doer of circumcision (subjective genitive)? Where there is doubt, translators should select one, and footnote the

---

this distinction has been the lot of demonic Spiritualism, and anthropocentric Liberalism.

other. In one *Star Trek* film,[191] Mr Spock, scientist and logician, was urged by logic and his captain's trust ("he feels safer about your guesses than [about] most other people's facts"), to *guess*. "Ah! Then I will try to make the best guess I can", he replied.

An educated guess—from Hebrew and Greek scholars—can outweigh uneducated certainties. The eunuch asked for educated help (Ac.8:31). Should we scorn the helping hand? Wrongly, postmodernism denies all certainty to words; rightly, it highlights guesswork in achieving meaning. Though both Carson and Payne have spoken of readers' sakes, they have taken different positions along a spectrum of interpretation, Payne unfairly denying the spectrum. Payne and Carson said that the old NIV/TNIV's bias was to over specify; only Payne unfairly concealed that the ESV's bias to under specify leaves meaning unclear and ambiguous. At best the argument is to compare versions text by text, short listing the more reliable ones, and getting to know them well.

The next chart examines genitives from a handful of versions. Based on Fee and Strauss' *How to Choose a Translation for All Its Worth*, 2007:3-9, 77-83, it is about *of* + *noun* constructions, that is, translating genitival nouns. Using 16 texts, I have tried to see how much effort has gone into removing ambiguity from genitives unambiguous in the Greek NT, as well as keeping ambiguity when the Greek NT is ambiguous. A general helpfulness, so to speak. It's not the issue that sparked the ESV, so I've not bothered to show the TNIV. I have thrown in a few other versions for added interest. Right = 2 marks, Wrong = zero marks; Wrong but footnoting the right, 1 mark.

## Genitive Chart

### Texts

The texts are Jhn.5:29; Jhn.6:45; Rm.1:7; Rm.1:17; Rm.6:4; 1 Cor.1:9; 1 Cor.3:9; Eph.1:13; Eph.1:17; Eph.1:18; Php.3:10; 1 Ths.1:3; 1 Ths.2:13; 1 Ths.3:2; Heb.1:3; Rv.1:1. I suspect that it's more likely that versions with low scores have been lazy or sleepy, rather than deliberately

---

[191] *The Voyage Home*

trying to preserve ambiguousness lest they dictate to those they were meant to serve. This limited chart is not in my Summary Chart.

**<u>Comparative Class Grades</u>**

| EV | Grade |
|---|---|
| NCV | A+ |
| NIV | A |
| NLT | A- |
| HCSB/NABRE | C |
| ESV | D |
| NKJV | U+ |

<u>Morphed Metaphor</u>?

"Metaphors were given by God, so should not be changed." This kind of argument goes back to the "if anyone takes away from" position. Yet what if metaphors, once meaningful, are no longer so? In other words, that once live metaphors have become dead? Why speak of sheep shearing where sheep are unknown? Is not translation the art of moving meaning from one format into another? *Which* metaphors, if any, have significantly lost their meaning, is open to debate, but it is wrong to jump from "this *one* is better in my English version", to "therefore *all* are better in my English version". If I ask you why you *walked by* an accident, you might begin to explain why you did not stop to help. Would you *walk by* a fire? The Greek *peripateō* isn't *literally* 'walk' or literally anything except *peripateō*. It can mean walk; it can mean 'keep in step'; it can mean 'journey'; it can mean 'regulate': the context, and to some extent the readers, will decide.

Are new Christians more likely to understand what's meant by "<u>walk</u> by the Spirit", or "<u>keep in step</u> with the Spirit" (Gal.5:25–ESV/TNIV); to "<u>walk</u> as children of light", or to "<u>live</u> as children of light" (Eph.5:8–ESV/TNIV)? Applied to a set English version, the argument that God's message is clear, if only we stick to it, is itself unclear. What do Christians, singing such as "I would seek *your face*, Yahweh", picture themselves actually doing, if God is invisible?[192] When they read that

---

[192] *Seeing* God's Face/Back is metaphor for unlimited/limited relational intimacy with God and his plans. For Moses, revelation followed this dialogue with

Moses saw God's back [parts] (Ex.33:23), what do they think he saw, and why did he wish to see such?

By saying that Scripture was clear, the Reformers meant "clear in its essentials to anyone really reading/hearing it faithfully put in their own language". They did not mean, clear to you in Hebrew even if you don't know Hebrew, or say that translating any given word in always the same way (for example the word *sarx*), would be more clear than translating a given word in varying ways. What does it mean? It depends on context. The Reformers' three steps: 1# good translation, 2# spiritual readership (*lay* or *clergy*), 3# finer points and deeper levels being the province of teachers: God has appointed teachers.

To generalise, we may say that Payne's attack too quickly jumped from particulars to generalities. The Latin phrase *abusus non tollit usum* highlights that improper use shouldn't condemn proper use. Should we throw out the baby with the bathwater, ditching good principles along with possibly bad practice? Sniping is a common problem between those who should be friends.

## *Sarx* Appeal?

As just said, the range of meaning that words have (their semantic range) can be seen in their varying contexts, so translating words is fitting clusters of meanings into cohesive strings. Translate context. Let's look at the English word 'ball'. 1# "I am having a ball"; 2# "Cinderella went to the ball"; 3# "She threw the ball." 1# might mean I am going to have a ball room dance party, or simply having a great time. If you know her story, where Cinderella went is clear, except to those who understand what a disco is but not what ballroom dancing is— "Cinderella went to a dance" might function better. Finally, did she throw a bouncy object, or arrange the dance-party? In, say, Dutch, should the word 'ball' be translated by the one word?[193] Even to

---

Yahweh: "'you have said that you know me well and are pleased with me. Now if you are, tell me your plans, so that I may serve you and continue to please you'... Yahweh said to Moses, 'I will do just as you have asked, because I know you very well and I am pleased with you'" (Ex.33:12-7 *passim*).

[193] The background etymologies to the word vary, so unlike with *sarx* one should talk of Ball 1 (dance), Ball 2 (toy orb). The English word is chosen simply to indicate how contexts help explain their components.

## Attack of the ESV

English readers the meaning might be unclear if simply using the same word. A particular criticism against the old NIV has been over the word *sarx*.[194]

The ESV, based on the RSV, makes great claims about its *literalness*. This means it attempts to keep closely to the Greek sentence structure, and fields few English variations on any given word. It doesn't mean that it can always be done, or that when done it works out best. The ESV stays closer than the TNIV to the general gloss for *sarx*. But the Greek word *sarx* does not always *mean* 'flesh', though flesh has been the traditional English default term ('gloss') for it. Its meaning must be based on context, but context sometimes isn't clear.

Should the primary aim be 1# to interpret the contextual meaning and then translate it into English,[195] or 2# to choose one English expression—or even transliterate the Greek—in every context, leaving it for readers to interpret? Both methods can misdirect but one must be chosen. The first method can lead to over specifying or wrongly specifying meaning, while the latter method can lead to under specifying meaning: both can mislead different audiences, although the former is more helpful to Bible readers, and the latter to Bible students.

---

[194] For example, Jay E Adams sadly took this line: *More than Redemption* 1997:110—cited in Scorgie, Strauss, and Voth 75. In his section quoted, he argued for 'sinful body', citing Rm.6:6. The old NIV/TNIV agree that 'sinful body' is the meaning in the context of Rm.6:6, but offer more sensitivity to other contexts than Adams would. He failed to note that he was interpreting *sarx* in one context and ignoring its semantic range.

[195] Transliteration? Take my name, Steve, Stephen. Though slightly modified by its host country, it is transliteration of the Greek *stephanos*. It's close in sound and semblance, but not in *sense*. To keep the sense, it should have been something like Winner, less militant than Victor. As it was, I share something with Estiennes, Estavans, Stefans and Steffies around the world, but we don't get congratulated each day. Versions balance between formal correspondence with the source, and functional correspondence. *Hallelujah* and *abba* are two transliterations usually kept in versions. But how many know that *hallelujah* should never be said to God?

Paul used *sarx* 27 times in *Romans*, and means different things in different places. The TNIV used 28 different words or phrases to translate it, mostly *sinful nature* (over 30 times) and *flesh* (16 times) (Scorgie, Strauss, and Voth 366). *Sarx* speaks of 1# the body's covering (1 Cor.15:39); 2# the human body (2 Cor.7:1); 3# human beings (1 Cor.1:2-9); 4# human ethnicity (1 Cor.10:18); 5# human sinfulness (Gal.5:1-7). And when contrasting humanity to God, it might carry the idea of mortality. 1 Cor.5:5 speaks of *sarx* being destroyed—does this mean the mortification of *flesh* that monks whipped their backs to attain? The ESV and HCSB read *flesh*, the REB reads *body*, the NJB reads *natural life*, the TNIV (likewise the NLT) reads *sinful nature* with the alternatives *flesh* and *body* footnoted.

Rm.11:14 causes particular problems for translating *flesh*—did Paul "move to jealousy his *flesh*"? If I told my GPs that I was moving to jealousy my own flesh, would they bind my body in a straightjacket? The KJV paraphrased this by reading "those who are my own flesh", and the ESV, following the RSV, used "fellow Jews". The TNIV and HCSB, "my own people".[196] "Gentiles by birth" (NIV) interprets well what Eph.2:11 means. Is "Gentiles in the flesh" (RSV/ESV), better? Is there even any long-term gain through working out, through much study and many readings, Paul's range of meaning in his use of *sarx*? Would Paul, who fitted himself into his audience, have wished me to sound like a foreigner by saying "I am English in the flesh", rather than "I am English by birth"?

True, the ESV can argue that *flesh* is the default term (gloss) before interpretation, and that it doesn't force any text into an interpretive straightjacket. It certainly needs less scholarship hours to produce. But is fuller interpretation a straightjacket, or a lifejacket? Many ESV readers, reading *flesh*, will probably assume that *human bodies* is always what's meant, *unless* they are saved by some reliable

---

[196] Some condemn the TNIV as if it promoted the anti-Semitist idea that Paul wasn't Jewish. But the context of Rm.11:14, in the TNIV, makes it very clear that he was ethnically Jewish. Real readers are unlikely to be mislead; proof-texters may wish to be misled.

interpretive lifejacket.[197] Translation will sometimes under-specify/under-interpret, sometimes over-specify/over-interpret, but it always *involves* some pre-interpretation/specifying—even saying that *flesh* interprets *sarx* is interpretation. The issue is *how well* translation does its interpretative task. Rendering *sarx* as *flesh* is as much an interpretive straightjacket as rendering *sarx* as *sinful nature*: to avoid the straightjacket the TNIV had footnotes.

<u>Sarx in Romans</u>

- Rm.14:21. The Gk. *krea* (meat) was put in Wycliffe-KJV terms as *flesh* in 14:21, and is further ignored.
- Except for 8:1 (further ignored), there is no textual disagreement *apropos sarx*. Only the WEB shows the gloss *flesh*, for all 27 references in the 23 texts.[198]
- Rm.7:14. The Gk. *sarx* (Latin *carnalis*), translated *flesh* (Wycliffe) but reverted to *carnal* (Tyndale-KJV).
- Where the KJV has *flesh*, the RSV has *flesh* 19 times, and alternatives 5 times. In the three places the KJV has *carnal* (once where the Bishops has *flesh*), the RSV has *carnal* once, and *flesh* twice.
- The ESV always reverts *carnal* (KJV) and *race* (RSV) to *flesh*. Other than that, it matches the RSV (*sarx* as Jews/human being/natural limitations/physical).[199]
- Various versions have fully dropped *flesh* (for example CEV/NOG/NLT), only mentioned in the TNIV in 8:3 (human flesh).
- The NIV has reintroduced *flesh* 15 times, consistently in ch.8 (13 times). *Sinful nature* (TNIV 13 times) has generally been replaced by *flesh* (11 times).
- Final tally: the ESV has *flesh* 23 times; the NIV has it 16 times.

---

[197] This easily falls back on the strange notion that the Bible presents sex as sin, rather than that which for saints is meaningful fun, yet which in sinful setting pollutes.

[198] Rm.1:3; 2:28; 3:20; 4:1; 6:19; 7:5,14,18,25; 8:3abc,4,5ab,6,7,8,9,12ab,13; 9:3,5,8; 11:14;13:14.

[199] In these places, 2:28; 3:20; 6:19; 8:1; 11:14, in line with the NU the KJV/WEB read *flesh*, likewise for disputed text in 8:1.

## Today's English Versions

### Sarx Chart C603

**Texts**

The texts are Rm.1:3; 3:20; 8:8; 9:5; 13:14; 14:21.

**Comparative Class Grades**

| C603 | Grade |
|---|---|
| CJB/EEB/ERV/FBV/GWT/MSG/NJB/NLT/NOG/REB | A+ |
| GNB/NCV | A |
| CEB/CEV | A- |
| ISV/TVB | B |
| NIV | C |
| LEB/NLV | C- |
| CSB/HCSB/NABRE | D |
| ESV/NASB20/NET/NWT | U+ |
| NCB/NRSV/NRSVU/RNJB/RSV/TLV | U |
| EJB/EOB/KJ21/KJV/LSB/LSV/MEV/NASB95/NKJV/WEB | U- |

**Summary**

The NIV's reintroduction of *flesh* might have been based on the idea that some misread 'sinful nature' to unbiblically mean that we had compartments, good and evil. Compartments, no, but, while I don't think that 1 Jhn.1:9 was written for Christians, surely 1 Jhn.1:7 was? How does the possibility, some would say the inevitability, of sin, relate to our nature? Spiritual renewal is a background process going on as we focus our lifestyle on God's moral light. I deem that while we're mortal, sinfulness remains an aspect of our nature, a tendency, some residual volitional alliance with the fallen Adamic nature: ah, to be "with the lord" shall be better.

For the general reader, I think the ESV should be less, well, fleshly. My beef is that the TNIV perhaps never shed enough *flesh*. For example, maybe committed to keep the metaphor of grubby clothes (how does one's sinful nature stain their clothing?), the TNIV/ESV translated *flesh* for *Jude* 23's *sarkos*. Yet the *sarkos* element on its own would have been clearer as something like "sinful lusts" (GNB), or "sinful lives"

(ISV). The NLT translates the stained clothing metaphor too, so can read. "hating the sins that contaminate their lives".[200]

I don't know, maybe the NIV, by narrowing the gap between the ESV, is like a wise explorer who, having gone so far, backtracks to live and bless in the town, rather than plodding on to death in the outback. Yet perhaps fellow travellers should follow the good explorers, not recall them.

## **Ale and Arty?**

I live where snow and Christmas meet—now and again. And Christmas Cards often, if not featuring robins, hark back not to heralds but the Dickensian or, perhaps nicer, Austenian days of carriages arriving at taverns: places of good cheer amid the snow— Jane Austen enjoyed her apple pies and home brewed beer. It's surprising what the term 'Christmas' conjures up.

The traditional Christmas story pictures Mary, aged 18-30, riding a [rent-a-] donkey with Joseph walking alongside to Bethlehem's overcrowded pub, only for them to be shunted off to its stable where Jesus was born on Dec.25$^{th}$, year zero. That after the *Gloria in Excelsis Deo* (Lk.2:14), the stable was soon full to busting with shepherds and three eastern kings, perhaps with snow on their boots,[201] and in the background robins singing, and cattle gazing at a halo or three. It's an artist's paradise.

An *inn* is in, but some of these ideas aren't in the KJV, and even a stable isn't stable. The ESV backs up the KJV, of Luke writing of an *inn* in Lk.2:7 and 10:34, but of a guestroom in Lk.22:11. However, the inn in or near Bethlehem (Jr.41:17), might well have closed by the C1, since Bethlehem was a minor village, 1-3,000 strong and off the beaten track.

---

[200] Dirty living dirties clothing; dirty ethics dirties lives. Jude alerted us to the spiritual yuck value of sin: "feel the yuck value, yet feel for the sinner," was his point.

[201] Such as in the carol in theistic *Wind in the Willows*, "Goodman Joseph toiled through the snow" (ch5).

## Today's English Versions

Unlike the ESV, some current versions have had a rethink—indeed Wycliffe put "chamber" ("guest chamber": Young's Literal Translation). The iconoclastic NWT has "lodging place" (so HCSB), the NJB "living space", the NLT "lodging", the CJB "living quarters" (so ISV). The TNIV was perhaps more accurate, with Lk.2:7 talking of a *guestroom* (so CEB/CSB/ERV). Lk.2:7 and 22:11 have *kataluma,* which seems in *Luke* to contrast to a public *pandoxeion* (10:34), as a private guestroom to a public guesthouse. Many of Joseph's relatives would have been living in Bethlehem, perhaps even his parents. The mentality of Jewish society was to lodge and be lodged with your relatives, not at the pub down the road. Having a *katalumata* was standard in houses, for visiting relatives and friends. And private houses had space—a cave, a barn, the house's ground floor—for visitors' donkeys and, if rich enough, for any family animals. So mangers were standard fittings.

Nor need we take *tē phatnē* (*the* manger) to mean Bethlehem's manger, so much as to emphasise the lowly birth. Archaeology has painted a better picture of C1 Palestinian life than the C16 enjoyed. Good interdisciplinary translation uses such background knowledge.

To finish the story, while shepherds visited the *newborn* Jesus, the magi (probably court magi)—how many we're not told—visited later, perhaps between two weeks and two years later, with an entourage for safety and dignity.[202] Soon after them, Jesus' family escaped into Egypt until Herod the Great died.

---

[202] Journey time from seeing an astronomical light on the birth night, would be about 2 weeks for the eager and wealthy. The magi were probably national ambassadors, able to move quickly, yet we are not told that the light (comet, conjunction of planets, whatever) occurred on the birth night. Some situational terms could indicate a later age for Jesus—a 'child', not 'baby', in a 'house', not a 'manger'. That Herod specified up to 2 years of age doesn't favour either dating, since had he known the birth had been 2 years earlier, he would have exempted the newborn, yet had he known that the birth had been only weeks earlier, he would have exempted the 2-year-olds. His historically documented paranoia may well have heard the magi say 'newborn', yet extended his order to cover 2-year-olds lest the magi had deceived him about the birth date—a case of overkill. Bethlehem was fairly backwater, but it's estimated that many as 20 boys under 2 years old were slaughtered (see Richard T France's *Matthew* (TNTC), 1985:8-7).

For all we know, Simeon might have died before the magi arrived, but he certainly didn't die waiting for them. Only eight days after Jesus was born, Simeon blessed God (ESV: Lk.2:28). Or did he? Here's another contrast between the ESV and NIV. Those who speak of *blessing* God, do so by contradicting the writer to the Hebrews, though they're backed by an English tradition. Heb.7:7 states as an axiom that blessings never go from the lower to the higher.

So, if we are lower, and God is higher, can we really bless him? Through differing forms, the basic Hebrew *BRK* functioned sometimes as *to bless*, sometimes as *to kneel* (to revere, praise). Possibly the Hebrew text came to lose its distinctive forms between kneeling before and being knelt to, between praising God and blessing people.[203] Be that as it may, it is generally agreed that the sense between God blessing humanity and humanity *blessing* God must differ, so versions should reflect this.

I have looked for phrases such as *bless the LORD* and *blessed be/is God*, to assess each version's policy. In general, quite a few, like the HCSB/NIV, are on the solution side, and quite a few, like the ESV/NABRE, on the problem side. A few minor blemishes with the better versions are fairly liveable even if not loveable, and should only prove a problem if folk proof text to 'prove' that we can bless God.

The ESV should, like any version, be argued for on its merits, not by *unjustly* attacking the old NIV/TNIV. It is good, even if *generally* inferior to the old TNIV, but what ails it?

---

[203] "Those finite verbs, then, that speak of God as 'blessed' may very well be qal forms artificially leveled by the Masoretes because the distinction between the verb patterns had been forgotten (for example 2 Chr.20:26; Ps.26:12; 103:1) and would mean 'kneel to, revere, exalt.' If such be the case, the distinction between 'bless[ed]' as God to human (piel) and 'revere[d], esteem[ed]' as human to God (qal; see NIV 'praise[d]' in such cases) would be apparent. Where the verb appears in a human-to-human context, the qal passive participle would indicate a meaning of 'praised, exalted,' thus 'blessed' (for example Gen.14:19), while the piel would signify 'bless' in the formal sense" (VanGemeren 756).

## Impossible Task, Needless Attack?

What if you had to betray either one friend or another, perhaps a confidence broken for the greater good, an appointment with one dropped for the good of the other? Life throws up such conflicts now and again. But with translation it goes with the job. Translators are traitors (*traduttore traditore*). Every translation will betray the text, the only questions are about how to soften the betrayal. The ESV implies that it beat the NIV/TNIV by being more literal. However, formal equivalence is not exempt from betrayal. Some possibly intended meanings will have to be lost, simply because total transfer from one language to another is impossible. Besides, while languages are alive, they change over time, and even words in one tribe may carry slightly different baggage than the same words in another tribe.

In remoulding one language text into another, translators juggle between formal and functional aspects. For instance, on Jr.17:7 the NET substituted a pronoun for God's name. It could have said, "Blessed is anyone who trusts in Yahweh, and whose confidence is in Yahweh". But what made fine Hebrew in Jeremiah's days, makes poor English in ours. To show that Yahweh spoke these words, the NET has, "My blessing is on those people who trust in me, who put their confidence in me." That's how Hebrew functions in English.

So, on the one hand the best-balanced translation will occasionally fail to offer enlightenment and communication. But on the other hand, the worst balanced translation might occasionally offer enlightenment and communication. Good Bible translators give us a very good idea of what Scripture says, factoring in all the essentials, even though dropping and adding some foreign elements.

Besides words modifying their meanings over time, word order also acts against pure translation, and must be adjusted from donor/source language to receptor language. At the end of the day the *function* of language is more important than the *form* of language, although the form sometimes is part of the function. For example, the form of poetry often shows the skill of the poet, their play on words. Simply to translate their 'meaning' without their art is like *saying* an artist has painted trees, without *showing* the glory of their picture.

# Attack of the ESV

Here's some translations from C16 Clément Marot's *A Une Damoyselle Malade*.

| 1 | 2 | 3 | 4 | 5 | 6 |
|---|---|---|---|---|---|
| Ma mignonne | My cute one | My darling, | Lover mine | Babe o' mine | My sweet maid, |
| Je vous donne | I give thee | I bid thee | Here's a sign | Gal divine, | You I wish |
| Le bon jour; | The good day; | Good day; | Of my love, | Here's a kiss, | A good day; |
| Le séjour | The stay | Thy stay in bed | Turtledove. | It ain't bliss | Your sickbed |
| C'est prison. | It's prison. | Is like prison. | You're not well, | Bein' sick. | Is a jail. |
| Guérison | Healing | Thy health | I can tell. | Get up quick, | Total health |
| Recouvrez, | Recover, | Recover, | All cooped up, | Take a spin! | Please regain, |
| Puis ouvrez | Then open | Then open | Buttercup? | Don't stay in | Then unlatch |
| Votre porte | Thy door | Thy door | How about | Where it's dark. | Your room's door |
| Et qu'on sorte | And that one leave | And go out | Going out? | For a lark, | And go out |

Column 2 is most 'formal', column 3 a little less so. Columns 3-5 better express the poem's feel, and Column 6 stands between the formal/informal biases. "The problem with a literal translation of the poem is that, even though it may convey fairly accurately its (cognitive) contents, it fails to reproduce its formal and emotive elements—the very things that makes the poem what it is" (Scorgie, Strauss, and Voth 46). Moisés Silva argued that *traduttore transpositore* is what translators are, namely, those who transform text by transposing it from one linguistic-cultural setting to another.

This is not new: "The KJV translators, for all their skill, failed to preserve countless features...that were in the original Hebrew and Greek texts. By the same token, their mere use of seventeenth-century English ensured that, at virtually every turn, they would add features absent from the original.... They responsibly interpreted the text, then transposed it to a different historical setting and thereby transmuted it into a form it did not have before...[making] it possible for millions to hear and understand its message" (Scorgie, Strauss, and Voth 47).

So-called *literal* translations are not necessarily more accurate. Consider *"I'm head over heels in love"*. Put literally into another language it could sound like I am a gymnast in love, or that I love gymnastics! Or, *"he bit my head off"*—sounds like someone was head-hunted! Robert Burns' girlfriend was "like a red, red rose". Obviously, she was smelly and had green leaves and prickles. These are only simple examples and there is much more to it.

Suffice to say that formal translation doesn't always pick up the inner life of language. Moreover, Greek word A should in some settings be translated as English word A, sometimes as English word B, and sometimes as English word C: translators might differ as to when to *use* English A, B, or C. It is better to avoid asking what the *literal* translation of a set word is. For example, many older Greek text books, when the masculine was often used in general speech to include girls and women, gave *adelphoi* as meaning *brothers*. More recent ones often have updated to today's general speech but still sometimes weigh towards the male gender though allowing that sisters can sometimes be included.

However, 'brothers and sisters' is the common use of *adelphoi* in the NT Letters, and there is not a built-in gender bias except in always including a brother. The NLT is annoying and misleading when, after correctly translating *adelphoi* as 'brothers and sisters', wrongly footnotes again and again that the Greek *means* 'brothers'. Though formally masculine, the Greek does <u>not</u> mean 'brothers'. In some contexts, it means 'brothers';[204] in some contexts it means 'brothers and sisters'. Perhaps where translating 'brothers' the NLT should footnote that the Greek *means* 'brothers and sisters'!

Context decides and there is no *literal* word for word equivalent. Rather than speaking of literal translation, it is better to speak of primary translation: "the distinction between literal and primary may seem a small thing, but it has far-reaching implications", such as

---

[204] For example Ac.15:1—sisters were not being circumcised! The NLT sidesteps away from 'brothers' by 'believers'—let the believers decide among themselves how it applies!

## Attack of the ESV

whether there is a built-in male bias for translation (Scorgie, Strauss, and Voth 134). We can analyse usage of a word and give its *primary* (majority?) meaning, a *try this first to see if it works*, but this should not be called its *literal* meaning.

On this something that in one culture only needs the shorthand of familiarity, might need the longhand of explanation in a different culture. Indeed, the NT sometimes added a word of explanation, as in "abba, that is, father" (Mk.14:36/Rm.8:15/Gal.4:6): Aramaic translated into Greek. Let's look at Mt.9:10.

In the KJV it reads that "...it came to pass, as Jesus sat at meat in the house, behold, many publicans and sinners came and sat down with him and his disciples." It might seem that Jesus sat on a chair but not at a table, alongside boozy carnivores and cads. Actually, the Greek (*anakeimai*) implies both a low table (not chairs) and food (not meat). Moreover, the fellow Jews (not boozers) were either explicitly or implicitly working with the Roman overlord.[205]

In the ESV it reads that "as Jesus reclined at table in the house, behold, many tax collectors and sinners came and were reclining with Jesus and his disciples." The table, visible to C1 Jews, is invisible to us unless it's translated in. Adding 'table' regains for us what Matthew said. To tell us that it was a low table could incline us to think it was lounging at an informal meal: it those days low table meant a socially formal meal. "Lying sideways at a low table for a formal private social meal" would be much freer than the text, but would nicely convey *Matthew*, but you can't always be turning one word into twelve.

Accuracy is sometimes easier for less formal versions, since they more readily add words to regain sense. The NASB95 and ESV amplify in

---

[205] *Publicans* (KJV) comes from the Latin *publicani* for public servants. Even *tax collectors* (ESV/NIV) fails to signal that in that Jewish culture they were licensed by and protected by Rome. Working for the 'enemy' tax collectors routinely made money on the side by overcharging tax at city gates. Fellow Jews hated them as extortionate collaborators with Rome, and some Zealots targeted them for execution. Had Britain been successfully controlled by Nazism, its tax collectors might have been similarly targeted by resistance movements. Linked with *sinners*, we might conclude that sinners were any who were happy to hang out with such traitors.

the posture to the table, but miss the nuance of the social status of the meal. The NKJV goes for the formal posture, dropping the historical particularity (how they did it) in favour of C1 Western particularity (how we do it)—'sat at the table'.[206] The GNB gets the nuance of a meal, but not what kind. The old NIV/TNIV mark more the formality, 'dinner', missing the nuance of posture. The NLT suggests a formal dinner, with invitations having gone to selected folk, but again drops the C1 posture.

There is so so much where, the ESV claiming the translational high ground, it fails to deliver the goods. As an enemy to the NIV, it fortunately fails. As an acceptable version, it succeeds, as did the RSV before it. Yet it continues to distrust the gender thing, concealing an important biblical part of inclusivity.

---

[206] Helping C21 understanding can be good, but there must be trade off. For example in the C1 context of the Passover Meal, understanding the reclining posture of the formal meal helps us understand that John wasn't lying on Jesus' 'bosom' (Jhn.13:23 KJV)—from which we have the expression 'bosom pals'. Rather, the text was worded for C1 audiences to know that John had the favoured position whereby, lying at table with Jesus behind him, he could partly roll over to confidentially ask Jesus Peter's signalled question, 'who?'. Jesus could whisper his reply without others overhearing, so they didn't understand why Judas, by a token honoured as a friend, was sent out. Had Peter understood, Judas might have lost both ears!

# Chapter 14   Gender Agenda?

Abandon ship, men and men first! In 1900, *The Christian Herald* included a witticism about a woman complaining to a clergyman that she felt excluded by his uni-gender talk. Why, she asked, did he not speak of gentlemen AND ladies, to which he replied that the one embraces the other. Charles Dickens likewise found some humour in unigender language, and using a "singular they/their...has been documented back to Jane Austen" (Bruce 1999:xv). Indeed, Carson's *The Inclusive Language Debate*, 1998, charted ebbs and flows of uni~ and bi~gender language in the Middle Ages.

In the West it is in. A generation on it might be out, but unless there is an overriding issue of truth, the issue is to speak where we are at. In a university pamphlet outlining acceptability, Johannes Kritzinger pointed out that exclusion and offence could unintentionally flow from sexism. I go further: the term *men and women*, excludes children, so in contexts that include children, "men and women", though not sexist, is ageist. Kritzinger argued that for some, even the term *man* (for example 'God created man') sparks misleading gender imagery, and, I might add, adult imagery. *Sageism* combines sexism with ageism. There is perhaps more scope on how we restructure, than on whether we restructure, and I unashamedly use *man* as shorthand for hu<u>man</u>ity, <u>man</u>kind, hu<u>man</u>kind.[207]

Yet if we see that our daily language should be more inclusive, yet not that we should include Scripture *translation* in this process, are we not excluding folk from Scripture, restricting access to God's written word?[208] We can fear getting bogged down in trivia and—especially for us older men relatively unaffected by sexism—convinced that the textual contortions sometimes required are a waste of time. Attaining to a bias-free and balanced way of thinking, writing, and speaking, is

---

[207] Unless tied to a masculine pronoun (he), in which instance I prefer humanity/it or mankind/it/they.

[208] Having some resemblance to Mt.23:13, ironically put in the NKJV as "you shut up the kingdom of heaven against men"!

not always easy. But to forego the effort, underplays the negative which sageist language can have and undermines the Bible.

In the days of the Jesus Revolution, there arose a new Moses, or, shall we say, David Berg, who claimed to be such. He attracted many to himself by his beliefs, and many more because he sent his women out to evangelise through prostitution. I met one such attractive fisher in the seventies, but somewhat reluctantly declined her fair bait. Of course, for social engineering you must give ideas you like, nice names, and give ideas you dislike, unnice names. Berg chose *Flirty Fishing* as the name to bless his girls as they went forth to multiply.

It was apparently the devilish System—not divine Scripture—which only allowed interpersonal sex between spouses, said Berg. His outfit, at that time called The *Children of God*, had a handbook which taught that kiss and convert didn't go far enough—clothes off when fishing for converts, and only then list them as part of your catch quota (http://xfamily.org/index.php/Flirty_Fishing (2010)). Jesus babies were a blessing! And they still called themselves, "children of *God*".

C S Lewis taught that human sexual intercourse was only proper within marriage—chastity or celibacy.[209] If Lewis was right rather than old fashioned, how did *The Children of God* justify flirty fishing? Easy: it was only obeying Jesus who said "I will make you fishers of men" (Mt.4:19).[210] Partly because of AIDS, 1987 saw the official end of its Flirty Fishing era, though it stood by its former policy as biblical and thus moral. Fishers of *men*? Even if Jesus had sexual evangelism in mind (historically he spoke only to guys without specifying technique), had he really made a *gender* point? Or, to be true to him, do we need more gender accuracy in translation? Loonies latch on to loose translation.

---

[209] When we exalt the human loves to overlordship (which Lewis said demonises them), lovingness becomes the ultimate ethical criteria and objectively dies.

[210] Fishing for men (CJB/EJB/ESV/KJ21/KJV/MEV/NABRE/NASB95/NKJV/NLV/NWT/REB/TLV/TVB/WEB), for men and women (MSG), for people (CEB/CEV/CSB/EOB/ERV/GNB/GWT/HCSB/ISV/LEB/NCV/NET/NIV/NJB/NLT/NOG/NRSV). Servetus argued that 'men' included women but excluded children (Calvin's *Institutes* 4.16.31).

What is inclusive language? Is it only using inclusive terms when the author assumed members of both sexes (Mark Strauss), thus a good term?[211] Or is it only using inclusive terms when the authorial aim is in reasonable dispute (Poythress and Grudem), thus a bad term? Poythress and Grudem (P&G) have said that it's right to use gender accurate language, but wrong to use inclusive language, since that takes us into disputed territory—they meant disputed by them. That all sounds fairly reasonable, until you ask whether today's dispute will still be tomorrow's dispute.

For example, Grudem initially argued that *adelphoi* <u>cannot</u> mean *brothers and sisters*. By translating *adelphoi* as *brothers and sisters*, the TNIV was therefore wrongly using inclusive language, since disputed. Then Grudem subsequently argued that *adelphoi* <u>can</u> mean *brothers and sisters*. So then, by translating *adelphoi* as *brothers and sisters*, the TNIV was therefore rightly using inclusive language, since undisputed—at least by Grudem. But if others still argue as Grudem once did, then the TNIV *was* using inclusive language, since disputed. If it only takes one to dispute, what will stand?

Who decides what is in dispute, and therefore what is inclusive language, if inclusive language means only gender neutral language that is in dispute, and so functions only as a negative term? Some ethics theorists say that what a person calls 'moral good' is simply what they happen to like—if my 'bag' is mass murder, then me calling it morally good is as valid (or invalid) as you calling it morally evil just because you dislike it. If, that is, there is no objective right and wrong.

Dostoyevsky's Ivan Karamazov showed a weakness in atheism, when he said that if you meet absolute evil, you should see that absolute goodness must exist: shadow proves light. If we deny absolute evil, we are in a moral void, which, if we would avoid God who crucifies human freedom, is the safe place to be. Demons likewise avoid that confrontation (Mk.5:7; Jas.2:19). Sadly, political legislators are often infected by this subjectivism: in ignoring deity, the hub position, they reject the only rational ground for objectivity, thus expose humanity

---

[211] Scorgie, Strauss, and Voth 119. Missing out the category of children, he was guilty of ageism, as was the NIVI's "fishers of men and women".

to carnage. For to reject the objective lord is to reject the objective law. Discrimination becomes "what we don't like", rather than wisdom in discerning right from wrong. That's bad. But isn't P&G's position the same, defining Inclusivity as "what we don't like"?

Is Strauss' definition better, even if problematic? What objective test always tells beyond reasonable doubt what an ancient author intended? Only all men, and in every people group over all time? Or including all women? Or maybe only a class of women (married, royal, outcasts)? And including children—children from every stratum of their society, and every society in their generation, or in every generation while their age lasted? We must work in probabilities and generalities, using knowledge of semantic ranges and contextual clues. It is detective work. It is linguistic work.

Inclusive language, like exclusive language, is neither a good nor a bad term. It can be appropriate or inappropriate, and translators must judge text by text, context by context. Inclusive language is using inclusive terms, whether or not the author meant such in their context, or would have meant such in ours. A good inclusive language English version is one that, submitted to God, uses top level linguistic skills to convey biblical relevancy without undermining what the author meant in their context or would have meant in ours.

Some guidelines are better than others, and some translation choices are better than others. Grudem once thought that *adelphoi* as *brothers and sisters*, had to be wrong. Grudem, converted by force of linguistic evidence, must now ask, in each *adelphoi* verse, In this verse about *brothers and sisters*, or only about *brothers*? Correct translation is not for lazy translators.

Over the centuries gender neutral talk, like the singular 'them' rather than 'he', has come and gone; masculine-bias talk has come and gone. Language lives with its speakers, constantly changing, sometimes for better, sometimes for worse. We sometimes significantly misunderstand someone simply because they have used a term their way, not ours. English language has changed a fair bit over the last 50 years, partly because after WW2 a new commercial importance was placed on youth as a source of spending power. Detaching them from parents increased their commercial value, and they came into various ideas of 'liberation', such as the hippy movement, liberating fish from

## Gender Agenda?

water. Developing their own sub-culture, they developed their own inner circle language.

This liberty, sometimes into the vice of slavery, led also to a feeling among women that equality was a 'right'.[212] We may support Feminism's Christian form,[213] and leave demons to support Feminism's antimarriage forms: God defines; man discerns. Feminism per se is not bad, though easily misunderstood and feared.

Resentments were raised about exclusive gender language, and bit by bit society subscribed to gender language change. In Christian circles, talk of Christ saving sinful *men* began to raise exclusive pictures of adult males of the human race being saved, whereas before in some contexts *men* was often assumed to include women and children. A generation arose that knows not Joseph.

In western society, many girls, with no wacky feminist drum to beat, hear the term 'men' as simply a number of adult males of the human race: boys can also feel excluded by the 'adult' idea behind 'men'. That is, talk about 'men' seems to exclude boys, girls, and women. Does the Bible exclude them? If not, should Bible versions *talk* as if it does? Scripture is relevant, must seem relevant, must be understandable.

This understanding has led various versions to seek inclusive gender accuracy. Sure, some seek gender inaccuracy to raise their Radical Feminist flag and fly their folly. Yet a number of responsible versions

---

[212] Rights theory is a legal fiction and a subsection of Moral Law. Sadly, it has often downplayed responsibilities that go with 'rights', and sought its idea of self-interests, against what is right. As a philosophy it is easily unbalanced, anomic, ethically damning, and ends in the tooth and claw of nihilism, of Mordor. What is right for humanity is not always a human 'right'. Rephrasing is often more ethical: for example not "I have a right not to be raped", but rather "it is not right to rape".

[213] For which see, for example, Elaine Storkey's *What's Right with Feminism*. This feeling of women's disempowerment goes back longer than the term *Feminism*. We can trace it into the Suffrage Movement, seeking political voting for women. Even in the King Arthur stories, where Sir Gawain marries the hideous hag, we read that power over men was the greatest yet secret desire of women. The ancient Greeks spoke of *amazones*, warrior women, a reactionary radical feminism, slayers of men.

have followed generally good guidelines. Sometimes they might go too far; sometimes they might not go far enough. To some extent, the perfect reading is impossible, because the perfect reader does not exist. But to a large extent, such creeping re-genderisation following language change, caused evangelical ripples, but not evangelical waves, because the versions doing it were not evangelical favourites.

And then, horror of horrors, the old NIV turned its attention to such things. Evangelical Bible rage was sparked off, mostly by evangelicals who, without reading it, 'instinctively' knew it was 'feminist' corruption. Or in other words, their gut feeling was to go with the knee-jerks of some respected leaders. A few minor NIV formats broached gender accuracy, but the USA evangelical base proved the main barrier to a global version, until the 2005 TNIV was allowed to run alongside the 1984 NIV, rather than to replace it.

The TNIV is now redundant,[214] but I have pitched it alongside the ESV, since the latter to some extent successfully pitched its sales as if contrasted to a Feminist dominated TNIV that was muting God's masculinity. And thus, by fair means or foul, the ESV managed to outsell the TNIV. They were the ones in the ring. Thus, the ESV managed to mute evangelism.

Let's be clear. God is not a man (ESV: 1 Sam.15:29). Come to think of it, he is not human (NLT), is not a human being (CJB), is not a mortal (NABRE), is not a mortal being (TVB).[215] Come to think of it, he is not biological at all. God has neither maleness nor femaleness. Both of the created sexes (a biological existence) carry gender strands from within

---

[214] Finally Zondervan threw in the towel, having gained too many enemies and failing to achieve too few friends in producing the NIVI, freezing the NIV to 1984, and in marketing the TNIV. At the end of the day unless under denominational pressure to accept a particular version, versions must defer somewhat to public taste. Even desirable changes of improved biblicality must bow to human pressures: the TNIV never achieved a critical mass of public support. The brand name 'NIV' has long been deemed safe for Evangelicals, and many TNIV gains transported into the NIV 2011. Both old NIV and TNIV were killed off in favour of an upgraded NIV.

[215] There is a sense in which God the son, therefore God, incorporated humanity by incarnation, becoming human with us. That is in the space-time continuum *ad infinitum*, but not defining God per se, the uncreated eternal.

his own nature, and are roughly defined by us as masculinity and femininity. Contrasted to his masculinity, are we not all feminine, at least weakly so? Some argue for egalitarianising the idea, *God*. They sometimes take the feminine portrayal of him to fully counterbalance the masculine portrayal of him, and perhaps turn the idea of 'him' into one of an 'it', a 'shim', or 'he/she' 'she/he', or 'father/mother', or some such.

They have some justification. For example, Paul and his team sometimes acted like a mother (1 Ths.1:7) and sometimes like a father (1 Ths.1:11). But gender is not just a social construct, nor is sexuality plastic, and even as in God's likeness human beings reflect an overlap of gender—more masculinity concentrated among men; more femininity concentrated among women—the overwhelming balance of Scripture concentrates on God's masculinity. To be biblical, so should we.

Which is one reason some don't like to be biblical, seeking instead an equalities god. But why is masculinity the biblical emphasis? Was it because it was written by men, because it was God's design, or—combining the two ideas—because it was God's design that predominantly men should write it and thereby naturally reflect a bias of emphasis which he himself wished conveyed (that is, men chosen to express masculinity)? The masculine concepts of spiritual warfare and of lordship are most pressing this side of the new age.

A high view of Scripture should hold it as having being written to God's design. I hold to a Complementarian position: men and women *complete* each other as distinct yet one (Gen.5:2). He called them Adam (CJB). I allow egalitarianism as a subservient idea (for example equal reasonable legal rights within workplaces), and leadership according to God's gifting. Evangelicals are by and large complementarian—guys and girls are equally precious to God, but within mortal society are not fully interchangeable, and some form of sovereignty/subservience between husbands and wives, analogous to the gender free relationship between God the Father and God the Son, is acted out on life's stage.[216]

In the USA, the bitter debate sparked off when Zondervan's *Committee on Bible Translation* (CBT) aiming to circulate a US NIVI (NIV Inclusive), thus opened up the way to opposition. The *Colorado Springs Guidelines* (CSG) arose, which roundly and unsoundly condemned the translation gender-theory of the CBT. Sadly, a leading light was Nazarene Dr. James Dobson (*Focus on the Family*), stirring up Bible rage. A document was signed by 12 leaders, many of whom Carson suggested were misguided by the idea that gender accuracy was an egalitarian attack on complementarianism, or had simply bowed to peer pressure. "Quite a number of them, I think, would make no pretence of having much grasp of Hebrew, Aramaic, Greek, translation theory, and linguistics" (Carson 1998:37).

This perhaps applied also to the Southern Baptist Convention, representing a 16 million membership (Dallas, 1997). It resolved to oppose "so-called gender inclusive language." It should be noted that the NIVI, succeeded by the TNIV, neither sought to downplay the idea of God's masculinity (main truth), nor to dwell on his femininity (minor truth), but merely to highlight justified gender-neutrality in his message to humanity. For example, though ageist, should it not be praised for showing that Jesus made his followers 'fishers of men and women' (NIVI), not just 'fishers of men'?

Southern Baptist, evangelical, and complementarian, Donald Carson, sought to mediate between CBT and CSG, siding mainly with CBT. Evangelical, Wayne Grudem, sought to stand by CSG. One criticism put, was that in seeking to sort out gender translation problems, number problems arose: for example, was God within 'every man who believed' (individualism) or simply in 'believing humanity' (corporality)? History may lump this with the mid-C20 Number/Reverence controversy of dropping Thee/Thine/Thou as singular reverentials, the sound of *holy language*.[217] You might like to read D A Carson's,

---

[216] Though not covered here, it is good to examine 1 Tm.2:12: www.cbmw.org/images/jbmw_pdf/10_1/teaching_usurping_authority.pdf.

[217] Only seeming 'holy language' to some because over generations the public have come to revere more the KJV's style, as it became more dated. The

## Gender Agenda?

The Inclusive Language Debate, and Poythress and Grudem's, *The Gender Neutral Controversy*.

Some terms in Scripture have been formally masculinised in earlier Western culture (for example *pas* as 'everyman' instead of its Greek meaning 'everyone') and are better nowadays translated as gender-neutral to convey their original meaning. On the other hand, the singular pronoun 'he/him' in gender-neutral texts is debated—does one give up the singular idea (an individual as an individual/many as individuals), perhaps using 'they' as doubling nowadays as plural and singular?

Theology can be at stake, where for example the idea of Christ dwelling in each individual 'him', could by insensitive inclusive pluralising sound like Christ dwelling communally in 'them' as a group. Does it change an individual message to a corporate message? To some extent a text's immediate context preserves us from certain misunderstandings, allowing gender and number accuracy to combine, but extra care does need to be taken to keep the message to each applicable individual, rather than to a conglomeration.

### **Nuances or Nuisances?**

Some suggest that important nuances, shades of meaning, such as individual salvation, are lost by inclusive versions. To argue against inclusivism, P&G spoke of four levels of reader approach. Namely, 1# the naive, 2# the theoretically informed, 3# the discerning, and 4# the reflective. In so many words, they firstly argued that most readers don't need inclusive language to get them to level three (intuitively discerning basic textual subtleties), because they are already there. Although they agreed that commentators help readers into level 4, it's as if they say that level 2 guidance (inclusive language versions) can subvert level 3 understanding. Sadly, they exposed themselves to the charge that

---

singular/plural distinction of thee/ye was already dated by the time of the KJV. Perhaps it would not have been used if the archbishop had not insisted that the Bishops Bible be closely used as its foundation document (Scorgie, Strauss, and Voth 211), the Bishops Bible itself locked into Tyndale's 1575 Middle English, where in fact you-singulars were used without reverence for celestials, terrestrials, and infernals.

they "spent much of the rest of [their own] book contradicting [their model] in practice" (Scorgie, Strauss, and Voth 122).

Though they did not make it clear, basic versions cannot work above level 2, though occasionally highlight level 2 issues, such as the fact that breath/wind/spirit (Ezk.37:5,9,14) all roughly translate the same Hebrew word (*ruach*). Should versions translate the feminine form *rûaḥ* as each context means, to get the best sense in English, or, say, translate as *spirit* each time to get the best sense of Hebrew wordplay?[218]

Putting the issue another way, how should versions translate, when to keep a *masculine* nuance is to lose, or suppresses, an *inclusive* nuance? Versions can't keep all nuances. Good translation is about faithfully and clearly conveying the priority ones, dropping only whatever conflicts with this aim. Even a modern Hebrew reader, reading biblical Hebrew, will lose cultural and linguistic nuances once second nature to Israelites.

Protesting injustice, Carson and Strauss rebuked P&G's pejorative language about *distortions/inaccuracies*, and the like, and implicitly questioning the integrity of certain Bible translators. "...Every time the decision goes against their favoured 'nuance', they accuse their opponents of distorting Scripture and introducing inaccuracies. At some point, one begins to suspect that it is their argument that is ideologically driven" (Scorgie, Strauss, and Voth 81).

Let's see one example of how P&G sought to slam functionalism. To debunk the NCV/NIVI/NLT/NRSV for adding/losing nuances P&G compared them to Pr.16:9 (RSV), citing the RSV as the 'literal' standard. They gaily ignored that *all* translation adds/subtracts nuances, and that the RSV's "a man's mind plans his ways, but the LORD directs his steps" missed nuances by translating *'āḏām* as *man* (it includes women and children), *lēb* as *mind* (it could be heart), and *yākîn* as *directs* (could be determines).

The ESV, though based on the RSV, actually opted for *heart* instead of *mind*, and adjusted *directs* to *establishes*, and misses nuances the RSV had. If it did not think the RSV perfect, why did not P&G also

---

[218] Likewise, the Greek word *sarx*?

## Gender Agenda?

indicate that the RSV was a flawed bag of nuances? Nuances the RSV/ESV miss, include the gender, and, to some extent age, *neutrality* of the text, and, in line with the other versions listed, the *nuance* of God's name.

In a bleat on quasi-Christian theology, C S Lewis referred to Alfred Loisy, Albert Schweitzer, Rudolf Bultmann, Paul Tillich, and Alec Vidler. "These men ask me to believe they can read between the lines of the old texts; the evidence is their obvious inability to read (in any sense worth discussing) the lines themselves. They claim to see fern-seed and can't see an elephant ten yards away in broad daylight" (Lewis 1975:111).

While I do not doubt the genuine Christianity of Poythress and Grudem, my betters by far, it is ironical that in arguing that readers instinctively know a generic 'he' from a non-generic 'he', they themselves failed to spot an obvious generic 'man' ten yards away in plain English.[219] For, like claiming to see fern seed but missing the elephant, they cited Liddell-Scott's Greek-English Lexicon to show that the Greek *anēr,* always meant a male human being in the NT.

True, it is used in distinction to 'woman', but when Liddell-Scott contrasted *anēr* to *God*, P&G overlooked that Liddell-Scott had actually highlighted its *inclusive* NT use, namely *mankind* as distinct from God (Scorgie, Strauss, and Voth 124). It is the tendency to misread the masculine case as generic—the thing that P&G say isn't very likely but did themselves—that inclusivists say requires inclusive versions.

P&G's forward by linguist Valerie Becker Makkai, says that no large scales *studies* had been done showing that gender talk has significantly changed. She did not say that there has been no large-scale *change*. At least one who assumed no significant change, and signed up to the Colorado Springs Guidelines, Andreas Köstenberger, defected. For in 1999, he discovered that Lauren, his 6 y.o., decided that *she* wished to be a fisher of women, not of men—she'd let her little sister fish for men (Lk.5:10).[220] How a younger generation were

---

[219] He has also argued that some, for example the NRSV, have gone too far in avoiding the masculine 'he'.

[220] www.biblicalfoundations.org/wp-content/uploads/2012/01/38-JETS-The-Inclusive-Language-Debate.pdf

misreading old gender language, convinced him that gender accurate versions were, after all, needful. Anyway, let's go to Colorado.

## **Giddy Guidelines**

The *International Bible Society* (IBS), founded in 1809 as the New York Bible Society for the socio-economic poor of New York, was a nonprofit ministry into Bible translation and distribution, and based in Colorado Springs. IBS merged with Operation Mobilization founder George Verwer's STL, is now rebranded as Biblica, and holds the copyright for the old NIV/TNIV. But way before that merger, when it was thinking of gender language update, it was summoned to a forum that feared an antimarriage form of feminism, accused of being in cahoots with the ungodly, and ordered to toe the line of James Dobson's *Focus on the Family*, and of *The Council on Biblical Manhood and Womanhood* (CBMW). The IBS reps had been snared.

> "In 1997, the Colorado Springs Guidelines were signed at a very difficult time when the primary concern of IBS leadership was to prevent further dissension within the Christian community. In retrospect we realized it was a mistake to sign the CSG. We reached this conclusion after thorough consultation and review of the guidelines with several respected translation experts from around the world. This review revealed the proposed guidelines were in many cases inconsistent, unduly restrictive, and would actually inhibit the ability of the CBT, and IBS, to perform our missions—to accurately translate the meaning of the original texts—and to provide God's Word to the next generation. Simply stated, the CSG, although well-meaning, does not conform to sound translation methodology widely accepted by a significant majority of evangelical linguists, translators, and scholars".[221]

In 2001 it formally withdrew its CSG endorsement. Through Zondervan, it published a frozen NIV 1984 and an unfrozen TNIV. The former, without ongoing support, was left to serve the traditional; the latter, the contemporary.

The CS Guidelines cover a number of contentious terms, which in short it says either must sound masculine, or at least should usually

---

[221] www.tniv.info/qanda.php

sound masculine. Carson 1998:111-3 argues that none of these terms must always be masculine, and that CSG's leeway for inclusivity is far more restrictive than ancient grammar requires and detrimental to today's younger Christians and non-Christians, alienating them from God. What is formally masculine grammar may well function biblically beyond the biological gender divide.

"The main points of contention involve masculine nouns—[traditionally put in English as] man, brother, father, son—and third-person masculine singular pronouns—[traditionally put in English as] he, him, his—all of which have traditionally been used in an inclusive sense".[222] The CSG fear seems to have been, and to be, that going down a more inclusive road mutes both deific masculinity and male masculinity, and is somehow less faithful, less reliable. A number of principles and particulars have been touched on. Let's briefly look at a couple more.

### CSG.B.1

May 1997: 'Brother' (*adelphos*) and 'brothers' (*adelphoi*) should not be changed to 'brother(s) and sister(s).'

Sep. 1997: 'Brother' (*adelphos*) should not be changed to 'brother or sister'; however, the plural *adelphoi* can be translated 'brothers and sisters' where the context makes clear that the author is referring to both men and women.

The revision concedes generics to the plural but not to the singular form. The ESV thus continues to say that Jesus allowed anger towards a sister but not a brother (Mt.5:22). It may expect every reader to assume that a spiritual sister is equally, or subserviently, meant. But must we be governed by Grudem's speculative and subjective criterion of a divine *male representative gender*? Does *adelphos* really

---

[222] www.cbeinternational.org/new/pdf_files/free_articles/TNIV_Kohlenberger.pdf

picture a representative male human to signify a generic principle covering brothers and sisters?[223]

A feminine form of *adelphos* exists, namely *adelphē* (for example Mt.12:50) but they are not simply grammatical opposites. The default masculine sometimes allows gender contrast, and is sometimes simply gender neutral (sibling), more open ended, than narrower *adelphē*. Singular masculines can also carry the gender inclusive plural. For example, consider "anthrōpos [masculine singular] shall not live by bread alone" (ESV: Mt/Lk.4:4), or in English, "a person ought not murder". Anyone who hates their *adelphos* (1 Jhn.2:11), is surely inclusive—any brother *or* sister.

Though we may not pass judgement on one another, we might be free to stumble or hinder a *sister* but not an *adelphos* (Rm.14:13), according to the ESV. Grudem affirmed the ESV *translation* here (Köstenberger and Croteau loc.1235). He argued that for translation, only the masculine is valid; that for *application*, only inclusive (guys and girls) is valid; that translation must not include application.[224] The ESV contains many such anomalies. The CSG must have some commendation for having had *some* flexibility in the light of biblical evidence, yet I'd welcome a radical rethink.

## CSG.B.2

This dislikes *huios* being translated as *children*. Wayne Grudem said that the NT writers used...

> "'children' (*tekna*) when they wanted to (as in Jhn.1:12, 'He gave them power to become children of God,' and Rm.8:1-7, 'bearing witness with our spirit that we are children of God.'). But in other verses the Bible spoke of us as 'sons,' and faithful translations

---

[223] P&G argued the idea of male imagery terms being God inspired, even of Hebrew and Greek gender structure being God-inspired, to teach transgender application under complementarianism.

[224] Grudem's assertion that *adelphos* 428 out of 428 times means "a male human being" (show me one exception) is countered by Carson 1998:130-3, where Carson notes how contexts show some *adelphos* use to be inclusive. Likewise, Grudem's point that "brothers and sisters" could have been written exactly that way in Greek, overlooked that it could be written alternate ways, for example by *adelphos* shorthand.

should not change this to 'sons and daughters' or 'children' as the NIVI did in Gal.4:7."

He said that in the latter passage, the rendering 'children', "obscures the FACT that we all (men and women) gain standing as 'sons' and therefore the inheritance rights that belong to sons in the Biblical world."[225]

Fellow Complementarian, Don Carson (1998:132), responded...

> "...this is methodologically mistaken. Just because some passages in the New Testament can distinguish between *huios* and *teknon* does not necessarily mean that the two words cannot share identical semantic ranges in pragmatic circumstances—for otherwise we have returned again to 'illegitimate totality transfer.' In other words, one must inspect usage in passage after passage to see if *huios* always means 'son' as distinct from 'child,' impelled, perhaps, by overtones of what it means to be an heir.

> "As soon as we do this, the position collapses. In Mk.12:19, Jesus was questioned about levirate marriage, which came into play when a man died leaving no *teknon* ('child,' and here surely an heir) to carry on his name. Zechariah and Elizabeth longed for a *teknon* to carry on the family name (Lk.1:7). The older brother in the parable of the prodigal son was addressed by his father, 'My son [*teknon*]...everything I have is yours' (NIV: Lk.15:31). Ac.7:5 says that God promised Abraham the land even though he had no '*teknon*'—which here must refer to an heir.

> "Paul could switch back and forth between *teknon* and *huios* in the same passage: 'because those who are led by the Spirit of God are sons [*huioi*] of God.... The Spirit himself testifies with our spirit that we are God's children [*tekna*]. Now if we are children [*tekna*], then we are heirs—heirs of God and co-heirs with Christ.... The creation waits in eager expectation for the sons [*huioi*] of God to be revealed.... The creation itself will be...brought into the glorious freedom of the children [*tekna*] of God'".

---

[225] An obvious clanger is ageism—Grudem meant "we all (as men, women or children)..." but like so many didn't really think about youngsters even though his context was about *children*—and *sons*.

Theologically there wasn't an agreed systematic difference between *huioi* and *tekna*. Paul preferred to use the former for us, while John preferred to use the latter. Both worded things to keep the distance between our relationship to the Father, and Jesus' one-of-a-kind relationship with him, and both worded things to witness that Christians and Jesus share the same family. By never teaching that Christians were *huioi*, simply *tekna*, did John teach that we lacked inheritance? Certainly not! Sometimes a footnote[226] will help where a male inheritance idea seems an explicit part of a *huioi* text.

CSG.B.2 also denies that the Hebrew singular masculine *ben* may be put as gender inclusive. Yet the apostle Paul did just this, putting 2 Sam.7:14's *ben* as "sons and daughters" in 2 Cor.6:18, and "no one, I think, would quickly charge Paul with succumbing to a feminist agenda" (Carson 1998:20).

## *Barnasa*

When talking of Is.7:14, I touched on initial historical meaning, which goes into translation. Likewise here. Does Heb.2:6 have a fuller messianic meaning (*sensus plenior*)? Firstly, consider what the psalmist's initial audience made of Ps.8. Their lord Yahweh was majestic throughout the world, beyond the world, beyond creation. They marvelled that he, having immortal angels vastly more powerful than humans, had made humanity almost their equal, and on earth masters. There was no eschatological messiah on the horizon, and so 'child of Adam/mortals/man' probably paralleled the thought of 'human beings/humans/son of man'—Hebrew parallelism. Was messianism a hidden nuance, something versions should bring out?

When Jesus was born, talk of messiah had become too politicised for public use. Neither Israel's monarchy nor Rome's emperors liked messianic king's epiphanies. The OT expression, often Anglicised as 'son of man' (Heb/Aram/Gk. *bēn 'āḏām/bar nasa/huios anthrōpou*), contained a strong down to earth, even negative, humanity theme (for example Nb.23:19; Job 25:6; Ps.146:3; Ezk.2:1), as well as heavenly glorification

---

[226] For example, "the Greek word for adoption to sonship is a legal term referring to the full legal standing of an adopted male heir in Roman culture" (TNIV footnote for Gal.4:5's 'adoption to sonship').

themes (for example Ezk.3:17; Dan.7:13), but seldom tapped into these ideas.[227] Jesus used this term of himself as an alias, a cryptic self-designation, but obviously not all OT uses referred to him: for example Nb.23:19 denies deity to the *bēn 'āḏām*. After his resurrection, it was transformed into the clear term *messiah*, no longer kept secret. Outside the Gospels it is extremely scarce.[228] The majority opinion is that Heb.2:6 is not about Jesus.

| | | |
|---|---|---|
| What is man *['ĕnôš]* that you are mindful of him, and the son of man [*bēn 'āḏām*] that you care for him? | Ps.8 | ESV |
| What is man [*anthrōpos*], that you are mindful of him, or the son of man [*huios anthrōpos*], that you care for him? | Heb.2 | |
| What are mere mortals [*'ĕnôš/anthrōpos*] that you are mindful of them, human beings [*bēn 'āḏām/huios anthrōpos*] that you care for them? | Ps.8/ Heb.2 | TNIV |
| What are human beings that you are mindful of them, mortals that you care for them? | Ps.8/ Heb.2 | NRSV |

For the ESV, John Piper argued that Heb.2 was a messianic intertestamental (intracanonical) link, and that the NIVI,[229] having at least seen that *masculinity* [and the singularity] should not be muted for Heb.2, foolishly muted it for Ps.8 (Carson 1998:179). Piper's words shows that even he thought that 'man/son of man' were masculine terms in their context, though they are not. On similar reckoning the ESV's Ps.90:3—"you return man [*'ĕnôš*] to dust and say, 'Return, O children of man [*bēn 'āḏām*]'"—happily mutes the masculinity and singularity of "sons of man"! CSG A--5 accepts that a masculine

---

[227] It's a good example of *illegitimate totality transfer* to imagine that *every* time it was used *every* one had loaded *all* of its possible meanings into the context. Jesus hid his identity within this wide range of meaning, beginning to show by his talk and actions, and concluding by his resurrection, what kind of son of man he was.

[228] In the NT, outside the Gospels, see Ac.7:56 and Rv.1:13; 14:14.

[229] An early stage of the TNIV, the NIVI confusingly only kept 'son of man' for Heb.2: the NIV has retreated into that confusion.

*referent's meaning* can transcend adult human males—that is, function is wider than form.[230] One good reason *for* inclusive language versions is *because* many wrongly assume such terms are always masculine!

Somehow, "What is man, that you are mindful of him, or Jesus, that you care for him?" just doesn't sound right. Most commentators follow Wycliffe,[231] arguing that Heb.2 simply cites a non-messianic passage that grasped the idea that contained the seed thought of man's (not just men's) future exaltation, and dwelt perhaps idealistically on man's earthly sovereignty (Gen.1:26)—faith over experience. Then it introduces Jesus, v9, as truly human, not an angel, and whose messianic exaltation spelt the start for a new kind of humanity that will see its full sovereignty when fully submitted to the Sovereign of sovereigns. Among other features is the parallelism of Hebrew poetry,

---

[230] The ESV also suffers from the confusion the NIVI showed between Ps.8 and Heb.2. For example for 1 Cor.2:14 it treats the masculine *anthrōpos* as a true generic—the natural *person*. Then it treats the masculine pronoun *autos* as what P&G called a *male representative* generic—*he*. But linguistically, nouns determine their pronouns, not the *vice versa* tail wagging the dog. Inclusive meaning has been clawed back, good translation spoilt. Often what the inclusive hand giveth, the exclusive hand taketh away. "The natural *person..him...*" might just as well be "the natural *man..him...*". Pace P&G, the Greek *autos* does not need a representative male image, since grammar isn't a biological animal (Scorgie, Strauss, and Voth 128). For example, in Greek, 'child' is in the neuter, but is not asexual. If a noun is truly *the man*, then *autos* would carryover the maleness—for example "the *man* (*anthrōpos*) came with his wife with *him* (*autos*)". Grudem could not imagine a Greek speaker using *autos* without them envisioning a male, because Grudem was thinking in English, not Greek. The English word *spirit* is feminine in Hebrew, neuter in Greek, and highlighted by Jesus as masculine (Jhn.14:26's *ekeinos* = *he*, masculine emphatic). The Spirit is not a creature, is beyond biology, and is, with the father and son, the source of all human genders. If *autos* must mean a masculine 'he', then Mt.5:15 says that people do not light a lamp [masculine] and put him [*autos*] under a bowl. Likewise, in the ESV Mt.16:25 reads that whoever wishes to save his life [*psuchē*—feminine] will lose her [*autē*—feminine form of *autos*] life. A lamp is not a he, nor a life a she. Grammatical gender is not biological gender.

[231] For Heb.2:6, Wycliffe had [man's son], but [son of man] for Ac.7:56/Rv.1:13; 14:14 as if for contrast.

## Gender Agenda?

where as shown above *'ĕnôš* (like *'āḏām*) is paralleled by the expression *bēn 'āḏām*, and *anthrōpos* is paralleled by *huios anthrōpos*. Likewise in Is.51:12, where man/the 'son of man' [*'ĕnôš/bēn 'āḏām*] dies/is made as grass (ESV). Note, from this perspective, the TNIV was right to exclude the expression 'son of man' from both Ps.8 *and* Heb.2. True to the historical self-designation of Jesus, as traditionally put, *huios anthrōpos* was kept as 'son of man' in the TNIV in the Gospels, Ac.7:56, and Rv.1:13; 14:14.

Barnasa Chart C604

**Texts**

The texts are Ps.8:4-5; Heb.2:6-8, with extra points for balance.

**Comparative Class Grades**

| EV | Grade |
|---|---|
| GNB/NRSV/NRSVU | A+ |
| CEV/EEB/NCV | B+ |
| CEB | B |
| MSG | C+ |
| CJB/FBV/NIV/NLT | D+ |
| TVB | D- |
| ERV/NET | U+ |
| CSB/EJB/EOB/ESV/GWT/HCSB/ISV/KJ21/KJV/LEB/ LSB/LSV/MEV/NABRE/NASB20/NASB95/NCB/NJB/ NKJV/NLV/NOG/NWT/RNJB/RSV/TLV/WEB | U |
| REB | U- |

## Overwriting Individuality?

In English grammar, for Person and Number we have...

|  | First Person | Second Person | Third Person |
|---|---|---|---|
| **Singular** | I | you (one person) | he/she/it |
| **Plural** | we | you (more than one person, perhaps all persons excluding speaker) | they/them |

Note that English only marks the Third Person Singular for gender, and no longer marks the Second Person for number.

"Is anyone among you ill? Let <u>them</u> call the elders of the church to pray over <u>them</u>..." (TNIV: Jas.5:14). Grudem joked that pluralising Jas.5:14 turns the picture from one sick person in a private home, into a multitude in a hospital. Others, equally jolly, joke that doing it the ESV way turns the picture from each sick person into just one sick ESV guy—do girls never get sick? "Is anyone among you sick? Let <u>him</u> call for the elders of the church, and let them pray over <u>him</u>..." (ESV).

We can all enjoy a chuckle, but we should not enjoy sick jokes nor mistake jokes for truth. Wycliffe would have had the priests visit, and a fair few versions only work with olive oil. The trick is not to not do, but if needs be to do better. Terms such as 'each one' and 'all such' could replace 'they', to be pedantic. "Anyone who is sick should call the church's elders [or, elders of the church]. They should pray for...the person in the name of the Lord" (NCV) would improve the ESV.

Grudem argued that the NRSV can wrongly suggest that texts are aimed at Christians, rather than the general public. For example for Gal.6:7, the RSV's "whatever a <u>man</u> sows", became the NRSV's "whatever <u>you</u> sow", and for Jas.1:20, the RSV 's "the anger of <u>man</u>", became the NRSV's "<u>your</u> anger": however the NIV has "human anger". Well, Paul and James urged Christians to apply general principles.

Against Grudem, although man's anger does not produce the righteousness that God desires, contextually James was speaking to his fellow Christians about Christians controlling their wayward anger (v19).[232] With Grudem, we may note that unlike the NRSV, the TNIV had "people reap", which seems aimed by Paul outside the Christian camp without excluding Christians. Grudem's point about application is valid, but judging each text on its merits is better than blanket condemnation. Sadly, the NIV11 reverted to sageism: "a man reaps what he sows", true, yet falling below even the ESV.

NT texts sometimes transform OT texts. Let us ignore the Septuagint factor, as well as fuller quotes and thus fuller issues. Didn't the deific

---

[232] The Greek *orgē* has a good side. Jesus had *orgē* (Mk.3:5). It may be OK within limitations (Eph.4:26). Jas.1:19 may imply a slowness to rule in righteous *orgē* and to rule out unrighteous *orgē*.

mind bless changes in Person? See Ps.68:18's "<u>you</u> have ascended... <u>you</u>...", to Eph.4:8's, "<u>he</u> ascended...<u>he</u>..." (Second Person Singular contextual gender to Third PS masculine).[233] Is.28:11 reads, "<u>he</u> will speak to this people", whereas 1 Cor.14:21 reads, "<u>I</u> will speak unto this people" (3PS masculine gender to 1PS contextual gender). Is.52:7 reads "the feet of <u>him</u> who", whereas Rm.10:15 reads "the feet of <u>those</u> who" (3PS masculine to 3PP inclusive). Even when the Hebrew text quotes itself, it can canonically vary wording.

This is not to say that since the canonical writers took liberties, any Tom, Dick, or Harriet, may do the same. It is to say that absolute formal equivalence, Person for Person, Number for Number, was not their more organic way of thinking, nor their readers'. The very art of translation—semantic pictures in another language—assumes some leeway. It does show that the NT did not necessarily think that some truth was lost if a text was reformatted. We must not jump the gun and shoot down any variation of Person or Number for the sheer sake of it. However, this does raise certain problems, even as by highlighting one point we dim another.

### Ps.34:19-20/Jhn.19:36

Ps.34 is a possible tie-in, in line with Lk.23:47. Does changing gender and number in Ps.34[234] lose the connection to the righteous man *par excellence*, as well as failing to help undermine the foreign myth of Jesus' body being broken?[235] No, but it probably puts it truer to the

---

[233] These 6 texts are per the MEV/NASB95/NKJV.

[234] For example, the CEV/NCV/NJB. The NLT/ISV follow nicely, using the singular to state the plural principle. Keeping the idea of an intended switch to a messianic individual, the ESV/HCSB/NKJV/NABRE/NIV. Both NIV and NABRE have reverted to messianic translation from TNIV and NAB.

[235] The TR feeds this 'broken body' myth, though not one of his bones was broken (Jhn.19:36). "This is my body *broken* for you" is a noncanonical misquote, a human tradition never contaminating the Gospel accounts, where one might most expect a genuine reference, only Paul's. Bread to be shared had to be broken, torn into pieces, indeed some say his body was *torn*, though not into pieces! Bread signifies several things, such as basic need, and particularly the unleavened flight from slavery to freedom. In the Passover, the lambs' bones were not broken (Ex.12:46/Nb.9:12; 1 Cor.5:7; 1 Pt.1:19). This was a sacrifice all the redeemed shared. Some say, what harm in keeping the idea, broken? I

original meaning, as well as better worded for today's audience. Hebrew often switched Number without switching meaning: in Ps.34 vv15,17 are plural, and 19-20 singular (though plural in the Septuagint). For v21 the Hebrew has a singular 'wicked' (Septuagint plural) followed by a plural pronoun (they). Ps.34 targeted the faithful in Ethnic Israel, and many NT fulfilments are based on the idea that Jesus' supremely fulfilled OT patterns. In short, had John Ps.34 in mind, he saw a deeper significance in a wide-ranging psalm that did not in its day highlight any individual.

## Attack on the ESV

In fairness I appreciate that the old KJV addressed its language norm, even though, since tied to the earlier Bishops Bible era, it was always going to be a bit old fashioned (McGrath 2002:269). I must address our language. This chart simply looks at a few verses to test a little bit for gender sensitivity. It is an important factor, especially in the West for the unchurched and under 40s, an age range ever increasing. It does not mean that versions scoring well do not overshoot accuracy into gender neutrality, in the sense of the ideology that humanity's gender differences more or less don't matter within Christianity. A bank that likes to say Yes can say Yes once too often.

**Column A**: Mk.4:23; 9:30; Jhn.6:51; Jhn.7:37; Jhn.10:9; Rm.8:9; 1 Cor.14:27; 2 Cor.5:17. Together they check that the Greek indefinite pronoun, *tis,* is taken to be *anyone* in inclusive texts, rather than *anyman*. If an immediate context claws back, zero marks. At times *anyman* is good translation (for example 1 Cor.7:18). Some historical settings may be unclear. I have sought texts that are clearly inclusive.

---

reply, what harm in changing it to "my body bled for you"? It's simply that true as it may sound, it is not what Jesus said so we should not say that it was. Incidentally, *breaking bread* together primarily meant sharing a meal, and by extension the holy meal they shared remembered Christ's death (1 Cor.10:16). Some church networks speak of the Eucharist as Breaking [of] Bread, but thankfully not as the Breaking [of] Body. The one word, *klōmenon,* possibly added by C4 Ambrosiaster, lodged itself into the Byzantine Empire and so became the Greek majority. For 1 Cor.11:24, p46, א, B, A, and C- Cyprian of Carthage, all witness to unbroken.

## Gender Agenda?

1# Mk.4:23's masc. pronoun must not claw back. 2# Mk.9:30 is straightforward. 3# Jhn.6:51 is eternal life crossing gender: the *shall have life* verb (*zaō*), is unmarked for gender; v54 must not claw back. 4# Likewise 7:37, with v38's masculine taken to mean believers (some notes deserve a half-mark). 5# Jhn.10:9 is fairly straightforward. 6# Rm.8:9 has *tis autou* but they are inclusive; translation of v12's *adelphoi* is neutral. 7# 1 Cor.14:27 should not be redefined by the masc. reflexive pronoun *heautō(i)* of v28. Bypassing the cultural factors behind Paul's call for silence, *Acts* showed that women could also speak in language they hadn't learnt. 1 Cor.14:34's silence was within leeway to pray and prophecy aloud (1 Cor.11:5), and both Paul and Luke allowed that glossolalia jumped the gender divide.[236] 8# newness in 2 Cor.5:17 jumps the gender divide, and must not be clawed back into the masculine.

**Column B**: Mt.5:22/Heb.2:11-2 tests that *adelphos* as 'brother and/or sister' (forbidden by CSG) and its plural 'brothers and/or sisters' (permitted by CSG), have been picked up as gender inclusive in these contexts. I sidestep whether "without just cause" is explicit in Mt.5:22, and along with Grudem I assume that Jesus forbade wrong anger towards one's wider family *sisters* as well as brothers. The background in *Leviticus* seems to agree. This nuance should not be lost in translation. Two marks right, zero marks wrong, one mark if a note 1# allows 'brother and sister', as although contextually insensitive it's partway there, or 2# if it degrades a good text by saying that the Greek is 'brother/s'. Heb.2:11 scored likewise. Scores are combined.

**Column C**: Jhn.14:23 may drop the formal singulars for meaningful plurals, if the plurals imply a focus on individual people indwelt, not Jesus and his father just joining a group. Masculine singulars, but with a note highlighting inclusivity, get one mark. Full inclusivity scores two marks, for at least attempting gender sensitivity. A focus on the individual level, for example 'anyone', plus inclusive plurals

---

[236] I tend towards the opinion that pneumalingualism is of the heart, not the mind, a touching God unimpeded by rationality, howbeit the freed spirit can sometimes be tuned into real human language. Likewise, as a violinist, Sherlock Holmes could easily switch from his usual careless scraping, to Mendelssohn's Lieder (*A Study in Scarlet*, ch.2).

such as "in them", holds both truths together, and scores three marks. An example of four marks: "all who love me...each of them".

**Column D**: Gal.6:7 tests nouns/pronouns. If the context of a masculine noun indicates inclusiveness, its pronoun should not redefine the noun as masculine. I sidestep whether *anthrōpos* in context relates to mankind generally, non-Christians particularly, or Christians particularly. The only issue is whether a consistent way has been sought to move a gender/age specific reading into a non~gender/age specific one. *Anthrōpos* and its pronoun, *touto,* must be gender accurate. Some let the tail wag the dog, for example "a person (gender accurate) harvests whatever he (as gender defining) sows"—zero marks.[237]

**Column E**: 1 Tm.2:4-5 should combine gender accuracy with age awareness, lest "mothers of Salem" rise up in protest! In short, eternal salvation extends to youngsters, so "men" bad, "men and women" better, and "people" best. If those he desires to save are immediately defined as *men* by v5, minus a mark, but 'man/mankind' are fine.

**Column F**: Jas.5:14, another text, like with Mt.5/Heb.2, checks that women and children are included. The one calling should not be gender specific, nor the one to be prayed for (*autos*). For this, the misleading footnotes of some will not be used against them.

---

[237] The pronoun must be masculine, to fit its masculine noun. But if the masculine noun is gender inclusive, so will the pronoun be. Grudem was able to crow when he saw the NIV's gender neutral dog wagged by its masculine tail. He cited Rm.14:22, and proclaimed himself baffled "that the 2011 NIV still used 'he' occasionally" (Rm.14:22; Köstenberger and Croteau loc.151-8). Just like the ESV. In fact, it does not 'still' use it, since earlier (TNIV) dog and tail were aligned; it has *reverted* to it. I suspect that the CBT, perhaps seeking *detente* (not for money but for mission), besides incorporating an ESV man, felt obliged to now and again downgrade translation: the text did not require it, but the text allowed it. Let us have peace to bless the people.

## Gender Chart C500

**Texts**

The texts are A (Mk.4:23; 9:30; Jhn.6:51; Jhn.7:37; Jhn.10:9; Rm.8:9; 1 Cor.14:27; 2 Cor.5:17); B (Mt.5:22/Heb.2:11-2); C (Jhn.14:23); D (Gal.6:7); E (1 Tm.2:4-5); F (Jas.5:14). Each column was been given a percentage equal weight.

**Comparative Class Grades**

| C500 | Grade |
|---|---|
| NRSVU/RNJB | A+ |
| GWT/NCV/NOG | A |
| CEB/CEV | A- |
| ERV/NLT | B+ |
| FBV/NRSV | B |
| GNB/NIV/TVB | B- |
| MSG | C- |
| EEB | D- |
| CSB/EOB/NABRE/NASB20/NET/NJB | U+ |
| CJB/ESV/HCSB/ISV/LEB/NCB/REB/WEB | U |
| EJB/KJ21/LSB/LSV/MEV/NASB95/NKJV/NLV/NWT/RSV/TLV | U- |

## Gender Glut?

Of the more gender accurate versions in our core comparison, let's take the CEV and review Michael Marlowe's review of September 2005, simply on the gender question.[238] It's good to be concerned that we get gender language accurate, and avoid getting it merely neutral. I shall compare the CEV on Marlowe's criticisms to 2 other versions which I have rated high for gender accuracy (NCV/NLT), along with the old TNIV, with the ESV/HCSB/KJV (two with stated policies against the TNIV's gender policy).

Marlowe's mistake on Eph.5:22 is painful—the KJV has *reverence*, while all others have *respect*. Did Marlowe fail to check? On Gal.3:28, Marlowe might be too stern. The range is "all one/the same/equal in Christ Jesus", and each English version preserves the meaning as

---

[238] www.bible-researcher.com/cev.html

spiritual, not social (Phm.16). Christian slaves were not socially equal to their masters.

Here the CEV fails on ageism, in that it speaks of men and women, rather than males and females, missing out kids. On 1 Cor.11:10, the KJV's "ought the woman to have power [*exousia*] on her head" is formally unclear, needing contextual reading. Whatever gender bias may be operating, the CEV does footnote being under authority, though it could have worded this in the masculine.[239] The ESV/HCSB "a symbol of authority [*exousia*] on her head" doesn't specify whether it's a symbol of her *intrinsic* authority, her *invested* authority from her husband, or her *husband's* authority. The NLT is emphatic: "she is under authority". Marlowe's criticism is a little unfair in the light of the spread of pro-masculine worded versions.

On 1 Tm.2:15, interpretation is complex. Marlowe has noted the unusually wide range of footnote options of the CEV, then implied that an option was overlooked because of intentional bias against submission. Perhaps the best interpretations are these. 1# Paul meant to balance with his talk of Eve's failing, the fact that women can be spiritually saved, even though giving birth still ran physical anguish brought about by the Fall. 2# Some women were being motivated by the idea that spiritual salvation for them meant spurning motherhood for ministry, pressured into seeking equality with, or superiority over, guys in order to redeem themselves in God's eyes, overcompensating for Eve's problems.

A bit like saying in his culture, "ease up girls, just being good wives and mums is fine with God except for any he calls for alternate jobs." It was a situational letter of which we don't know the full situation, so like one side of a telephone conversation, cannot fully understand Paul's input. For this text, functional equivalence, based on in-depth

---

[239] There is a definite gender neutral policy within the CEV. Eg, 1 Tm.2:8 is, I think, the only version to avoid saying men (*andras*). Paul was addressing a given situation, where it seems that guys and girls both had their particular problems to be sorted. For the guys, it was their attitude in prayer, perhaps sniping at each other to God. As a situation letter, it seems that gender accuracy requires this gender issue kept, even though the principle obviously is not gender specific.

exegesis, is a must. Near to Marlowe's point is perhaps an imperfect NLT footnote, yet the CEV should be commended for pointing out several of the ideas about this text, though missing the one about God being happy in general with women simply playing the wife/mother, as befitted their society.

The CEV (and sadly the REB) renders Gen.2:18 as *partner*, rather than *helper*, and against correctivism I side with Marlowe. Marlowe has a fair point on Col.3:18/1 Pt.3:1: the others have 'submit', the CEV has 'put husband first', which tends towards egalitarianism more than 'submit'. I welcome biblical complementarianism and egalitarianism, but maybe the CEV has stretched the meaning of these texts. On 1 Tm.3, the CEV alone reads as gender neutral—except for vii which is feminine! Even if the principles were phrased in one gender but open to both, at most a footnote might be made to hint that maybe women were permitted to be overseers. The CEV has concealed an important difficulty.

Verdict: Marlowe's charge of feminising the text is sometimes unjust, ignoring the wider evidence of Bible versions. In short, I suggest that the CEV has generally acted responsibly and presents good gender accuracy, but at times (for example Gen.2:18; Col.3:18/1 Pt.3:1; 1 Tm.3) has pressed gender inclusivity into the text, whereas the NCV/NLT/TNIV have not.

## **Hail Mother God?**

Is "Our Mother who art in heaven", good translation? Bear in mind that talk about destroying God, or feminising God, are popular misuses of language. God is God and cannot be destroyed, feminised, or otherwise changed by any action on our part—the unmoved mover. What we can do is to destroy, feminise, whatever, our concept of God. Books like Cornelius Hunter's *Darwin's God*, and Antony Flew's *There is a God*, should be entitled *Darwin's Concept of God*, and *God Is*, respectively. Concepts of God there are a many, but God is ultimate being, the brute fact. Too often we speak the polytheistic contexts of the bygone world, rather than translating within our world. God cannot become an endangered species: "the one who rules in heaven laughs. The Lord scoffs at them" (Ps.2:4 NLT). Let's summarise the issues by dialogue.

John: "The Bible likens God to a mother (for example Is.66:13; Dt.32:18), and the Hebrew for 'Spirit' is a feminine gender, so God is equally our mother."

Jean: "A number of other texts are similar, and female creatures have their feminine attributes from God. But these texts are far far less than the tip of an iceberg, compared to the exceedingly predominant masculine biblical imagery about God, and many uses of *ruach* were masculine."

John "I know this, but my point is that since there *was* minority feminine imagery in that male dominated society, should that imagery not be more equally balanced in our more gender balanced society? Indeed, may better balance have been God's trajectory, the buried seed now bearing much fruit?"

Jean "Incidentally beware of the magic genie of Trajectory Hermeneutics. OK, you picture humanity as once male dominated but with evolutionary seeds of gender equality? Even so this doesn't explain why the OT theology was masculine dominated, since surrounding peoples had remarkably *female* orientated theologies—goddesses abounded. For instance, Jeremiah rebuked the stubborn feminist theology of his people (Jr.44:16-7). If Ancient Israel and Judah were patriarchies, at least they were significantly countercultural patriarchies that rejected feminine options. Isn't it better to say that masculine imagery dominated in spite of feminist theological tendencies among the ancients, because it more truly shows the masculine (not male) balance of God?"

John "Perhaps OT theology avoided feminising the idea of God simply to avoid the feminist *excesses* of surrounding peoples? Maybe prophets kept feminism as an inner belief, fearing the truth would be misunderstood and misapplied by their people."

Jean "The OT prophets don't seem to have been shy of facing difficulties and saying what they believed."

| | |
|---|---|
| John | "OK, maybe, but let's look at how language functions. Do we agree that metaphors are not merely colourful speech, but allow deeper insights beyond the level of literal language? If so, then masculine images need not imply masculinity. For example, "Yahweh is my shepherd" (Ps.23) is masculine in a society where only boys and men shepherd flocks, but in a culture where only girls and women shepherd flock, the meaning would translate as "Yahweh is my shepherdess". It's not the gender of the metaphor but its meaning of care and protection that counts, isn't it?" |
| Jean | "Metaphor can function like this, but it doesn't mean that we should ditch the metaphor's gender—sometimes gender might be part of the inner meaning. For example, Eph.3:14-5 plays on the terms *patēr* (father) and *patria* (fatherhood, representing family headship?). Gender role models do seem to reflect in the minor key the divine intent, indeed the divine society, rather than to be projections of the lower into the higher (1 Cor.11:3).[240] There seems a sense in which masculine gender is meant to represent intrinsic masculine concepts, and so implies that the gender form can be revelatory. Paul's motherly side (1 Ths.2:7) seems a diminutive form of the majority apostolic (non-motherly) weight he could use. If Scripture is canonical, and Scripture has no example of praying to *Mother God* as our mother in heaven, can we pray to such a concept without adding to or vitiating Scripture?" |
| John | "Hum, I'll give this a little more thought." |

Some think that attributes are neutral, genderised according to cultures; others think that gender is a transcultural attribute. Both sides can accept that God is the divine fount of masculinity and

---

[240] In *The Silver Chair* (C S Lewis), the Queen of the Underworld says that what's claimed as upper realities, such as the sun and lion, are really imaginary projections from the real world of lanterns and cats. Another relevant Narnian story is *The Horse and His Boy*, in which Bree the horse dismisses the lion-ness of Aslan as merely a metaphor for strength—until he feels a lion's whisker as Aslan touches him.

femininity, but sincerely divide over how to express this in a culturally relevant way yet faithful to biblical revelation. Some say that our public talk should be masculine, with private prayer life a matter of private conscience (*Themelios* 2004.29.2.24). Some dethrone masculine talk and enthrone feminine talk, not for sincere biblical reasons, but through psychological rejection of human male dominance. They thus enthrone corollaries such as *Ms* designation (no girl or woman should tolerate this), *partner* (no married couple should tolerate this) as an equal value umbrella for any IPS status, and may even idealise homosexual relationships (no biblicist should tolerate this)—three expressions of the 'politically correct' dive into immorality, linked with postmodernism's distaste of all absolute standards except its own. Sadly, some tarnish some versions with this anti-Christ brush.

# Chapter 15   Good Diversity

There are hundreds of partial and complete English versions we could look at. I only look at a few, highlighting either historical significance, or current market interest. One big date is 1881, when the RV NT hit the world: it was more accurate yet less readable than the KJV, but the new model of text typing behind its accuracy was a significant improvement factored into translation. Other things being equal, this means versions after 1881 should have a better NT text. Another big date is 1947, when Qumran began to reveal a Hebrew OT more than 1,000 years earlier than the OT Masoretic Text available. Building on these, versions after 1947 can have a better text.

But changes can be a trade-off between accuracy and acceptability. Versions can have a short shelf life because they lack monopoly power and we are so spoilt for choice. Those who favour such as the NIV usually don't dismiss other fine versions. The KJV itself went through many struggles, even aided by king and Anglicanism, to outlive other fine versions and indeed to finally get public approval. Anglicanism promoted the KJV throughout the British Empire, quelled the Geneva, and promoted Onlyism, even as the Vulgate had subjugated other Latin versions under Papal mandate.

Enough, the monopolies of Rome and Canterbury have had their say. Now we are in the age of people power, where one man was able to inspire a network to birth the NIV. Many more versions have been birthed in a context constantly sprouting new versions of merit. Onlyism needs time for an outstanding, or dominant sponsored version, to utterly dominate the market into a generation that no longer knows earlier times, and can think that what they have is unshakeable. Global politics and State ecclesiastical backing no longer seem likely to coincide in such a way, especially in an era of people power. Perhaps never again will a Bible version become the test of orthodoxy or church/State politics. Nor is it advisable. As the KJV translators, citing [St.] Augustine of Hippo, said, "variety of Translations is profitable for the finding out of the sense of the Scriptures" (Köstenberger and Croteau loc.330).

Rather than being Onlyist in usage, a good policy is to have a main English version pitched with a slight bias to functional equivalence, then to have another slightly more formal, another slightly less so, and perhaps a current paraphrase to help contemporise the message. Do you take a Bible to church? If so, why not take one version one week, and another another week—circulating usage avoids narrow mindedness. Do you use a tablet in church? Select different versions each week. Ideally, use those from fairly different traditions, as comparing differences helps to highlight issues. I would suggest not using the outgoing gender style for public use—such as the RSV and 1984 NIV: why needlessly distance women and youngsters for whom also Christ died? Various comparisons have already been made, showing that not all versions are of equal value. Let's look at a few more, to help with short listing versions to use, and then conclude.

## Is *John* Up To Date?

For up-to-dateness, I've made a chart built around something similar by Andreas J Köstenberger, a once listed ESV supporter.[241] Using *John* (on which Köstenberger has a major commentary) as a benchmark, I consider various aspects where current knowledge of Greek, texts, archaeology, and current issues, can be put to good use by translators. This chart can indicate the policy positions of each version.

In my chart...

**A# 1:5** tests movement to better translation, useful exegetically.

**Scores**: from 3 marks for *conquest/master* (with comprehension in footnotes), to zero for *comprehension* (without conquest in footnotes).

**B# 1:10f; 3:19**, tests sensitivity to Greek connectives, by looking at how *kai* is now understood to sometimes have an adversative sense, such as 'yet/but/even'.

**Scores**: part sensitive (1 mark), fully sensitive (2).

---

[241] Some of our English versions are of different date: for example, his NLT had "Passover feast" in 18:28, but the 2004 edit has only "Passover". His chart might also lack some final double checking: for example on p349 the ESV is listed with the NIV, HCSB, etc., as average on 7:53ff., but on p360 charted as *below* average. Likewise p348 seems to rate the TNIV as only on par with the NRSV and NLT on 1:18, yet unlike them got an *above* average mark.

**C# 1:19; 5:15; 7:1** et al, tests sensitivity over woodenness to hoi Youdaioi, which can range in John's context from Jewish leadership, to Judeans, to the ethnic Jews in the areas under discussion.

**Scores**: any English version that links some references to leadership and some to laity in the text, get 4 marks per mention. To at least footnote the distinction, or the parochial nature of the population, 1 or 2 marks. A uniform 'the Jews', zero marks. No bonus for footnotes merely highlighting the classical reading.

**D# 1:39; 4:6,21; 19:14** look at translating timing into our terms. Eg, the 'seventh hour' is roughly our 1pm, not our 7am.[242]

**Scores**: functional and wrong (based on Roman administrative midnight to midnight 'clocks') is misleading, scoring 0; Formal = 2; Functional and right (based on Jewish/Roman *people* 'clocks') = 5, or 4 if, irrespective of context, text lacks an am/pm value, or is a rough approximate (eg "early afternoon"). Any constructive footnote gets a bonus: a mere mention of Roman time is neutral.

**E# 2:4; 8:20**, alerts readers to the special time (*hōra*) for Jesus' death.

**Scores**: *mission time* (0); a mere *time* (2); a suggestive *hour* (4); an indirect note (+1); a direct note (+2); a good note (+2); no note required (10). The highest score was 16, and the lowest 2, so all final scores were dived by 14%.

**F# 3:3,4,7** looks for perception of the friendly riddle set by Jesus to Nicodemus (ben Gurion?). Jesus served up an ambiguous *born anew* (EOB). Smiling, Nicodemus returned a 'you cannot be serious' *born again* (NABRE), to which Jesus volleyed with *spiritual birth* (CEV) you ninny. Game, set, and match. All good fun of course, and Nicodemus

---

[242] Conventional reckoning: in fact 7 hours after dawn, which varies according to the time of year. Each day simply had roughly twelve units of time, judged before mechanical and electronic watches. In daylight terms, an *hour* raged between 50 minutes (mid-winter) and 70 minutes (mid-summer), but could mean a cataclysmic time.

would remain an honest spectator until Yeshua, overcoming Death, proved himself champion. Good footnoting gains marks.[243]

William Tyndale admitted that he wasn't born again. Was he a Christian? Evangelicalism, *eu-angelion,* means Good News-ism, and *Born Again* is its defining term, for some a holy cow. Yet to note that it was a Nicodemean jest (4) in itself requires but a small change in expression (7). That done, change should go deeper. Nicodemus was being primed that though he was in God's earthly kingdom, by human birth (1 Chr.28:5; Ex.19:6), not even Jews could be in God's messianic kingdom, except by spiritual birth consequent to the cross. That would be the only kingdom that eternally mattered. Today the dialogue leaves many Evangelicals with a riddle. Namely, if ultimate eternal life was hitherto accessible by all people, and henceforth it would only be accessible to those who became Christians, why call that limitation good news?[244]

From the C16 I'd say that Geneva/Bishops/Reims were rubbish, all flattening out the wordplay (BBB). Slightly better the KJV by not having Nicodemus use exactly the same expression (BØB). The best of the rest were Tyndale/Coverdale/Matthew, since they limited the 'born again' to the chump Nicodemus, and fed him from the start the ambiguity of 'born anew' (ABA). The Great, though it limited the 'born again' to the chump Nicodemus, from the start fed him the answer of 'born from above' (CBC). I have at least shown that Bible translation offered varied, of which the C17 KJV was but one voice.

**G# 5:2; 19:13,17,20; 20:16** tests small detail search analysis, looking for a clear sense that Aramaic, not Hebrew, was the common Semitic language of the C1 Jews. In *John* there is a definite Hebrew-only term, but that's simply an old name (9:7). A few other terms could have come from either Hebrew or Aramaic (for example 11:16's 'twin'). But a few *new* terms definitely come from Aramaic only (1:42, 19:17), which

---

[243] Incidentally, *born again* shouldn't be used in 1 Pt.1:23. There the KJV ditched Reformation's Tyndale—Bishops (born anew) in favour of Rome's Martin (born again).

[244] My *Salvation Now and Life Beyond* redefines Evangelicalism, cutting this Gordian Knot. Hint: the Evangelical definition of salvation based on Christ remains, and a new definition has been added by Christ.

seems to clinch what John meant by *hebraisti*. We can see in *Daniel* how Aramaic impacted the Jewish people, as later did Greek. It seems that Hebrew was only known among the learned, so *hebraisti* should indicate Aramaic as the more common language to Palestinian Jews, some whom preferred it to Greek. Still, a footnote should flag up slight uncertainty.

**Scores**: three marks for translation as *Aramaic* (plus footnote), down to zero for *Hebrew* (without footnote). In this text I also deduct ½ mark for translating (in text or footnote) *stauros* as *stake*, no penalties for *cross*, and a bonus for *crossbeam*. Of special demerit is the NABRE whose painful notes typically picture John as clashing with the Synoptics and mistaken in wording, as if theologically created without regard for history or linguistics.

**H# 7:53**— looks for this section to be shown mainly by notes, to be a cuckoo in John's the nest. Possibly Lukan, it rings true (authentic) and is good to keep, but not as an intruder into John's Gospel, where John moved straight from 7:52 to 8:12—he predated our chapter-verse numbering.

**I# 12:32** looks for the idea that Jesus' death would remove religious apartheid—spiritual husk before globally individual regeneration.[245] It must not be put in sexist, ageist, terms: worded well in their days, older versions must now lose a mark. It must not allow the idea that eternal life is to be for every human being, since whether or not true, the context was not about that but about opening up salvation's message to people of all races/peoples: redemption accessible to all, but about ultimate take-up by all people of all races (Universalism).

**Scores**: no marks for highlighting the dual meaning of 'exalt' (that is, glory and execution), but special commendation to footnotes in such as the HCSB and NIV, and cross references in the ESV. From lowest:

---

[245] *Regeneration* was twice used in the KJV (Mt.19:28—birth of a new age; Tts.3:5). For individuals (Tts.3:5), unless taken as conversion, the term is better dropped. Paul's point was that in life we need to birth (*genesis*) again (*palin*), this time spiritually by the spirit. Numerous versions drop the Latinised term in favour of rebirth, or new birth. Biblically *palingenesias*, does not mean regeneration as a body repairs itself, so is not about ongoing holiness, simply birth into holiness.

men/everyone/all people/all people (+ footnote)/all peoples. "Men of all sorts" is sageist but a bonus mark.

**J# 13:1; 18:28; 19:14** should not support the old idea that John's dating contradicted the Synoptics' account. The basic Passover Meal didn't come after Jesus' Last Supper, which began a week of celebration. That week's sabbath, to be prepared for (19:14), was as all Passover sabbaths, especially special. All Gospels record Jesus having a Passover Meal after the Passover Lambs had been officially slain on Thursday afternoon (Nisan $14^{th}$), and were being eaten hours later by Jesus and his disciples that evening (Nisan $15^{th}$). The Passover Meal was on the preparation day for the Passover Week's sabbath, which began on our Friday evening. Some terms must be clarified to reveal their function. In English read 13:1's *heortē...pascha* not as a Feast but as Passover *Festival/Celebration,* 18:28 as Passover *Feast-week/Celebrations,* and 19:14 as Passover *Week's Friday daytime,* or *Passover Week's Sabbath,* preparations (best NCV/NIV84).[246] The NABRE/NET footnotes mislead

## Johannine Chart C400

### Texts

As above, and as usual conflated into a class grade.

### **Comparative Class Grades**

| C400 | Grade |
|---|---|
| NIV | A+ |
| NET/NLT | A- |
| CEV/EEB/ERV/NABRE | B+ |
| CEB/ERV/ISV | B |
| NCV/NRSV/TLV | B- |
| FBV/GNB | C+ |
| ESV/LEB/REB/TVB | C |
| NCB/NWT | C- |

---

[246] Incidentally a slight penalty for saying or suggesting that John's $6^{th}$ *hour* (Jhn.19:14) meant sentencing at 6am. This follows Westcott on putting on Roman administrative glasses (midnight to midnight days), instead of seeing through Jewish glasses (dusk to dusk days) and seeing that Jesus died the day after the Passover lambs and the day before Passover Sabbath.

| | |
|---|---|
| CJB/EOB/GWT/MSG/NOG/NRSVU/RNJB/RSV | **D+** |
| GWT/HCSB/NASB20/NJB/NOG/NRSVU/WEB | **D** |
| RNJB | **D-** |
| NKJV | **U+** |
| MEV/NASB95 | **U** |
| EJB/KJ21/KJV/LSB/LSV | **U-** |

## **Philosophy or Polytheism?**

Introducing philosophic monotheism, a synthesis of unfolded biblical revelation of God as three persons. But this is undermined by hidden polytheism, common talk in Christian circles, as it was under Sinai. Should we use a capital to cover up polytheism, an idea within the Bible that there is more than one god, or should we see it, face it, and upgrade? Is there a God, or is there a god: G or g? Does it matter? I think so.

It is a human tradition: not all are bad; not all are good. The ancient scripts did not have capitals to bother about. Nor did they have any textual way to differentiate the term, GOD, between higher and lower uses (Ps.82:6). Differences have been introduced in later transmission, and in translation, so differentiating is not sacrosanct, even if useful.

Capitalisation can be foolish. "Why does this Man talk like this? He is blaspheming!" (ABCE: Mk.2:7). Here, the Amplified Bible aimed to justify a capital of man, "because of what He is, the spotless Son of God, not what the speakers may have thought He was", a mere man. In wrongly itching to capitalise so-called reverential pronouns, it went against the irreverential source, namely, the *grammateis* (a.k.a. scribes, professionals who could read, write, and interpret scripture, and usually sided with the pharisees but occasionally (Mk.12:28,34) with Jesus). A few versions, such as the NKJV, continue this folly of making opponents sound like proponents, and the updated Amplified Bible gave it up, conceding that man was man, not Man. Indeed, he is he, not He.

A trend to capitalise pronouns kicked off in the C19 (but with a 1770 hint by John Worsley). We can contrast the 1769 KJV with the NKJV: Contrasting Mk.1:7 and v10, the NKJV has [he preached], and [He saw], to differentiate between John and Jesus. If in fact it was John who saw, the NKJV has misinterpreted. You can see the itch for reverential pronouns. Likewise with Mk.1:13: "And He was...". On this, the KJV has, "And he was".

So with representing what the people of Sinai actually believed by a small g, god, rather than capitalising as God "because of what He is, God, not what the speakers may have thought He was", a god. A good principle of biblical interpretation, is to first try to see what the text meant in its original context. By systematic theology, we can now see that their idea was, by God's design, undeveloped, leaving scope for the revelation of the new covenant into both a strong monotheism and a tripersonal monotheism at that. But let's *see it* as undeveloped.

"And Joshua said to all the people, 'Thus says Yahweh, the **G**od of Israel: Long ago your ancestors—Terah and his sons Abraham and Nahor—lived beyond the Euphrates and served other gods" (NRSV: Jos.24:2). Since the text speak of *other* gods, what justifies representing Joshua as capitalising the god of Israel, his god, but not seemingly equal gods, other than them seemingly being foreign? Joshua spoke in polytheistic terms, the common theology of their day, even as the scribes spoke of Jesus as a man, not a Man. "And Joshua said to all the people, 'Thus says Yahweh, the god of Israel: Long ago your ancestors—Terah and his sons Abraham and Nahor—lived beyond the Euphrates and served other gods."

And if we allow this as undeveloped theology, why do we persist in speaking about God being our god, a type of god? Should we not, from biblical theology systematised, restyle our talk within philosophic monotheism, and speak not of my god being good, but God being good, etc? But our Bibles say otherwise. Poor translation?

Translation standards can, and sometimes should, highlight the source position. So if suboptimal OT records show worship of Yahweh as if one god among many—they were myopic—I hold that this should not be covered up by falsely saying that Yahweh was a **G**od, rather than Yahweh was a god. Yet English translators strain out the Israelite's unclean camel, by giving us an unclean capital Gnat to swallow. Is it too irreligious to admit that most Israelites, being polytheists, were wrong, since polytheism is wrong?

I admit that when Luke recorded that they *buried* Stephen (Ac.8:2), Luke was wrong, since only Stephen's discarded body was dead, not Stephen himself. It was envelope language. We should neither keep his false aioniology, nor speak of deceased *people* as buried.[247] That's like saying that the drivers share their vehicles' fates, lying around in scrap yards. Though Bultmann was bad in practice, when he argued for remythologising, he had a point. Theologising translation can help. Sometimes we should ditch man's envelope which God's letter came within, once we have formed his data into systematic theology.

So, the term *god*, in some contexts, should be capitalised. As an absolute, for instance: God is. But in a relative setting, a smaller g conveys the idea: ultimately there is one *god*, God, and the *gods* of the nations are idols, though poetically *gods*, an unexplored link. The latter fitted ancient society when polytheism was a shared language. But why, in the light of monotheism, are some still happy to speak within the shadow of polytheism? Many of our songs have an our-god is... structure, reflecting and reinforcing polytheistic (multiple gods) talk. My-*god* is wonderful, your-*god* is precious, our-*god* is healer, etc., or is a wonderful/precious/holy-*god*, etc. How's yours today?

Some say there are over 800 million divinities in Hinduism. In Western talk, *this* god/*that* god talk, can sound like a throwback to polytheism, the idea of many more or less equal gods and goddesses. Do we affirm Hinduism? No, but basically as a Roman Catholic once said, "we do not even believe in a god, for this would imply a possible or conceivable multiplication of gods: but only in God" (Tyrrell 76). The OT is a mixture of contexts, and probably reflects different levels of understanding, though levels always present. At a popular level, the philosophy about God wasn't the focus, but rather the strict loyalty of the rescued vassal to God as their god—more practical than theoretical. Yahweh was their god, and Ba'al and Mot were others' gods—follow thou me! Basic lessons for basic people.

---

[247] Ac.8:2: Had "godly men buried Stephen" (NIV), or "buried Stephen's dead body" (EEB)?
1 Kg.22:37: After the king died, was only "his body..taken to Samaria" (NLT), or had "they buried him there" (NIV)?
*Ruth* 1:17: Did Ruth say, "I will be buried" (NIV) in Israel, or "my body will be buried" (New International Reader's Version (NIrV) in Israel?

## Today's English Versions

Yet a sub-theme was that philosophically, Yahweh alone was God—he alone had created the universe. Quite possibly Ethnic Israel had grammatical and/or theological safety mechanisms that maintained philosophical monotheism alongside practical monotheism. I can ride with *our god* translation within the OT, where it belongs, though some texts could justifiably ditch it.

We are like Abraham, as regards geography (Heb.11:13). There is no Christian nation in God's plan, though nations may be Christianised. With the ethnicity factor removed, I look to a global perception being shown by English versions. It can be done, and can be done consistently. Since Pentecost, the message has not been about others being under their gods and us under our god. It is from that point in history that I feel we should factor into translation what is called philosophical monotheism, even if some poetical polytheism was sometimes used, particularly 2 Cor.4:4's "god of this world".[248]

Let us speak as people of the new covenant. Why not say, *God, who is mine*, instead of *my god*? Muslims speak of the *Christian* god, Christians talk of the *Islamic* god. 1+1 = 2, but both sides say there is only 1 god. This doesn't add up. Christianity and Islam have different concepts about God, not different gods. For my money, "...the god of peace" is better as "God, the source of shalom" (CJB: Rm.16:20). "God is not a god of confusion", is better as "God is not the author of confusion" (KJV: 1 Cor.14:33). And "the Lord, the god of the spirits of the prophets", is better as "the Lord God, who inspires the prophets" (NLT: Rv.22:6).

---

[248] Not even he was really a god, though poetically god of the world. Sure, the NT contains archaic speech patterns about idols, *et al*. Nevertheless, it does not ride on the simple idea that Rome has its gods but Christians have their covenant god. Gal.4:8 taught Gentile converts to reject such silly ideas. And 1 Cor.8:6 underlines that while Gentiles talked irrelevantly about gods and divine lords, yet Christians were into true meaning—one lordship, Christ, who revealed one kingdom, his father's.

PS: I like the CEV for 1 Sam.2:2; 1 Chr.17:20, etc: "No other god is like you", alone erring on the side of common sense. But it missed a trick for Jnh.1:6, where several versions sensibly have [your god].

## God-types Chart C605

**Texts**

The texts are Rm.3:29; 15:5; 15:13; 15:33; 16:20; 1 Cor.14:33; 2 Cor.1:3; 2 Cor.13:11; Eph.1:17; Php.4:9; 1 Thes.5:23; Heb.13:20; 1 Pt.5:10; Rv.1:6; 2:7; 3:2, 12; 4:11; 5:10; 7:3,10,12; 12:10; 19:1,5,6; 21:3,7; 22:6.[249]

**Comparative Class Grades**

| C605 | Grade |
|---|---|
| EEB | A+ |
| CEV | A |
| NLT | C- |
| GNB | D |
| CJB/GWT/MSG/NLV/NOG/TVB | U+ |
| ISV/NCV/REB | U |
| CEB/CSB/EJB/EOB/ERV/ESV/FBV/HCSB/KJ21/KJV/LEB/LSB/LSV/MEV/NABRE/NASB20/NASB95/NCB/NET/NIV/NJB/NKJV/NRSV/NRSVU/NWT/RNJB/RSV/TLV/WEB | U- |

---

[249] Sadly some add in polytheism: eg 1 Pt.1:16; 1 Tm.6:15 (CEV).

# Book Conclusion

This brings together a number of things I've looked at, crossing various divides. Of the charts I have made, I've combined a number here to better compare versions on these big issues.

A. That on God's name (page 110) tests a safety feature against the West's slide into Sabellianism. Phonetically *the LORD* of most versions sounds the same as *the Lord* that is highlighted as Jesus in the NT, sounding as if the OT *LORD* is no more and no less than Jesus. This idea needs a clear phonetic distinction to prevent its growth. Trinitarianism clarifies that Yahweh is eternal and triune: three persons of one being, the three members of one society.

B. That on God the son (page 122) indicates orthodoxy, the Alexandrian witness, and up to date translation.

C. That on marriage (page 149) tests that the English versions are sensitive to the original culture, and perhaps also offer more biblical insight on marriage, largely lost by sacerdotalism/sacramentalism—neither church, temple, nor state, 'marries/divorces' couples, though ideally interface with such. Middling versions move confusingly between marriage, and engagement, cultures.

D. That on *John* (page 205) tests a number of issues under this roof, making sure that what *John* says is not misrepresented in our culture. A high score here is likely to reflect a high attention to detail throughout the version.

E. That on gender (page 194) indicates sensitivity to gender and age, and also to what the source languages *actually* say. It warrants simply that they go far enough, not that they have not gone too far.

F. That on miscellaneous has combined some charts I have deemed important, yet in some sense secondary, if only in the sense that they might not jump out at one unless doing particular studies.

# Book Conclusion

## Summary Chart: C000

The charts summarised are **A** (Chart C100: *God's ID*); **B** (Chart C200: *Deificity of God's son*); **C** (Chart C300: *Marriage*); **D** (Chart C400: *John's Gospel*); **E** (Chart C500: *Gender accuracy*); **F** (Chart C600: *Miscellaneous*: page 135 (Chart C601: *Incarnation*); page 150 (Chart C602: *Covenant*); page 161 (Chart C603: *Sarx*); page 188 (Chart C604: *Son of man*); page 210 (Chart C605: *God-type*)). Comparative percentages have been used for each column.

## Results

The highest version here is the NLT at 401 marks, and the joint lowest is the NLV at 130. I have recalculated the lowest as being zero (130 minus 130), and reduced the highest to 271 (401 minus 130). All scores have then been divided by 271%, turning them all into comparative percentages. In the chart below, 'J' means Joint Place.

| 100-95 | 94-90 | 89-85 | 84-80 | 79-75 | 74-70 | 69-65 | 64-60 | 59-55 | 54-50 | 49-45 | 44-40 | 39-27 | 26-14 | 13-00 |
|---|---|---|---|---|---|---|---|---|---|---|---|---|---|---|
| A+ | A | A- | B+ | B | B- | C+ | C | C- | D+ | D | D- | U+ | U | U- |
| A1 | A2 | A3 | B1 | B2 | B3 | C1 | C2 | C3 | D1 | D2 | D3 | U1 | U2 | U3 |
| 4.3 | 4 | 3.7 | 3.3 | 3 | 2.7 | 2.3 | 2 | 1.7 | 1.3 | 1 | 0.7 | 0 | 0 | 0 |

| Rank | EV | A | B | C | D | E | F | T | T-130 | % | GM |
|---|---|---|---|---|---|---|---|---|---|---|---|
| 1 | NLT | 57 | 89 | 7 | 87 | 82 | 79 | 401 | 271 | 100 | A+ |
| 2 | NIV | 50 | 80 | 41 | 100 | 71 | 57 | 399 | 269 | 99 | A+ |
| 3 | NJB | 100 | 67 | 85 | 46 | 31 | 58 | 387 | 257 | 95 | A+ |
| 4 | NRSV | 50 | 85 | 30 | 74 | 75 | 69 | 383 | 253 | 93 | A |
| 5 | ERV | 59 | 80 | 30 | 79 | 83 | 47 | 378 | 248 | 92 | A |
| J6 | NCV | 50 | 77 | 30 | 72 | 92 | 55 | 376 | 246 | 91 | A |
| J6 | NOG | 100 | 78 | 15 | 45 | 92 | 46 | 376 | 246 | 91 | A |
| 8 | CEB | 50 | 73 | 15 | 79 | 88 | 68 | 373 | 243 | 90 | A |
| 9 | CEV | 50 | 71 | 4 | 81 | 88 | 76 | 370 | 240 | 89 | A- |
| 10 | NRSVU | 50 | 76 | 37 | 48 | 96 | 61 | 368 | 238 | 88 | A- |
| 11 | NET | 54 | 100 | 41 | 89 | 29 | 54 | 367 | 237 | 87 | A- |
| J12 | NABRE | 55 | 59 | 93 | 77 | 27 | 44 | 355 | 225 | 83 | B+ |
| J12 | RNJB | 50 | 58 | 81 | 41 | 100 | 26 | 356 | 226 | 83 | B+ |

| | | | | | | | | | | |
|---|---|---|---|---|---|---|---|---|---|---|
| J14 | CSB | 50 | 81 | 56 | 81 | 36 | 45 | **349** | 219 | 81 | B+ |
| J14 | EEB | 50 | 78 | 0 | 79 | 42 | 100 | **349** | 219 | 81 | B+ |
| 16 | LEB | 100 | 70 | 59 | 61 | 19 | 37 | **346** | 216 | 80 | B+ |
| 17 | GNB | 50 | 63 | 0 | 68 | 72 | 91 | **344** | 214 | 79 | B |
| J18 | ISV | 50 | 73 | 44 | 82 | 19 | 59 | **327** | 197 | 73 | B- |
| J18 | TVB | 63 | 63 | 4 | 64 | 73 | 62 | **329** | 199 | 73 | B- |
| J18 | MSG | 52 | 66 | 19 | 52 | 56 | 81 | **326** | 196 | 72 | B- |
| J18 | GWT | 50 | 78 | 15 | 45 | 92 | 43 | **323** | 193 | 71 | B- |
| J18 | NASB20 | 50 | 82 | 81 | 49 | 29 | 28 | **319** | 189 | 70 | B- |
| 23 | RSV | 50 | 70 | 100 | 50 | 4 | 38 | **312** | 182 | 67 | C+ |
| J24 | ESV | 50 | 63 | 78 | 63 | 17 | 30 | **301** | 171 | 63 | C |
| J24 | HCSB | 73 | 71 | 44 | 47 | 19 | 47 | **301** | 171 | 63 | C |
| 26 | NCB | 50 | 78 | 59 | 57 | 26 | 25 | **295** | 165 | 61 | C |
| 27 | LSB | 100 | 70 | 81 | 00 | 4 | 21 | **276** | 146 | 54 | D+ |
| J28 | REB | 50 | 58 | 11 | 63 | 26 | 64 | **272** | 142 | 52 | D+ |
| J28 | WEB | 100 | 76 | 33 | 47 | 15 | 0 | **271** | 141 | 52 | D+ |
| 30 | FBV | 5 | 61 | 7 | 66 | 79 | 41 | **259** | 129 | 48 | D |
| 31 | NKJV | 50 | 59 | 93 | 28 | 2 | 14 | **246** | 116 | 43 | D- |
| 32 | TLV | 27 | 73 | 37 | 70 | 6 | 25 | **238** | 108 | 40 | D- |
| 33 | NWT | 75 | 00 | 56 | 55 | 4 | 45 | **235** | 105 | 39 | U+ |
| J34 | CJB | 31 | 34 | 4 | 50 | 26 | 84 | **229** | 99 | 37 | U+ |
| J34 | EJB | 54 | 64 | 93 | 09 | 8 | 1 | **229** | 99 | 37 | U+ |
| 36 | EOB | 50 | 69 | 26 | 50 | 27 | 5 | **227** | 97 | 36 | U+ |
| 37 | MEV | 50 | 62 | 74 | 24 | 2 | 14 | **226** | 96 | 35 | U+ |
| J38 | KJ21 | 54 | 53 | 93 | 03 | 0 | 4 | **207** | 77 | 28 | U+ |
| J38 | KJV | 54 | 53 | 93 | 03 | 0 | 4 | **207** | 77 | 28 | U+ |
| J38 | NASB95 | 50 | 64 | 52 | 18 | 2 | 21 | **207** | 77 | 28 | U+ |
| 41 | LSV | 31 | 56 | 93 | 11 | 4 | 5 | **200** | 70 | 26 | U |
| 42 | NLV | 0 | 41 | 0 | 53 | 13 | 23 | **130** | 0 | 0 | U- |

# Book Conclusion

**Comparative Class Grades**

| Summary | Grade |
|---|---|
| NIV/NJB/NLT | A+ |
| CEB/ERV/NCV/NOG/NRSV | A |
| CEV/NET/NRSVU | A- |
| CSB/EEB/LEB/NABRE/RNJB | B+ |
| GNB | B |
| GWT/ISV/MSG/NASB20/TVB | B- |
| RSV | C+ |
| ESV/HCSB/NCB | C |
| LSB/REB/WEB | D+ |
| FBV | D |
| NKJV/TLV | D- |
| CJB/EJB/EOB/KJ21/KJV/MEV/NASB95/NWT | U+ |
| LSV | U |
| NLV | U- |

Among their peers, I rate a fifth of them as Unsatisfactory, redundant because we have better. However, the NLV should be respected as designed for a specific missionary project, not as a global version, and the KJV, initially unpopular, served well for long and preserves something of a bygone language for a bygone Bible. It has a niche constituency for some, even if unsatisfactory for the general public. High on my wish list would be that the MEV/NKJV, representing the TR model, a model for now worth keeping, will upgrade to gender accuracy. That could improve their grades and better serve their constituency and evangelism. All could do better. Many have been subject to the penalty of the zero, the lowest scores having been levelled to a zero, not as worst possible, but as worst in their group.

Here let's turn to Robert Louis Stevenson's *Kidnapped*, chapter 11, where, fearing the English, Alan Breck Stewart added a button and sprigs of pine and birch, to some cross shaped wood, as an urgent letter to kinsman John Breck. Smiling, David Balfour asked why Alan simply didn't write a note. Simpler, sure, said Alan, but John would have to go to school for two-three years, and Alan might get weary waiting for the reply. Well, unless we will go to school, spend time learning Hebrew and Greek, we must do with the English versions available, the buttons and birch, shaping them with theological sense. Indeed, even being able to translate does not guarantee most accurate translation. Yet translations of the Bible have great riches in them and cover the basics. We can pine over their deficiencies, yet enjoy their efficiencies.

My tests have some subjectivity in them, which does not always flow with objectivity. But then, what tests would not? I have tried to fit the tests to the facts, and not the facts to them, and to score reasonably. If you completely disagree, you can still benefit from the charts, taking low scores as high, and top scores as worst scores! Only provide reasonable justification. And style is something I have not tested for: tastes and needs vary. On balance, I would suggest having perhaps four versions from this chart that score very highly on at least four issues.

A summary of English versions and the six big issues charted above:

| | |
|---|---|
| ≥50% on 6 issues | None |
| ≥50% on 5 issues | CEB/CEV/GNB/MSG/NCV/NIV/NLT/NRSV/TVB |
| ≥50% on 4 issues | CSB/EEB/ERV/ESV/ISV/LEB/NABRE/NCB/NET/NJB/NRSVU/REB/RNJB/RSV |
| ≥50% on 3 issues | EJB/EOB/FBV/GWT/KJ21/KJV/LSB/MEV/NASN20/NASB95/NKJV/NOG/NWT |
| ≥50% on 2 issues | CJB/HCSB/LSV/TLV/WEB |
| ≥50% on 1 issue | NLV |
| ≥50% on 0 issues | None |

## Comments

A variety of versions is good. If I were allowed exactly 10 versions for my bookcase—and/or accessible on electronic devices—my ten English Versions would include the NKJV and NABRE as protected status, as well representing the RC and TR positions: commendably the NKJV includes footnote correctives to the TR text; uncommendably the NABRE touts many cringeworthy notes, often

## Book Conclusion

unscholarly and sceptical: it would be better ditching its notes. From the Roman stable I prefer the NJB, but I would sacrifice accuracy, and perhaps style, for accessibility, especially on version compare sites.

I would choose next the A-graded, so long as they fall below 50% in no more than one issue. Thus, I include the CEB/CEV/NCV/NIV/NLT/NRSV. Below that, I would have the ERV/NET, being A-graded, though they fall below 50% on two issues.

So, the CEB/CEV/ERV/NCV/NABRE/NET/NIV/NKJV/NLT/NRSV. They cover a range of formal and functional approaches, as well as strengths and weaknesses, and levels of reading. However, overall I find the ERV/NCV weak for study, where formal links are important.

The selection could easily be otherwise. Any who wish to may simply rejig the stats, rating high what I rate low. Bible use is always better than Bible rage. Why, I wonder, being so blessed with a wealth of versions, do we so easily make less use of the Bible than Christians in China, where the Bible is not such an easy come by. Still, my task now comes towards its end. Younger age groups are probably best on versions that treat gender and language as current, the Bible as relevant, yet are not too trendy. Those worst for marriage tend to be too eager to contemporise, and I lament the NLT, otherwise so engaging. Older age groups might be happier with more traditional styles. Generally, one should look for what fits their style within high levels of accuracy. For discussions with non-Christians, it is sometimes worth checking the text in a few of versions.

*Gloria in excelsis Deo*

**Works cited:**
Tokunboh Adeyemo's *African Bible Commentary*: 2006
Jane Austen's *Pride and Prejudice*: 1980
Geoffrey Bromiley's *Theological Dictionary of the NT*: 1985
F F Bruce's *History of the English Bible*: 1986
Stan Bruce's *Introduction to NT Greek*: 1999
Henry Bett's *The Hymns of Methodism*: 1945
D A Carson's *The King James Version Debate*: 1985
D A Carson's *The Gospel According to John*: 1991
D A Carson's *The Inclusive Language Debate*: 1998
Owen Chadwick's *A History of Christianity*: 1995
J D Douglas' *Illustrated Bible Dictionary* (IVP): 1994
Walter A Elwell's *Evangelical Dictionary Of Theology*: 1985
C Stephen Evans' *Philosophy of Religion*: 1982
Fee and Stuart's *How to Read the Bible for all its Worth*: 1994
W H C Frend's *Creeds, Councils and Controversies 337-461*: 2000
Wayne Grudem's *Systematic Theology*: 1994
E W Ives' *God in History*: 1979
William Kay's *Pentecostals in Britain*: 2000
Craig S Keener's *Commentary on the Gospel of Matthew*: 1999
Nobuyoshi Kiuchi's *Leviticus*: 2007
Andreas J Köstenberger's *John* (BECNT): 2004
Köstenberger and Croteau's *Which Bible Translation Should I Use?*: 2012
C S Lewis' *English Literature in the C16*: 1954
C S Lewis' *Fern-seed and Elephants*: 1975
C S Lewis' *Christian Reflections*: 1981
C S Lewis' *The Pilgrim's Regress*: 1978
C S Lewis' *Mere Christianity*: 2002
I Howard Marshall's *Acts* (TNTC): 1992
Elmer A Martens' *God's Design*: 1994
Walter Martin's *The Kingdom of the Cults*: 2003
Alister McGrath's *In the Beginning*: 2002
Alister McGrath's *The Dawkins Delusion?*: 2007
Bruce M Metzger's *The Bible in Translation*: 2006
Douglas J Moo's *James* (TNTC): 1985
Alec Motyer's *Isaiah* (TOTC): 2005
Chawkat Moucarry's *Faith to Faith*: 2001

## Book Conclusion

Mouw and Noll's *Wonderful Words of Life*: 2004
Mark A Noll's *Christianity in America*: 1983
Geoffrey Parrinder's *Africa's Three Religions*: 1969
Mark A Pike's *Mere Education*: 2013
Gail A Riplinger's *New Age Versions*: 1994
David Schaff's *The Life of Philip Schaff*: 1897
Scorgie, Strauss, and Voth's *The Challenge of Bible Translation*: 2003
George Tyrrell's *Lex Orandi*: 1903
Willem A VanGemeren's *New International Dictionary of OT Theology and Exegesis*: 1997
James White's *The King James Only Controversy*: 1995
John White's *The Golden Cow*: 1979
Mark Yarhouse's *Understanding Gender Dysphoria*: 2015

# The Word's Gone Global

## Selective Index

### 2

21st Century King James Version/KJ21 · 61, 95, 215

### A

Abraham · 115, 133, 184, 209
Act of Uniformity · 56
Adeyemo, Tokunboh · 149
al Razi, Fakhr-ul Din · 16, 17, 18
Alexandrian Text Family · 18, 25, 26, 40, 49, 66, 76, 85, 86, 88, 89, 94, 113, 115, 136, 137, 141, 142, 143, 211
Alexandrinus/A · 72
American Standard Version/ASV · 69, 84, 144
Amplified Bible · 84
Apocrypha/Deuterocanon · 25, 26, 32, 38, 48, 60, 66
Augustine of Hippo/Saint Augustine · 200

### B

Bancroft, Richard · 54, 64, 65, 66
Barker, Robert · 60, 61, 71, 80
Beza, Theodore · 39, 45, 46, 47, 49, 58, 59, 74, 91, 136
Bishops Bible · 30, 33, 34, 35, 42, 46, 47, 53, 54, 59, 64, 74, 84, 90, 97, 106, 107, 131, 160, 178, 191
Broughton, Hugh · 64, 65
Burgon, John William (Dean) · 65, 66

### C

Calvin, John · 35, 42, 46, 48, 119, 133, 145
Christian Standard Bible/CSB · 163, 215
Colorado Springs Guidelines/CSG · 177, 180, 181, 182, 183, 185, 186, 192
Committee on Bible Translation/CBT · 145, 146, 177, 181, 193
Common English Bible/CEB · 24, 95, 111, 163, 215
Complete Jewish Bible/CJB · 123, 161, 163, 175, 176, 209, 215
Constitutions of Oxford, the · 28
Contemporary English Version/CEV · 95, 111, 148, 160, 190, 194, 195, 196, 202, 215
Council of Trent · 36, 64
Council on Biblical Manhood and Womanhood/CBMW · 181
covenant · 16, 19, 36, 38, 54, 59, 83, 100, 102, 105, 108, 121, 130, 131, 148, 150, 151, 209, 212
Coverdale, Miles/Coverdale Bible · 30, 31, 32, 33, 45, 47, 93, 104, 106, 107, 109, 129

### D

Darby, John Nelson · 58, 76, 84, 92, 105, 129
Douay-Rheims · 30, 34, 35, 58, 72, 104, 106, 107, 129

## E

Eastern Orthodox Bible/EOB · 23, 24, 65, 148, 202, 215
Easy-to-Read Version/ERV · 95, 141, 153, 163, 215, 216
eclecticism · 57, 60, 113, 142
Elzevirs · 39, 47, 48, 49, 50
English Jubilee Bible/EJB · 61, 215
English Standard Version/ESV · 33, 84, 95, 147, 148, 150, 151, 152, 153, 154, 155, 156, 158, 159, 160, 161, 162, 163, 164, 165, 168, 169, 175, 179, 180, 182, 183, 186, 187, 188, 189, 190, 191, 193, 194, 195, 201, 204, 215
Erasmus, Desiderius · 23, 30, 31, 39, 42, 43, 44, 45, 46, 47, 48, 49, 50, 58, 59, 64, 72, 74, 75, 91, 92, 93, 129, 136

## F

Flew, Antony · 196
Focus on the Family · 177, 181
Formal Equivalence · 29, 101, 147, 150, 158, 165, 166, 167, 182, 190, 192, 216
functional equivalence · 24, 29, 109, 147, 158, 165, 195, 200, 202, 216

## G

gender · 73, 84, 88, 146, 147, 153, 167, 170, 171, 172, 173, 174, 175, 177, 178, 180, 181, 182, 183, 185, 187, 189, 190, 191, 192, 193, 194, 195, 196, 197, 198, 201, 211, 212, 214, 216
Geneva Bible · 30, 32, 33, 35, 41, 42, 47, 49, 50, 51, 53, 54, 55, 56, 64, 65, 71, 76, 84, 87, 90, 97, 104, 105, 106, 107, 119, 122, 200
God's Word Translation/GWT · 120, 215

Good News Bible/GNB · 71, 84, 120, 134, 153, 161, 169, 188, 215
Great Bible · 30, 32, 33, 45, 58, 104, 106, 107
Great Isaiah Scroll · 111

## H

Holman Christian Standard Bible/HCSB · 108, 125, 148, 151, 156, 159, 161, 163, 164, 190, 194, 195, 201, 204, 215
homosexualism · 79, 80, 81, 82, 83, 84, 85, 199
huiology · 211, 212

## I

incarnation · 11, 12, 44, 78, 113, 130, 131, 132, 175, 212
International Standard Version/ISV · 84, 111, 112, 120, 125, 135, 148, 151, 153, 162, 163, 190, 215
Islam/Muslim · 13, 14, 15, 16, 17, 34, 43, 105, 109, 141, 150, 209

## J

James 1, King · 33, 40, 53, 55, 81
Jerome · 25, 26, 32, 33, 36, 37, 38, 43, 63, 64, 74, 91, 92, 93, 104, 108, 115, 133, 136
John · 13, 30, 42, 58, 78, 91, 92, 98, 114, 115, 119, 128, 153, 185, 191, 202, 203, 204, 205, 211, 212, 217
Judaic · 15, 16, 17, 36, 103

## K

Kenyon, Sir Frederic · 18
King James Version/KJV · 12, 23, 29, 30, 31, 33, 35, 39, 40, 41, 42, 44, 45, 46, 47, 49, 50, 51, 52, 54, 55, 56, 57, 58, 59, 60, 61, 63, 64, 65, 66, 67, 68, 69, 70, 71, 72, 73, 75, 76, 78, 79, 81, 83, 84, 85, 86, 87, 88, 89, 90, 91, 92, 93, 94, 95, 97, 98, 99, 101, 103, 104, 105, 106, 107, 110, 113, 114, 116, 117, 119, 120, 121, 122, 123, 124, 125, 126, 127, 128, 129, 130, 131, 132, 133, 135, 136, 141, 142, 143, 144, 145, 159, 160, 162, 166, 168, 169, 177, 178, 191, 194, 195, 200, 203, 204, 209, 215
KJV Advocatism/KJVA · 88
KJV Onlyism · 47, 57, 58, 60, 61, 75, 76, 85, 93, 102, 103, 113, 117, 123, 124
Köstenberger, Andreas · 180, 201

## L

Laud, William · 56
Lexham English Bible/LEB · 94, 95, 101, 120, 153, 215
Luther, Martin · 22, 26, 30, 31, 34, 43, 64, 93, 104, 129, 154

## M

Majority (Byzantine) Text/MT · 23, 24, 35, 37, 38, 39, 40, 42, 43, 46, 49, 50, 57, 58, 59, 60, 72, 74, 89, 91, 92, 113, 128, 129, 132, 133, 136, 137, 141, 142, 143, 191
marriage · 76, 77, 82, 83, 130, 132, 147, 148, 149, 150, 151, 171, 174, 181, 184, 199, 211, 212, 216
Martin, Gregory · 5, 34, 35, 203

Matthew's Bible · 30, 32, 45, 106, 107
Message/MSG · 95, 151, 153, 210, 215
Modern English Version/MEV · 61, 111, 149, 153, 190, 214, 215

## N

Names of God Bible/NOG · 120, 160, 215
Nestles-Aland/United Bible Society (NU) · 23, 40, 51, 58, 59, 72, 76, 92, 122, 132, 133, 136, 137, 142, 143, 144, 145, 160
New American Bible · 107
 NABRE/2010 · 30, 72, 95, 111, 116, 120, 125, 129, 133, 134, 148, 156, 164, 175, 190, 202, 204, 205, 215
New American Standard Bible
 1995 · 153, 168, 190, 215
 2020 · 144, 215
New Catholic Bible/NCB · 215
New Century Version/NCV · 95, 120, 134, 148, 153, 156, 179, 188, 189, 190, 194, 196, 205, 215, 216
New English Bible/NEB · 107
New English Translation/NET · 135, 205, 215
New International Version/NIV · 41, 45, 46, 58, 59, 60, 62, 67, 68, 71, 73, 75, 76, 77, 78, 79, 80, 81, 83, 84, 85, 86, 90, 91, 94, 95, 107, 108, 116, 117, 118, 119, 120, 123, 124, 125, 126, 127, 128, 129, 144, 145, 146, 147, 148, 150, 152, 153, 154, 155, 156, 158, 159, 160, 161, 162, 164, 165, 169, 175, 177, 181, 184, 189, 190, 193, 200, 201, 204, 205, 215
NIVI/1995 · 175, 177, 184, 186, 187
New Jerusalem Bible/NJB · 30, 72, 90, 103, 120, 129, 134, 148, 159, 161, 163, 190, 215
New King James Version/NKJV · 23, 50, 51, 95, 136, 148, 153, 156, 169, 170, 190, 214, 215

New Life Version/NLV · 95, 130, 134, 135, 161, 212, 214, 215
New Living Translation/NLT · 95, 108, 120, 125, 148, 156, 159, 160, 162, 163, 167, 169, 175, 179, 190, 194, 195, 196, 197, 201, 209, 212, 215, 216
New Revised Standard Version/NRSV · 95, 120, 130, 135, 179, 180, 186, 188, 189, 201, 215, 216
New World Translation/NWT · 95, 97, 98, 109, 111, 116, 120, 123, 163
New York Bible Society/International Bible Society · 145, 181
Nueve Versión Internacional/NVI · 90

## O

Origen · 12, 25, 45, 58, 74, 85
Orthodoxism/Eastern Christianity · 20, 21, 22, 23, 24, 26, 35, 37, 54, 133

## P

polytheism · 206, 208, 209, 210, 212
Puritans · 33, 41, 42, 53, 54, 55, 56, 71, 91

## R

Reina Valera Revisada/RVR · 90
Revised English Bible/REB · 151, 159, 196, 215
Revised Standard Version/RSV · 23, 33, 66, 130, 144, 145, 148, 158, 159, 160, 179, 180, 189, 201
Revised Version/RV · 49, 65, 66, 69, 70, 75, 98, 136, 141, 142, 200
Rogers, John
   Matthew's Bible · 32

## S

sageism · 49, 189
Sarx · 157, 159, 160, 161, 212
Satan/satanic · 11, 68, 73, 74, 76
Scrivener, F H A · 49, 50, 59
Septuagint/LXX · 12, 23, 24, 100, 101, 103, 115, 132, 189, 191
Sinaiticus/א · 44, 65, 72, 74, 137, 142
Smith, Julia Evelina · 33, 97
Son of man/Barnasa · 185, 188, 212
Stephanus · 18, 23, 39, 45, 46, 47, 48, 58, 59, 74, 91, 125, 136

## T

Tetragrammaton Chart · 105, 110
Textus Receptus/TR · 23, 35, 39, 40, 42, 43, 46, 47, 48, 49, 50, 51, 57, 59, 60, 65, 72, 73, 75, 76, 86, 88, 89, 92, 113, 115, 125, 126, 129, 136, 141, 142, 143, 190, 214, 215
Themelios · 199
Today's New International Version/TNIV · 33, 83, 84, 152, 153, 154, 155, 158, 159, 160, 161, 163, 164, 172, 175, 177, 181, 185, 186, 188, 189, 190, 193, 194, 201
Trajectory Hermeneutics · 197
Trinitarian Bible Society/TBS · 48, 49, 50, 51
Tyndale, William/Tyndale Bible · 5, 30, 31, 32, 45, 47, 49, 57, 58, 59, 64, 93, 103, 104, 105, 106, 107, 108, 160, 178, 203

## U

USA · 55, 56, 69, 175, 177

## V

Vaticanus/B · 43, 44, 65, 72, 137, 142, 143, 191
Voice · 120, 175, 215
Vulgate · 12, 25, 26, 29, 30, 33, 35, 40, 41, 43, 44, 45, 46, 59, 63, 64, 91, 92, 93, 103, 104, 106, 107, 129, 133, 134, 200

## W

Webster, Noah · 97
Wesley, John · 30, 46, 48, 58, 62, 65, 75, 92
Westcott and Hort · 18, 49, 65, 66, 75, 76, 77, 79, 81, 82, 94, 137, 141, 142
White, John · 85, 90
Whittingham, William · 33
World English Bible/WEB · 65, 84, 103, 110, 153, 160, 215
Wycliffe Bible Translators · 19
Wycliffe, John/Wycliffe Bible · 5, 19, 28, 29, 30, 32, 45, 46, 58, 59, 64, 72, 96, 103, 104, 105, 106, 128, 129, 133, 160, 187, 189

## Y

Yahweh/God's name · 14, 48, 58, 100, 101, 102, 103, 104, 105, 106, 107, 108, 109, 110, 111, 119, 129, 131, 132, 133, 137, 150, 156, 157, 185, 198, 208, 209, 211, 212

Like or loathe any of my books? Please feedback to Amazon.

## Books by this Author

## Theology

**Israel's Gone Global**

Israel's Gone Global traces salvation through the term, Israel. Was the covenant with the people-nation of Yakob-Yisrael, crossed out? How eternal is covenant? To examine that, we examine marriage. Can a covenant partner be truly divorced? Has Yeshua-Yisrael mediated a spiritual covenant with a spiritual Israel? Is evangelism of ethnic Jews needless, a priority, or neither?

No one could have everlasting life but for the cross, but has it always been globally accessible? Might any who die as Atheists, Hindus, or Islamists, make heaven? And is eternal life joyful? Is everlasting life fun?

Tackling the question of people who die in infancy (or as adults who never heard the gospel), we consider whether it is fair if only those who don't die in infancy get a chance of eternal damnation (if infant universalism), or alone get a chance of eternal heaven (if infant damnation). Does predilectionism make best sense of biblical revelation?

Opportunities to enjoy eternal life spring from the new covenant—reasons to rejoice. But what about salvation history before that covenant?

∞

**Singing's Gone Global**

Singing's Gone Global, briefly explores the background of singing, before and into ancient Israel. It examines the impact songs have on those who sing, and on those who listen, touching on spiritual warfare. It looks at how nonsense songs neither make sense to evangelism, nor to the evangelised, and asks, "Is there a mûmak in the room?"

Oddly some songwriters simply misunderstand prayer. Part two covers the basics of the trinity, focusing on the spirit in order to understand types of prayer (eg request, gratitude, adoration, chat), leading in turn to a better understanding of our heavenly father, our brother, our helper, and ourselves in Christ's likeness.

Next we look at some common problems. Part three focuses on problems such as buddyism, decontextualising, misvisualisation, and unitarianism. Diagnosis can help Christ's 'bride' to recover from suboptimal and unbiblical songs (Eph.5:18-30).

Giving a Problem Avoidance Grade (PAG)—an A+ to Unsatisfactory scale—in part four we examine specific songs. Weapons forged (Part three), the mûmakil can be attacked, seeking to save and be saved.

Subsequently the book concludes by showing how Christmas carols may be tweaked to better serve our weary world, rejoicing that joy to the world has come.

∞

## The Word's Gone Global

The Word's Gone Global, examines Bible text (trusted by early Islam) and introduces textual critique. It looks at the Eastern Orthodox Bible and the Latin Vulgate. Did the Reformation improve text and translation? Were Wycliffe, Tyndale, and Martin, helpful?

Why did the New International Version begin, and why does it enrage? Why did complementarians Don Carson and Wayne Grudem, clash? Is marketing hype between formal and functional equivalence, meaningless? Which version or versions should you regularly read?

In English-speaking circles, Broughton wished to burn Bancroft's King James Version, yet many KJV proponents—think Gail Riplinger and Peter Ruckman—wish to burn all alternatives. More heat than light?

Grade Charts cover 30+ English versions on issues such as God's name, God's son's deity, marriage, gender terms, anti-polytheism, and issues in John's Gospel such as whether Tyndale was 'born again' and John antisemitic, and whether he disagreed with the other Gospels—all No!

∞

## Books by this Author

**Prayer's Gone Global**

Prayer's Gone Global, begins with ancient civilisations and prayer (the Common Level). Then it narrows into Ancient Israel and prayer (the Sinai Level). Then it deepens and widens into Global Israel and prayer (the Christian Level). Deity is revealed as trinity: Sabellians mislead.

Relating to the trinity includes the Holy Spirit. We should of course work with him, but should we worship him, complain to him, chat with him? Above the spirit stands the often forgotten father—oh let Jesusism retire.

Authority is another issue. Are we authorised to decree and declare? Is binding and loosing actually prayer, or is it evangelism? Is it biblical never to command miracles? Do we miss out on the supernatural which Jesus modelled for us, too fearful of strange fire to offer holy fire?

You can freshen up your prayer life—ride the blessed camel, not the gnats. Listen to Saint Anselm pray, and C S Lewis and 'Malcolm' discuss prayer, and be blessed.

∞

**Revelation's Gone Global**

Revelation's Gone Global, is a telling of John's future, as if by a then contemporary named Sonafets speaking to his church about how John's apocalyptic scroll related to their days, and about what was still future to John.

Encouragement is a big theme. Roman persecution was an unpredictable beast which ferociously lashed out here and there—what church or Christian was safe? But God stood behind the scenes, allowing but limiting their enemy, and messiah walked among the churches, lights to the world.

Victory lay neither with Rome nor demons, but with God, and with the warrior lamb who had been slain. Victory was guaranteed, and would finally be enjoyed.

Exhortation was given to believers, to play their part while on the mortal stage. They were to walk in the light, and not to let the show down by straying.

Angels of power, actively working out God's will, far exceed the puny forces against God and his church. His wrath was not pleasant, but could be redemptive until the new age begins.

C S Lewis' essay, The World's Last Night, is briefly examined to enjoin a calm awareness of the ongoing battle we are in, and the brightness to come when the king returns.

∞

## The Father's Gone Global

Focusing from God as father, to the specific person of God the father, The Father's Gone Global looks at the biblical parent/child pattern from Genesis, through Sinai, and into the Church.

Abba as a new covenant word expresses deep filial affection even under deep anguish in our Gethsemane battles. Coming through God's belovèd son, it speaks into the church and into our lives.

Though to many the 'forgotten father', human parents/fathers should 'put on' God the father, and his children should 'put on' his son. We forget him to our cost.

Human applications aside, what is the Eternal Society? Is filial relationship modelled by God the son incarnate? Are we to be always obedient to our father and guided by the spirit?

Eschatologically the father will be supreme, but even now he is the one to whom the son points. Christian life should relate to God our father, God our brother, and God our helper, prioritising the father.

Renewal of the church is vital for our confused world, but renewal which downplays the father falls short of the good news which Christ created and the spirit circulates. May this book play its part.

# Books by this Author

∞

## Salvation Now and Life Beyond

Salvation Now, divides the doctrine of salvation into the four main levels of common humanity, the old covenant, the new covenant, and life beyond.

A big weight is put on the term, Israel, as God's master plan. This too has four levels, meaning a man, a people, a new man, and a new people, respectively.

Various ideas of what Christianity, the new covenant for the new people, is good for, and how we get into it and best enjoy it, are examined, and a faith-based inexclusivism is suggested.

Everlasting life is seen as the ultimate goal of salvation, universal meaningfulness and love beyond all fears and pains.

∞

## Revisiting Revisiting The Challenging Counterfeit

Revisiting The Challenging Counterfeit, is an extended review of Raphael Gasson's 'The Challenging Counterfeit' (1966). Raphael was an ethnic Jew whose spiritual journey included many years as a Christian Spiritualist minister.

Today, when psychic phenomena captures the imagination and the bank accounts of popular media, it is useful to unearth the witness of one who had well worn the T-shirt of a medium with pride, only to bury it in unholy ground as a thing of shame and of sorrow and of wasted time.

Challengingly, his book exposes what true Spiritualism is. He had nothing but high praise for Spiritualists, and deep condemnation for Spiritualism. For he had discovered true Spiritualism to be itself a fake of true Spirituality, a mere Counterfeit that, in deposing death in the mind, enthroned it in the soul.

Counterfeit phenomena covered include apparitions, Rescue Work and haunted houses, materialisation of pets, psychic healing, Lyceums, clairvoyance, and OOBEs—to name but a few. This book surveys his exposé of Spiritualism's offer of fascinating fish bait, false food falling short of real food for the soul. Though it takes issue with

Raphael on a number of points, his core insights are powerful and timely, helping us to avoid—or escape from—a Challenging Counterfeit, and to discover true spiritual currency.

∞

## Revisiting The Pilgrim's Progress

Revisiting The Pilgrim's Progress, is a re-dreaming of John Bunyan's most famous dream. An ex-serviceman and ex-jailbird, he found fortune, freedom, and fans worldwide.

This dream journey is substantially Bunyan's from this world, and into that which is to come. It is not a fun story, but it has lots of danger, and joy, and reflection on some big life themes.

Profoundly, sinners who become pilgrims become saints. But that can make life more difficult. One big question is, Is it worth it? One big temptation is, Turn back or turn aside. And if you see others do so, that makes it harder not to. Bunyan was tempted. And he discovered that not deserting, can lead to despair. But he also discovered a key to liberty.

Pre-eminently, it is a story of grace which many follow. Grace begins the journey, helps along the way, and brings the story to a happily ever after. Are all fairy stories based on heaven?

∞

**Fantasy**

## The Simbolinian Files

From Simboliniad, a crystal planet long gone, came the vampire race, the wapierze, thelodynamic shapeshifters seeking blood. Most oppose Usen, King of the Light, so side with the Necros. Seldom do the Guardians intervene. These files, secretly secured from various insider sources, reveal something of what they have done, and will do.

∞

## Vampire Redemption

Artificial intelligence, created by superpowers to save man, questions man's worth, and becomes The Beast. Escaping into the wild, many discover a wilderness infested by zombies and diabolical spirits. Who will help? Father Doyle? He's tied up with the mysterious Lilith.

# Books by this Author

Tariq? He's tied up with Wilma. Can the bigoted old exorcist deliver him from evil?

Radical problems can require radical solutions. But does man really need hobs, elves, and the more ancient of days? In the surrounding shadows, vampires and demons form an alliance, raising the stakes against Whitby and Tyneside. Powerful vampires live shrouded within Whitby, speaking of life beyond this galaxy. Is salvation in the stars? Is Sunniva, the despised woman of Alban, worth dying for? Big questions, needing big answers. Not even Guardian Odin can foretell man's fate and, as silent stars go by, one little town must awake from its dreams.

Though The Beast slumbers purposeless and undisturbed, in the far west a global giant slowly opens its yellow eyes and threatens to smother the earth in fire and ice. There is one chance only.

∞

**Vampire Extraction**

Bitterly long their imprisoned spirits lay, fast bound to Earth's drowsy decay. To the Simbolinian race, there was no hell on Earth, for Earth was hell, and Usen the cosmic jailer. Was it so surprising that as vampires they stalked Usen's children for blood? Most chose the Kingdom of Night, wary of both the Kingdom of Necros and the Kingdom of Dawn.

As queen of the Night, Lilith's story streams through the summer sands of Sumer, and through the green woods of Sherwood. It flags up both dishonour and joy, and cuts across the paths of Ulrica the Saxon and Robin the Hood, as tyrannies rise and fall in merry England. Bigotry seldom has a good word to say about Usen, nor about mercy. Reluctantly, Lilith examines what it means to show mercy, to show weakness. Wulfgar had enslaved Ulrica: is it mercy to let her burn; should mercy have spared Lona? Could Hamashiach turn daughter into sister? Could Count Dracula be turned from his madness? Has Draven really betrayed his mother? Life has many questions.

Tales picture ideas, letting us walk through the eyes of others to better see ourselves. This story exposes subplots behind common history. How these chronicles came to be written up is, in the spirit confidentiality, not for the public eye. What truth is within you must judge. Discrimination is a gift from Beyond, from which the words still echo: mercy is better than sacrifice. Indeed mercy can be sacrifice. Judge well.

∞

## Vampire Count

Vampires were not always earthbound, nor are all evil, but being victims of Usen's Eighth Law, his Children became their fair game. Yet the Night Kingdom was divided: some veered to the Necros; some to the Dawn. Who was wrong; who was right?

Long ago one incited his people to racial violence against elven and human kinds. Ever he strove to be king of the Night, and unto Necuratu the Dark Lord he gave the dragon shape. He made war upon the ancient Middle East, even the Nephilim War. Against him the Light raised flood and division.

At last his own people, paying the price of his rampage, bound him in deep sleep. Yet the millennia seemed meaningless to him: even the rising of Hamashiach hardly disturbed his dreams. At last awoken, he and his brides stalked the hills of Transylvania. Only the fear of Lilith—and after her unforgivable sin, Queen Rangda—chained their bloodlust.

Dracula sought escape and autonomy. By cunning and devious means, he immigrated to London via Whitby. Pursuit followed swiftly, with a shadowminder helping a circle of human headhunters, though they sought the death of all vampires.

∞

## Vampire Grail

Wulfgar is a vampire, a thelodynamic creature from another galaxy, now locked into our world by one called the Cosmic Jailer. He hides a tormenting secret from his queen, Lilith, which the Necros use as blackmail. She will only go so far with the Necros against Hamashiach—Wulfgar must go further.

Unknown to the Darkness, to bury Hamashiach is to plant the Light. From the buried seed springs life, and humanity must reimagine itself. Longinus turns to The Way, the nexus of the Seventh Age. His spear goes on a special mission to the island of Briton, where Wulfgar lives again.

Logres is centred on Avalon, but raises up Arthur, a man of mixed race, to carry its flag and to protect against the Saxons. But its main enemy is the Darkness, which ever seeks to extinguish the Light it hates and fears.

Finally, it seems as if the Darkness has won, and the dark ages descend. But does the Light not shine in the Darkness? Must Wulfgar remain in the Night?

∞

**Vampire Shadows**

Dark vampires, hidden within the ancient empire of Khem, fall out with the king who, stirred up by the Necros, enslaves the Sheep People. But Iahveh, the shepherd-divinity, is stirred up, and stirs up a hidden hero to force a way out.

Apprehensively the two vampire-magicians join the Sheep of Iahveh, on their long and deadly trek in search of a promised land. Can any survive?

Warily they ask deep questions. Is Usen evil, as prejudice says? Is he possibly a good jailer? Are his unusual regulations, meaningful? They risk ending up in death.

Neverendingly the Sheep's sorry story drags out in interminable peregrination. Weary of wandering, most would settle for some green pastures and untroubled waters. But as they well know, that would take a miracle.

www.ingramcontent.com/pod-product-compliance
Lightning Source LLC
Chambersburg PA
CBHW071452040426
42444CB00008B/1300